INTRODUCTION
Invitation to Wisdom Ways

In the last decade or so, spirituality has become a key topic not only in theology but also in commercialized forms of self-help groups and diverse New Age movements. The *Wall Street Journal* reports that spirituality and the search for meaning are a billion-dollar business. Leading companies everywhere are turning to the power of spirituality as they look to convey business goals and to inspire people to do their best for excelling in the global market place.

Since the bible is one of the main resources for traditional spirituality, it is important to explore different understandings of spirituality and to inquire into the links between a critical feminist spirituality and the global feminist struggles for liberation and well-being.[1] However, the bible can not simply be taken as a feminist source or resource insofar as it has been indicted by feminists for inculcating patriarchal, or better kyriarchal (i.e., lord, slave-master, father, elite male domination), values and visions. Yet, whether as a source of well-being or of dependence on authority, the bible is still central in many wo/men's[2] lives. Its visions of justice and love still inspire many wo/men in their struggles for dignity and well-being. If the spiritual challenge for all of us is today to recuperate and regain the capacity for becoming outraged about injustice and for caring about the well-being of every wo/man on the globe, then feminists cannot afford to jettison the bible and to disregard its power in wo/men's lives.

Engaging in a feminist biblical spirituality, therefore, means learning how to read/understand the bible from the standpoint of a feminist theory of justice and a feminist movement for change. Hence, feminist scholars and activists in religion have developed new ways of interpreting the bible (and other culturally influential texts) in order to prevent biblical knowledge from being produced in the interest of domination and injus-

---

[1]See María Pilar Aquino and Elisabeth Schüssler Fiorenza, eds., *In the Power of Wisdom: Feminist Spiritualities of Struggle* (London: SCM Press, 2000).

[2]For an explanation of this way of writing woman/women, see the glossary.

tice. We not only engage in the activity of feminist biblical meaning-making as "interpretation" that is not just concerned with giving the text its "due" in and through a correct "exegesis" or a "close reading." We are also concerned with analyzing the contextualizations of such interpretations in wo/men's lives that are embedded in structures of domination.

In this book I invite you to probe and engage the possibilities for articulating a feminist biblical spirituality that sustains rather than mutes struggles for self-esteem, survival, and transformation. Since for many wo/men the bible still functions as a spiritual authority, *Wisdom Ways* seeks to assist those who read the bible (or any other malestream text) in exploring how their own biblical understanding remains caught up in kyriocentric discourses, as well as to help them get in touch with the bible's wellsprings of justice and visions of sacred life-giving power. Whether you are a bible reader, never have been one, or have stopped reading the bible, I invite you to become a critical, i.e., self-determining, subject of interpretation and spiritual vision. The task is not to identify oppressive or liberating texts and visions once and for all, but rather to learn how to "discern the spirits" at work in biblical texts and to identify their life-giving or death-dealing functions in different contexts; it is to learn wisdom/Wisdom's ways of deliberation and accountability.

As I have suggested in *But She Said*[3] and *Sharing Her Word*,[4] feminist biblical inquiry is best understood as a practice in the horizon of Divine Wisdom, as searching for Her presence and sustenance on the way, as learning Her ways or as engaging in the steps and moves of Her spiraling circle dance of interpretation. To walk in the ways of Wisdom is to walk in the ways of justice. To read/hear the bible "in the way of wisdom/Wisdom" means to interpret it in terms of justice and well-being; it means to become wise and sagacious. Hence, I invite you first of all to join in the feminist struggles and Wisdom movements for self-affirmation and justice. I do not want to persuade and cajole you into reading the bible. Nor do I want to teach you the "correct" reading, to demonstrate the correct "application" of scholarly interpretations to your situation, or to persuade you to accept my or any other interpretations without question. Rather, I invite you to learn how to interpret the bible in the paradigm of wisdom/Wisdom. The metaphor of wisdom as quality and mentality and Wisdom as a biblical female figuration of the Divine is key for understanding this book.

Since biblical studies usually distinguish between "exegesis" and "appropriation," between "interpretation" and "application," you may be ac-

---

[3]Elisabeth Schüssler Fiorenza, *But She Said: Feminist Practices of Biblical Interpretation* (Boston: Beacon Press, 1992).

[4]Elisabeth Schüssler Fiorenza, *Sharing Her Word: Feminist Biblical Interpretation in Context* (Boston: Beacon Press, 1998).

customed to such a two-step model of interpretation. However, I do not subscribe to this dichotomous hermeneutical[5] model. According to such a dualistic model, one first comes to an "understanding" of a text or tradition and then in a second step "applies" one's interpretation to contemporary questions and issues. In this model one engages in exegesis and interpretation so that one can "appropriate" the text for contemporary living.

Instead I propose a different model. I conceive of the task of the feminist interpreter in rhetorical-emancipatory terms. Rhetoric is aware that texts seek to persuade and to argue; they are address and debate, rather than objective statement and explanation. Moreover, the biblical scholar does not have the task of "popularizing" and "applying" the results of research so that they can be appropriated by the general reader. Rather, I argue, feminist biblical scholars are part of a social movement and hence must articulate the values and perspectives of this movement as theoretical frameworks for critical investigation and study of the bible. Whether you are a believing bible reader or a reader who appreciates the bible as a cultural treasure, becoming a feminist interpreter means shifting your focus from biblical interpretation construed as an ever better explanation of the text to biblical interpretation as a tool for becoming conscious of structures of domination and for articulating visions of radical democracy that are inscribed in our own experience as well as in that of texts.

Wisdom Ways wants to introduce you to the practice and process of such feminist "meaning making" that is seeking deeper understanding and profound insight not just into the bible but also into the self and the world in order to engage in struggles for survival and justice. Hence, I invite you to journey with me on the way to Wisdom's open house. Some of you may be experienced travelers, while others may never have read the whole bible, but have been committed to feminist struggles for justice. Others again may be familiar with biblical interpretation but until now have not seen the importance of struggling against all forms of domination for right biblical understanding. Yet all of you seem to be interested in learning more about feminist biblical studies, since you have started to read this book.

I imagine that you picked up this book because you wanted to join me in the journey to the open house of Wisdom, although you may still long for the familiar and protecting walls of home. We may have met at the occasion of one of my many lectures and travels. Or you may have picked up this book not because you have ever heard of my work or read anything on feminist hermeneutics but because you are in a college or seminary introductory class to biblical studies, and this primer is listed among the required or recommended readings. Or you may be a professor or a high school teacher looking for introductory materials either to the

---

[5]I understand hermeneutics as the theory and practice of interpretation.

bible or to feminism or to both. Or you may not have anything to do with the academic world but you are reading this book nevertheless because either you are interested in the bible or you want to know more about feminist theology. You may be discussing the proposals of *Wisdom Ways* in a bible study group of your church or synagogue or have chosen the book for your wo/men's reading group.

Ideally, I imagine you as a feminist activist and intellectual who passionately cares about justice for wo/men because she is inspired by the biblical vision of equality and well-being for all. For whatever reasons, you have joined me on the road to the open, radical, democratic, and inclusive space of Divine Wisdom. By picking up this book, you have taken the first step in the spiraling circle dance on the way to Wisdom's open house, which is without borders and exclusions.

At first glance you may be disappointed, because this is and is not one of the many "how to" spirituality handbooks that are flooding the market. On the one hand, *Wisdom Ways* seeks to introduce those who want to learn how to "do" the work of feminist biblical interpretation to this emerging new field of critical biblical studies. On the other hand, *Wisdom Ways* challenges you to give up long-held convictions, such as the views that the biblical text is an unclouded window to the historical reality of wo/men, that G*d has written it, that it is a historical source-text providing data and evidence which document wo/men's reality, or that it contains biblical injunctions and prescriptions as timeless revelation and fixed norms given once and for all. *Wisdom Ways* challenges you to give up these preconceived notions and to see the bible as a perspectival rhetorical discourse that constructs theological worlds and symbolic universes in particular historical-political situations.

After much debate on how to write this book, I came to see the following options: I could write a survey of different feminist hermeneutical positions, a textbook detailing the results of feminist biblical research, or a somewhat watered-down scholarly work on feminist hermeneutics and rhetoric for popular consumption. Finally, after a long walk along the beach contemplating the ever-changing light and ever-moving waves of the sea, which image for me the ever-touching presence of Divine Wisdom, I decided this: I would try to suggest to you hermeneutical frameworks or lenses for seeing Wisdom dancing like the sun brilliantly dances on the surface of the waters. Such hermeneutical methods and moves could also be understood as providing shoes for walking in Wisdom Ways.

Nevertheless, I do not want to give you ready-made prescriptions as to how to do feminist biblical interpretation. Instead, I invite you to become a subject of interpretation and to recognize the tools for engaging in a critical approach to reading and interpreting biblical texts. The statement of Audre Lorde that "the master's tools will never dismantle the

master's house" has become a commonplace in feminist discourses. This statement is true if one understands the tools of inquiry as rules, norms, and regulations for how to do intellectual work. However, methods and ways of inquiry can also open up new questions and render problematic established answers, norms, and rules. Used as "tools" for deconstructing the "master's house," methods of inquiry can serve to reconstruct a new and different house, the open house of Wisdom, as long as we discard the master's intellectual frameworks and theories and do not use them as plans and blueprints.

However, *Wisdom Ways* does not want to speak solely to students and readers who are feminists. It seeks to persuade also those who until now have resisted the designation "feminist." It wants to address those who are interested in the emerging field of emancipatory biblical criticism—a field or, as I would prefer, a practice—that feminist biblical studies has initiated, shaped, and pioneered. Moreover, biblical studies is not just a field of inquiry that is accountable to academy or church but rather an intellectual praxis, a spiraling circle dance that is not limited to the academy or the seminary but creates its own publics, movements, discourses, and audiences.

Since it is not widely recognized that feminist biblical studies have greatly contributed to the articulation of new and different ways of reading the bible, I want to remedy such lack of knowledge by introducing the exciting new area of emancipatory studies, to which the field and practice of feminist biblical studies belong. The new emerging paradigm of biblical studies, I have argued elsewhere, must be named and recognized as engaging in "emancipatory rhetoric," rather than simply being "ideological," "postcolonial," or "cultural." This is because, like malestream historical criticism, so also ideology criticism as well as postcolonial and cultural biblical criticism have for the most part not made *wo/men* subjects of interpretation, connected intellectuals, or historical agents central to their theoretical frameworks. Neither have they sufficiently recognized the importance of gender analysis for biblical studies or developed an ethics of interpretation that always takes wo/men's experience into account when analyzing social location and the operations of power within discourse.

Moreover, although the expression "reading" is usually favored today over the traditional notion of "exegesis," I prefer the word "interpretation" to both "reading" and "exegesis." A focus on the activity of interpreting rather than on that of exegesis or reading seems to be more appropriate because many wo/men in the world are still illiterate or barely able to read. This does not mean that I want to endorse the romantic notion that "oral culture," "stories," and "storytelling" are more feminist than reading and writing. The fact is that most wo/men in the world are illiterate because they are too poor or prohibited from going to school because

of their gender. Studies have shown that illiteracy contributes to higher unwanted pregnancy rates and to low economic status. The association of literacy with freedom as well as the ambiguous and duplicitous potential of literacy come to the fore in the story that Ella Butler, who was forced to labor on a plantation in Louisiana, shared in an interview: In the days of slavery, when the white folks went away, they sprinkled meal before the door of the food storage place and wrote on the meal with their fingers or a stick so that no one could go in and steal food without stepping on the writing before the door. This gesture of writing in the interest of domination and exclusion was soon subverted because, as Butler ironically states, "That's the way us learn how to write."[6]

In contrast to "reading," the practice of interpretation can be pursued by all, whether they are literate or have professional training, and it affects the meaning of both oral and written "texts." The shift from reading to interpretation, from gender analysis to feminist analysis, initiates the shift from a text-centered to an emancipatory methodology of conscientization. To interpret the bible "in the ways of Wisdom" has as its goal to engender right action and to achieve the "good life."

In short, I am concerned here with engaging in a social critique and political analysis of biblical traditions and contemporary discourses that is verified pragmatically through its contribution to an increase in liberation and well-being. Since through the feminist movement I have come to understand myself as a critical interpreter, my work seeks to explore wo/men's central questions in light of critical theory and analyzes them as conditioned by structures of oppression and dehumanization.

This is what I mean by a rhetorical interpretive criterion. A textual reading or contextual analysis must be judged as to whether it is empowering to wo/men in their struggles for survival and transformation. This pragmatic criterion for ethical and theological evaluation is justified because feminist studies in general and feminist biblical studies in particular owe their existence and inspiration not to the academy but to social movements for change.

To sum up my point: In contrast to books written in the genre of biblical introduction, *Wisdom Ways* is interested not so much in explaining *what* we read in the bible but in exploring *how* to interpret critically in the interest of wo/men. It does not take the bible alone as its object of study but also the ways in which wo/men understand the bible (or any other text and tradition) and how such meaning-making affects our self-perception, our understanding of the world, and our visions of life and well-being. In

---

[6]Grey Gundaker, "The Bible as and at a Threshold: Reading Performance and Blessed Space," in *African Americans and the Bible: Sacred Texts and Social Textures,* ed. Vincent Wimbush (New York: Continuum International, 2000), 757.

short, in this book I invite you to explore with me what it means to engage in a critical interpretation/reading of scripture (or any other text) for liberation.

Wisdom's Spiraling Dance

In order to make it easier for you to engage the spiraling dance of feminist biblical hermeneutics and learn how to interpret in a feminist critical way, I have attempted to write as clearly and accessibly as I can. Moreover, I have tried to avoid cluttering up the text with too many footnotes or with minute technical debates. However, to write clearly does not mean to simplify complex issues in order to make them more palatable. My goal is not consumer satisfaction, nor is it the repetition of scholarly arguments in a popularized fashion. Rather, my goal is to encourage readers to critically explore and question both feminist biblical studies and the bible. Hence, one cannot completely avoid using technical terms, e.g., hermeneutics, exegesis, or semiotics, because such technical language often is a shorthand expression for complex problems.

After finishing a basic draft, I shared the manuscript with participants in my Gospel Stories of Wo/men class. Their critical and constructive feedback has immensely improved the text and helped me to clarify or reshape my argument. It has inspired and encouraged me to publish it as soon as possible with all its limitations. Most of the notes have been added not so much in debate with existing scholarship but in response to students' queries. Thus, *Wisdom Ways* exemplifies in a small way how biblical interpretation is done in the radical democratic[7] space of Divine Wisdom.

To those interested in a more technical discussion, I recommend my other more technical works, in which you will find extensive footnotes and bibliographies documenting the ideas that I put forward here. For those who do not have access either to a library or the internet or who do not

---

[7]I have added "radical" to "democracy" in order to indicate that what I have in mind is not representative government nor majority rule but the root-sense (radical is derived from *radix* = root) of democracy or, better, grassroots democracy, which means the exercise of power by people who are all equal. Again by equality I do not mean sameness. Rather, radical equality means the abolishment of the existing dehumanizing inequalities engendered by domination so that justice is done and diversity is celebrated. Another way of defining equality is found in Jean Jacques Rousseau, *On the Social Contract,* book 2, chapter 10: "With regard to equality, this word must not be understood to mean that degrees of power and wealth should be exactly the same, but rather that with regard to power, it should be incapable of all violence, and never exerted except by virtue of status and the laws; and with regard to wealth, no citizen should be so opulent that he can buy another, and none so poor that he is constrained to sell himself."

have the means to purchase another book, I have appended a short dictionary or glossary. If you need more information, I recommend that you consult an annotated study bible, encyclopedia, or biblical dictionary that will explain and translate scholarly language, recognizing that such explanations always import certain understandings and views of the world.

It is important to familiarize yourself with the use of technical language, such as hermeneutics, and its unspoken methodological assumptions. In order to break down the barrier between expert and everyday language, feminists must be able to speak both dialects. Such knowledge enables us both to enter a conversation on complex and difficult questions of interpretation and to recognize the hermeneutical frameworks they transport. Since technical language is often used to keep those who do not belong to the "guild" of biblical scholars or preachers ignorant outsiders, it is important to democratize such language and to make it available to everyone interested. Many wo/men students have shared with me that they have been discouraged from using technical terms and have been told that they need not encumber their pretty heads with them. Thus, avoiding rather than explaining technical "scientific" language can function as a powerful weapon for maintaining the exclusion and ignorance of wo/men. Such a dodging of technical scholarly language has an even more pernicious effect if it is used for reinforcing practices of feminine cultural socialization that make wo/men "second-class citizens" in society, religion, and the academy while at the same time extolling their "feminine" virtues.

Instead of empowering so-called popular audiences, the academy often denies them the tools to investigate the ideologies, discourses, and knowledges that shape wo/men's self-identity and determine their lives. Instead of enabling students to become critical thinkers, education in general and biblical education in particular often contribute to their self-alienation and adaptation to the values and mores of kyriocentric (i.e., lord, slave-master, father, elite men centered) social, academic, and religious communities. It is therefore of utmost importance that those on the margins of academy and church become bilingual and learn how to use the language of the academy in their own interests.

Although feminist biblical interpretation is rarely cited or acknowledged as pioneering intellectual work in standard reference books, dictionaries, commentaries, and overall discussions of the field, it nevertheless has made great inroads into biblical studies. Thirty years ago feminist biblical studies were unheard of. I am often asked with whom I studied feminist theology and my response is unfailingly this: When I studied in the 1960s, feminist theology and feminist studies did not exist. Hence, we had to invent them! Now, thirty years later, feminist studies are a richly blooming field of inquiry.

I can remember that in the late 1960s, when the so-called "second wave" of the wo/men's movement first emerged on the scene, I devoured everything that appeared on any wo/men's or feminist topic. In the 1970s, I could still read anything that appeared in the area of feminist theology or feminist studies in religion. In the 1980s, I was no longer able to keep informed and to read everything that appeared in feminist critical studies but could still keep abreast of most of the publications in my own area of expertise, biblical studies. In the 1990s, I have had a tough time reading the literature appearing even in my field of special-ization, Christian Testament Studies. This enormous proliferation of feminist intellectual work in general and in biblical studies in particular is grounds for celebration. Elizabeth Castelli[8] has aptly characterized the variegated intellectual voices of feminist biblical studies with the metaphor of *heteroglossia*, which means "speaking in other different tongues." Although this expression is derived from Bakhtin, it also al-ludes to the biblical notion of *glossolalia* (which means speaking in tongues) as a gift of Spirit-Wisdom.

Without question, in the last twenty-five years feminist biblical stud-ies have been established as a new area of inquiry with its own publica-tions. It is taught in schools, colleges, and universities and is practiced by many scholars in different parts of the world. Although there are diverse and theoretically different articulations of feminist biblical studies, most of them would agree on the following three points, whereas the fourth point is still contested.

- The bible is written in androcentric-kyriocentric language and serves patriarchal or, better, kyriarchal interests.
- The bible came into being in patriarchal/kyriarchal societies, cul-tures, and religions.
- The bible is still proclaimed and taught today in patriarchal/kyriar-chal societies and religions.
- In and through a critical feminist interpretative process, the bible can function as spiritual vision and a resource in struggles for emancipation and liberation.

However, to tell the story of the emerging field of feminist biblical studies as a success story obscures and hides the negative underside of this achievement.

---

[8]Elizabeth A. Castelli, "Heteroglossia, Hermeneutics and History: A Review Essay of Recent Feminist Studies of Early Christianity," *The Journal of Feminist Studies in Religion* 10/2 (1994): 73–98; see also Janice Capel Anderson, "Mapping Feminist Biblical Criti-cism," *Critical Review of Books in Religion* 2 (1991): 21–44.

First, scholarly articles and books, as they have become more and more sophisticated, also have become increasingly specialized and arcane. While academic studies on "women" or "gender" in the bible proliferate and sometimes explicitly claim to be feminist, one rarely can find in such academic works any reference to a wo/men's movement for change or any connection with the actual daily struggles of wo/men. Value-free and objectivist academic frameworks do not allow for the articulation of a goal of change and transformation. They do not allow one to understand social location as integral to the research process. At the most, they allow for the personal, individualistic, confessional voice of the scholar or preacher but rarely for a critical analysis of how biblical texts and interpretations function in maintaining structures of alienation and domination.

Second, feminist biblical studies are for the most part the success story of white Euro-American Christian scholarship. Although womanist biblical scholars have been on the scene of biblical studies since the 1980s, there are still very few African-American biblical wo/men scholars. Jewish feminist biblical scholarship has greatly increased in the 1990s, yet, with the exception of Amina Wadud-Muhsin's work,[9] Muslim feminist biblical scholarship is almost non-existent. In celebrating our success story in biblical studies we must not overlook the fact that articles and books by Latina, Australian, Asian, Native American, Maori, and other indigenous feminist scholars in North America and around the globe are still scarce. Only a very few wo/men of the former European colonies have had access to biblical studies and even fewer have advanced to the level of full professors or have the means to publish their work. This, however, is due not so much to the racism and elitism of Euro-American white feminist scholars, as some seem to think, as to the elitist character of the academy and the fact that global capitalism is built on the exploitation of wo/men. Hence, because of kyriarchal structures of domination, very few wo/men of disadvantaged groups or countries have achieved access to education and higher studies. Moreover, we must not forget that the majority of those who are illiterate are wo/men.

Third, not even in the white European and North American academy, where one finds a good number of highly educated wo/men, are feminist biblical studies widely recognized as an important field of study. If, for instance, one looks at and searches through introductory books and reference works to the bible and biblical studies, one very rarely will find a competent discussion of feminist biblical studies as an established area of inquiry. Feminist scholars are still daily written out of history and their

---

[9]Amina Wadud-Muhsin, *Qurán and Woman* (Fajar Bakhti, 1992) and her article "In Search of a Woman's Voice in Quránic Hermeneutics," in *Women's Sacred Scriptures,* Concilium, ed. Kwok Pui-lan and Elisabeth Schüssler Fiorenza (Maryknoll, N.Y.: Orbis Books, 1998), 37–44.

work is consigned to the margins. This is not due to the self-ghettoization of feminist biblical scholars as some have suggested. Rather, it is due to the kyriarchal structures of the field.

Moreover, applicants for doctoral programs typically are not selected if they express interest in a feminist studies approach. Scholars still have a difficult time receiving tenure or academic and/or ecclesiastical recognition if they have published in the area of feminist biblical studies or feminist theology. Students are still told not to write their dissertations on feminist topics if they want to succeed. Senior scholars are put down rather than honored because they allegedly have done "strident" feminist work. In short, the marginalizing and silencing tendencies of kyriarchal academic and religious structures that have barred wo/men from higher education and the study of theology in past centuries are still in place, even though they are now directed against feminists and no longer against wo/men who play "by the rules."

Fourth, even worse is the co-optation and appropriation of feminist work. Many academic works and popular books claim to be feminist because they write about wo/men or the feminine in the bible. Critical reflection is often lacking on how such work on "wo/men" or the "feminine" re-inscribes or reinforces kyriarchal structures of domination. One of the reasons is, I suggest, that advisors of doctoral students (Doktorväter!) still tell brilliant young wo/men that they first have to criticize the work done by first-generation feminists. Then they have to resort to the work of a leading male theorist for articulating their own more sophisticated feminist research. In light of such co-optation, it is no wonder that feminist work is in danger of becoming more and more determined by the academy and the questions and methods it allows.

For instance, a couple of years ago I chaired a panel session on writing a feminist dissertation at the annual meeting of the Society of Biblical Literature, the oldest biblical society in North America. Four bright young wo/men detailed their dissertation work. While affirming their exceptional accomplishment, the senior scholar who responded nevertheless had to point out that none of the dissertation projects presented was actually feminist in an explicit and critically reflective way.

In short, the emerging field of feminist biblical studies not only lacks the participation of feminist scholars from diverse social locations, but it also is in danger of being further marginalized in favor of biblical gender studies that fit better into the functionalist value-neutral, objectivist ethos of the academy. Moreover, because it speaks in many different tongues and overlapping voices, feminist biblical interpretation sometimes produces a cacophony of voices rather than a consistent argument in support of struggles for liberation. Instead of conceptualizing feminist biblical studies in terms of an academic field or a theological discipline that

serves ecclesiastical or academic institutions, I have suggested that we should cultivate feminist biblical inquiry as moving in the power of Wisdom to serve wo/men's struggles for survival and well-being.

Creating the Circle to Dance

Hence, it is necessary to take biblical reading out of the privatist spiritual realm of the individual solitary reader and constitute a forum, that is, a public space where the *ekklesia*, the radical democratic assembly, can debate and adjudicate the public meanings of the Scriptures. While Christian biblical interpretation often is individualistic and solitary, traditional Jewish interpretation as practiced by feminists provides a radical democratic model for learning to walk in the ways of Wisdom. According to traditional Rabbinic understanding, study and interpretation of Scripture lead to the redemption of the world because they bring G*d's presence into it. Hence, investigating and interpreting Scripture are sacred activities.

We usually think of reading and interpretation as an act of passive reception and individualistic self-contemplation rather than as a way of communication and communal identification. For the Rabbis, however, reading was, according to Barry Holtz,

> a passionate and active grappling with God's living word. It held the challenge of uncovering secret meanings, unheard-of explanations, matters of great weight and significance. An active, indeed interactive reading was their method of approaching the sacred text called Torah and through that reading process of finding something at once new and very old.[10]

Traditional Jewish Torah study, called Havruta, requires a social context. The Talmud commands: "Make yourself into groups to study the Torah, since the knowledge of the Torah can be acquired only in association with others" (Berekoth, 63b).[11] Echoing this tradition, Jesus, who in Matthew's gospel is identified with Wisdom-Sophia, promises: "Where two or three are gathered in my name, I am in the midst of them" (Mt 18:20). Torah/bible reading is not, as in the modern tradition, something individualistic and private. Rather, according to this Wisdom tradition, Torah that is personified and identified with Divine Wisdom in Jewish Wisdom writings speaks to people in groups who together "turn the text again and again" in order not only to discover ever new textual meanings in their own historical

---

[10]Barry W. Holtz, ed., *Back to the Sources* (New York: Summit Books, 1984), 16.
[11]Naomi M. Hyman, *Biblical Wo/men in the Midrash: A Sourcebook* (Northvale, N.J.: Jason Aronson, 1997), xxv–xxxix.

contexts but also to learn what it means to live "the good life" and to walk in the ways of Wisdom. Biblical meaning must again and again be reconsidered, questioned, debated, adjudicated, and reformulated.

In the horizon of this wisdom/Wisdom practice of interpretation I envision you working with this book in a group or forum that constitutes a feminist radical democratic public space of critical debate, creative imagination, and substantive conversation. Critical group discussions should have two focal points: your own social-religious location and interests, and biblical texts and their possible meanings. The goal of such debates and exploration is not to ascertain the true, single meaning of a text as a given "fact" but to render problematic both texts and interpretive perspectives, in order to adjudicate how much texts and interpretations foster values and mindsets of domination or mentalities and visions of liberation.

Ruth Cohn, who as a Jew had to immigrate to the U.S. during National Socialism, proposed a political "pedagogy for everyone" called "Theme-Centered Interaction" (TCI), which was capable of mobilizing people against National Socialism and other oppressive regimes. She wanted

> to encourage people, who do not want to tolerate such suffering, not to "give up" and to feel powerless, but to use their imagination and their potential for action, in order to declare and practice their solidarity, as long as we still sense autonomous powers in ourselves.[12]

TCI is not a "neutral method" but rather seeks to embody the political vision and radical democratic goal of a more just world. It consists of four elements that constitute the group process and are all of equal importance:

- The person (the I) who turns to herself, to others, and to the theme. The first requirement, "be your own chairperson," conceptualizes the group as radically democratic. It encourages self-esteem, initiative, and autonomy.
- The group members (the We) who form a group in and through their concentration on the theme and their interaction with each other, which opens the door to genuine participation and involvement.
- The theme or task (the It) which is taken on by the group. TCI values every individual contribution to the task and facilitates communication of that contribution. For instance, to explain why one is asking a certain question avoids artificial debates.

---

[12]Quoted in Antje Röckemann, "In Spiralen fliegen. Bibliodrama und TZI (Themen-zentrierte Interaktion) interkulturell," in *In Spiralen Fliegen. Bibliodrama und TZI Interkulturell,* ed. Margarete Pauschert/Antje Röckemann (Münster: Schlangenbrut e.V., 1999), 10.

- The context (the globe) in both a narrow and broad sense as that which influences the group and is influenced by it. The "globe" can mean the particular circumstances, for instance the environment of the room, or the political-cultural and natural cosmos that includes historical memories which we have internalized as "heritage." The principle of "disturbances and passionate involvements" takes precedence. The "*disturbance* principle" allows for the method of kyriarchal critique, whereas the technique of *amplification* not only enriches the interaction triangle (the individual, the group, and the theme) with personal experience and biographical data but also shows the impact of socio-political structures and cultural-religious worlds on it. Hence, German feminists who have combined the methods of TCI and bibliodrama, i.e., the dramatic rendering of biblical texts, place special emphasis on this fourth element, "the globe."

I myself have incorporated group work into my classes. Autonomous groups prepare and present projects that either engage a chosen feminist perspective (e.g., queer, mujcrista, womanist, or Asian feminist) or a critique (e.g., of violence against wo/men, the international sex-trade, or Roman Catholic ordination politics) as the "lens" for interpreting a particular biblical text. Such groups not only achieve solid knowledge of the text and standard methods of interpretation but also acquire alternating leadership skills, practice "hearing each other into speech," and develop creative hermeneutical teaching and communication skills.

If you cannot form such a radical democratic group forum, I recommend that you team up with a study partner who has a similar level of knowledge, set aside a regular time for study, choose a text, and identify a feminist theoretical perspective with which to look at the text. It is important that each of you has a copy of the text. Take turns reading it aloud, discuss what you have noticed or the questions you want to ask, consult commentaries, and make the connections to emancipatory struggles. And remember, there are no right or wrong answers but only right questions. With Naomi Hyman I invite you to consider the following ancient commentary:

> "And acquire yourself a friend." How so? This teaches that a person should acquire a friend to eat with, drink with, read Torah with, study Mishnah with, sleep with, and to whom all secrets will be told—secrets of Torah and secrets of everyday affairs. (Avot de Rabbi Nathan, Ch. 8)[13]

---

[13]Hyman, xxv.

If you are a part of a class or group that is too large, have the whole group meet and then break into pairs. After a specified time reconvene as a large group, share your different insights and interpretations, and debate their implications for the struggles for justice and well-being.

Such a feminist study approach of critical "conscientization" is similar to but distinct from the approach used by wo/men's consciousness-raising groups. In such consciousness-raising groups the individual and her experience stand in the center of attention. So as not to undermine her self-confidence, no critical questions interrogating her experience are allowed. Affirmation and solidarization rather than critique and debate are the goals of such consciousness-raising groups. In comparison, Latin American conscientization groups are focused not just on individual affirmation but much more on critically exploring systemic oppression and the paths to liberation.

A radical democratic forum is also similar to but different from traditional bible-study groups, which often have as their goal the inculcation and acceptance of biblical texts and traditions. Insofar as they start from the assumption that the bible is the revealed word of G*d, they begin with a hermeneutics of empathy and obedience rather than with a hermeneutics of suspicion and critical debate. Such groups are also similar to but different from academic study groups that focus on biblical texts and use discussion questions in order to "test" whether malestream scientific methods and results of interpretation have been internalized. Moreover, for the sake of objectivity, such study groups often eschew any critical reflection on the experience and social location of biblical interpreters as well as on the contemporary significance and impact of biblical texts.

The first task, then, before you continue reading this book is to initiate such a study partnership or group-forum for critical debate and mutual friendship. If you are already working in a group, you might want to discuss whether your group constitutes such an *ekklesia* (assembly/congress) of critical debate and creative vision. If you are working in a class that does not require group work, get together with some of your classmates and form such a group. If you are a professor, try to get together a group of colleagues who are interested not just in questions of biblical specialization but in a critical theoretical exploration of the issues at stake in biblical interpretation as conscientization.

If you are forced to remain an individual reader, you may want to call up some of your friends or neighbors to form a study partnership. Or you might want to go to the internet and create a radical democratic forum by initiating a "virtual" feminist study-team or discussion group. If you are not able to do any of these things, make sure that you constitute such a virtual forum in your own imagination and stage a running argument and continuing conversation between the different voices and perspectives

that populate your mind. One-dimensional thinking must be replaced with a radical democratic form of thinking that cultivates different perspectives and creative imagination.

Essential for the constitution of a radical democratic feminist group-forum is the presence of true differences in social location, religious confession, political outlook, and feminist persuasion. Although a critical articulation of differences makes group work often difficult and full of tension, it must be valued as positive and integral to radical democratic feminist practices of articulating emancipatory knowledge. Radical democratic approaches also must question the dominant mode of reasoning and knowledge production in the Eurocentric malestream paradigm of knowledge that separates reason from feelings and emotions in order to produce detached impartial knowledge. They must insist on a process of conscientization that enables us to walk/dance in the ways of Wisdom.

In her book *Feminism Is for Everybody,* the cultural feminist critic bell hooks also has called for a revival of revolutionary consciousness-raising practices of the 1970s. Revolutionary consciousness-raising is based on the conviction that we have to change ourselves if we want to change oppressive structures of domination such as racism, homophobia, sexism, class bias, or colonialist hegemony.

> Importantly though, the foundation of this work began with wo/men examining sexist thinking and creating strategies where we would change our attitudes and our belief via a conversion to feminist thinking and a conversion to feminist politics. Fundamentally, the consciousness-raising group was a site for conversion. To build a mass-based feminist movement, wo/men needed to organize. The consciousness-raising group...was the place where seasoned feminist thinkers and activists could recruit new converts.[14]

Hooks points out that the feminist movement was mistaken as "anti-male" because it did not create such consciousness-raising groups for boys and men who also needed to examine their internalized (hetero)sexism. She argues further that in the 1980s revolutionary consciousness-raising was replaced by "liberal reformism" and "life-style based feminism which suggested that any wo/man could be a feminist no matter her political beliefs."[15] The "success" of academic women's or gender studies contributed to the demise of revolutionary consciousness-raising, "insofar as the classroom replaced the consciousness-raising group as the primary

---

[14]bell hooks, *Feminism Is for Everybody* (Boston: South End Press, 2000), 8.
[15]hooks, 11.

site for the transmission of feminist thinking and strategies for social change" and "the movement lost its mass-based potential."[16]

Like bell hooks, I envision the revitalization of revolutionary consciousness-raising in and through the creation of feminist wisdom/Wisdom groups that come together to engage in biblical interpretation as a spiritual practice of conscientization, conversion, and commitment to walking in Wisdom's ways of justice.

Unlike many introductory works to biblical studies, this book does not just want to answer the question of "*how to exegete*" or "*how to read*" the bible. Rather, it is concerned with the question of how to *interpret* the bible from a feminist perspective and in an emancipatory way. After this introduction, I explore a feminist discursive wisdom/Wisdom space of learning in the first chapter and attempt in the second chapter to lift into consciousness the various ways in which engagement with the text may be blocked. The third chapter argues that feminist biblical inquiry is rooted in and must remain accountable to social movements for change, and the fourth chapter provides a feminist social analytic for exploring the social locations of biblical interpreters and of biblical texts. While the fifth chapter elaborates the different methodologies or "dance steps" developed in feminist biblical studies, the last chapter sums up my explorations by looking at the hermeneutical "moves" or strategies that are integral to wisdom/Wisdom's circle dance, spiraling with the different turns of a critical feminist inquiry for liberation.

To the end of each chapter I have appended three "dance" exercises: First, for those who want to deepen their understanding of biblical interpretation for liberation, I have suggested for further reading a chapter from one of my books that discusses a biblical text and the different ways one can approach textual interpretation. Second, I have suggested "moving step" questions that invite you to debate and practice the ideas and proposals presented in each chapter. These questions do not have only one "right" answer or a definite solution but challenge you to continue moving in Wisdom Ways. Finally, I have added worksheets which are meant not to "test" your knowledge but to compel you to practice the steps and movements of the hermeneutical spiral-dance. They provide suggestions for further discussion and assistance in clarifying and working through complex issues. Group leaders and teachers can utilize them for deepening the arguments presented in each chapter.

Since I want to offer a hermeneutical tool-kit rather than methodological prescriptions or progressive arguments, it is not necessary—or even advisable—to read the chapters sequentially and in a linear fashion. For instance, you may want to consult sections of chapter four whenever you

---

[16]hooks, 10.

need an explanation of key concepts and categories. Because each individual chapter forms a unit of its own, you may be interested in reading later chapters earlier and early chapters later. Rather than engaging in a continuous reading, you may want to work through the book in a spiraling fashion, since all chapters in different ways circle around the practice of a critical feminist emancipatory interpretation and look at it from different angles. The goal is not just to convey information but to contribute to conscientization.

The metaphor of the circle dance seems best to express the moves and movements of Wisdom at work in such a feminist process of consciousness-raising. Dancing involves body and spirit, it involves feelings and emotions, it takes us beyond our limits and creates community. Dancing confounds all hierarchical order because it moves in spirals and circles. It makes us feel alive and full of energy, power, and creativity. This metaphor of movement and dance suggests that feminism is not a core essence that can be defined but that it is best embodied in a movement for change and transformation.

A critical feminist biblical interpretation, I argue in this book, is best located in the radical democratic space of Divine Wisdom, which is open to the winds of change, the cleansing rains, and the warming sun. To re-imagine biblical interpretation as a spiraling circle dance and Spirit movement in the open space of Divine Wisdom invites us to join the movement of Spirit-Wisdom. As Linda Ellison put it after having read the manuscript of this book:

"Dancing in the House of Wisdom" or "Waltzing in Wisdom Ways" [means] stepping and twirling—creating an interpretive, communal dance and breaking out of the rhythm of the rigidity of culturally ascribed dance steps. I visualize a diverse group of wo/men dancing in a circular formation inside the pillars of an open-air house—their dance circle open, ready to accept the reader inside. The dance could be edifying to the mind, body and spirit of the reader.[17]

Won't you join this twirling, moving, spiraling dance of feminist biblical interpretation in the "imagined" and practiced radical democratic space of Divine Wisdom?

---

[17]Linda Ellison, Midterm Paper for Gospel Stories of Wo/men, Fall 2000.

Deepening Movement

Elisabeth Schüssler Fiorenza, *Sharing Her Word: Feminist Biblical Interpretation in Context* (Boston: Beacon Press, 1998), 105–136.

Moving Steps

- How did you come to pick up this book? *Wisdom Ways* suggests many different audiences. Reflect on your own reasons for picking it up and reading it. How did you feel after reading the introduction and discovering what the book is all about? Do you feel anxious about continuing with it? Why?

- As you begin this book, reflect on why you do or do not call yourself a feminist. Develop a timeline of your own life and the development of your own spiritual awareness. What events were most important to you along this journey? How did malestream interpretation affect how you viewed yourself in G*d's eyes? What motivates you to understand the bible from a feminist perspective?[18]

- What is your experience with the bible? Do you read the bible? Do you feel overwhelmed, comforted, challenged, or angered by it? Why are you interested in learning to interpret it? What is the relationship of the bible to politics? Share one positive and one negative experience with the bible and its authority.

- Naomi Hyman states: "We write because in the writing we find places for ourselves in the white spaces between the black letters."[19] Have you ever experienced moments when you felt left out of a text, experience, or dialogue? How were you able to insert yourself? How did you make your voice heard? Can you envision using these same tools to interpret biblical texts as a wo/man?[20]

- Do you plan to form a group or find a study partner? What are the difficulties in doing so? What emotional objections do you have to group work? What is your experience of working in groups?

Movement Exercise

Utilizing worksheet 1, prepare an explanation of what feminist biblical interpretation consists of. Use examples from your own experience.

---

[18]Thanks to Elizabeth M. Zachry, Gospel Stories of Wo/men, Fall 2000, for this question.

[19]Hyman, xviii.

[20]Thanks to Yolanda Denson Lehman, Gospel Stories of Wo/men, Fall 2000, for this question.

Mapping Feminist Biblical Studies

I. The Bible

- What do you know/feel about the bible?

- What would you like to know?

II. Biblical Studies

- What do you know/feel about biblical studies?

- What would you like to know?

III. Feminism

- What do you know/feel about feminism/gender/women's studies?

- What would you like to know?

IV. Feminist Biblical Studies

- What do you know/feel about feminist biblical studies?

- What would you like to know?

CHAPTER I

Mapping Wisdom's Terrain

When Lucy Tatman started doing research for an article on "Wisdom" for a feminist dictionary project, she encountered an almost total silence on the subject. While there is an abundance of spiritual reflection and liturgical celebration of Wisdom, she could not locate a sustained theological exploration of the topic. More distressingly, Tatman was not able to find the words which she wanted to say. While reading Katie G. Cannon[1] she realized that she could not write a theological definition of Wisdom until and unless she heard Wisdom's story as told by wo/men. Only then could she begin to speak and write the story of Wisdom, which she concluded with the following paragraph:

> Once upon a time there was Wisdom. There was Wisdom, and she was present everywhere with all the intensity and all the desire of all there was. And once the Word was spoken she and she alone dived into the spaces between the words, blessing the silence out of which new worlds are born. Now as it was in the beginning, Wisdom is hearing all creation into speech. She alone knows something of its possibilities.[2]

In the past two decades feminists have rediscovered and recreated the submerged traditions of Divine Wisdom in all their splendor and possibilities. Feminist theologians have discovered anew the creativity of wisdom/Wisdom and have searched for Her presence in the spaces "in-between," the blank spaces between the words of the bible. They have sought "to hear Wisdom into speech," to use the expression coined by Nelle Morton, one of the first feminist theologians and teachers of wis-

---

[1]Katie Geneva Cannon, *Black Womanist Ethics* (Atlanta: Scholars Press, 1988). Katie G. Cannon, *Katie's Canon* (New York: Continuum, 1995).

[2]Lucy Tatman, "Wisdom," in *An A to Z of Feminist Theology,* ed. Lisa Isherwood and Dorothea McEwan (Sheffield: Academic Press, 1996), 238.

dom/Wisdom, who recognized that "Wisdom is feminist and suggests an existence earlier than Word."[3]

Wisdom's Province

In the bible, "Spirit (Ruach)"—"Presence (Shekhinah)"—"Wisdom (Chokmah)" are all grammatically feminine terms. They refer to very similar female figurations in the Hebrew Bible[4] who express G*d's saving presence in the world. They signify that aspect of the Divine which is involved in the affairs of humanity and creation:

> For within her is a spirit intelligent, holy, unique, manifold, subtle,
> Active, incisive, unsullied, lucid, invulnerable, benevolent, sharp,
> Irresistible, beneficent, loving humans,
> Steadfast, dependable, unperturbed,
> Almighty, all-surveying, penetrating,
> All intelligent, pure and most subtle spirit.
> For Wisdom is quicker to move than any motion;
> She is so pure, she pervades and permeates all things.
> She is a breath of the power of G*d, pure emanation of divine glory;
> Hence nothing impure can find a way into her....
> Although alone, she can do all;
> Herself unchanging, she makes all things new.
> In each generation she passes into holy souls,
> She makes them friends of G*d and prophets;
> For G*d loves only those who live with Wisdom.
> She is indeed more splendid than the sun,
> She outshines all the constellations;
> Compared with light, she takes first place,
> For light must yield to night,
> But over Wisdom evil can never triumph.
>   (Wisdom 7:22-25, 27-30)[5]

Traditional theology has focused on the Spirit, who is in Latin grammatically masculine. Jewish feminists have rediscovered a spirituality of Shekhinah because she plays a significant part in some Jewish traditions, and Christian—especially Catholic—feminists in turn have elaborated the female figure of Divine Wisdom (which in Greek is called Sophia and in

---

[3]Nelle Morton, *The Journey Is Home* (Boston: Beacon Press, 1985), 175.

[4]I use Hebrew Bible instead of Old Testament and Christian Testament instead of New Testament because Old and New Testament are Christian expressions that announce the superiority of Christianity over Judaism.

[5]I am quoting from the text of the Revised Standard Version (RSV) and/or the Jerusalem Bible but I have generally changed masculine language for G*d and humans.

Latin Sapientia). Several books of the bible speak about Her, but some of these books are not found at all or only in an appendix in Protestant versions of the bible.[6] Divine Wisdom-Chokmah-Sophia-Sapientia plays a significant role in Orthodox theology but less so in modern Western theology.

In biblical as well as in contemporary religious discourses the word "wisdom" has a double meaning: It can either refer to a quality of life and of a people and/or it can refer to a figuration of the Divine. Wisdom in both senses of the word is not a prerogative of the biblical traditions but is found in the imagination and writings of all known religions. It is transcultural, international, and inter-religious. It is practical knowledge gained through experience and daily living as well as the study of creation and human nature. Both word meanings, that of capability (wisdom) and that of female personification (Wisdom), are crucial for articulating a feminist biblical spirituality that seeks to fashion biblical readers as critical subjects of interpretation.

Wisdom is a state of the human mind and spirit characterized by deep understanding and profound insight. It is elaborated as a quality possessed by the sages but also treasured as folk wisdom and wit. Wisdom is the power of discernment, deeper understanding, and creativity; it is the ability to move and to dance, to make the connections, to savor life and to learn from experience. Its root meaning comes to the fore in the Latin word *sapientia,* which is derived from the verb *sapere* = to taste and to savor something. Wisdom is intelligence shaped by experience and sharpened by critical analysis. It is the ability to make sound choices and incisive decisions.

Wisdom, unlike intelligence, is not something with which a person is born. It comes only from living, from making mistakes and trying again and from listening to others who have made mistakes and tried to learn from them. It is a perception of wholeness that does not lose sight of particularity, relativity, and the intricacies of relationships. Wisdom understands complexity and seeks integrity in relationships. It is usually seen as using the left and right brain in a union of logic and poetry, as bringing together self-awareness and self-esteem with awareness and appreciation of the world and the other. Wisdom is neither a specialized discipline nor a discrete field of study. It is a radical democratic concept insofar as it

---

[6]The following books that are called by Protestants "apocryphal" or "deuterocanonical" are usually printed in Protestant bible editions in an appendix placed after the Christian Testament. They are found in the Roman Catholic, Greek, and Slavonic canon: Tobit, Judith, Wisdom of Solomon, Ecclesiasticus, also called the Wisdom of Jesu Ben Sirach, Baruch, 1 and 2 Maccabees, 3 Maccabees (only in Greek and Slavonic bibles), 4 Maccabees (only in an Appendix to the Greek bible), 1 Esdras (in the Greek bible; = 2 Esdras in the Slavonic bible), Prayer of Manasseh (in Greek and Slavonic bibles; as an appendix in the Vulgate, the Latin translation of the Catholic bible), Psalm 151 (following Psalm 150 in the Greek bible), and additions to the books of Daniel and Esther.

does not require extensive schooling and formal education. Unschooled people can acquire wisdom and highly educated people might lack it.

Wisdom, however, is most fascinating to feminists as a representation of the Divine in female "gestalt" or form. She is a divine female figure who in extra-biblical traditions is represented by a variety of Goddesses and Goddess traditions. The biblical texts about Divine Wisdom-Chokmah-Sophia-Sapientia retain the subjugated knowledges and the submerged language of the Goddess within Christian tradition just as the Divine Shekhinah-Presence does within Judaism. Although the feminist scholarly search for the footprints of Wisdom-Sophia in biblical writings encounters a host of historical-theological problems, it is nevertheless commonly accepted that the biblical image of Wisdom-Chokmah-Sophia-Sapientia has integrated Goddess language and traditions.

Whereas the biblical Wisdom literature generally has been seen as kyriocentric literature written by and for elite educated men, more recent feminist studies have argued that post-exilic wo/men in Israel and Hellenistic Jewish wo/men in Egypt conceived of Divine Wisdom as prefigured in the language and image of Egyptian (Maat, Isis) or Greek (Athena or Dike) Goddesses. According to a very well-known prayer, all the different nations and people use divine titles derived from their own local mythologies when they call on the Goddess, Isis. They do so in the full knowledge that Isis is one, but encompasses all. Like the Goddess, Isis, so Divine Wisdom uses the "I am" proclamation style for announcing her universal message of salvation:

> Wisdom speaks her own praises,
> In the midst of people she glories in herself....
> I have grown tall as a cedar in Lebanon, as a cypress on Mount Hermon;
> I have grown tall as a palm in Engedi, as the rose bushes of Jericho;
> As a fine olive in the plain, as a plane tree I have grown tall....
> I am like a vine putting out graceful shoots,
> My blossoms bear the fruit of glory and wealth.
> Approach me, you who desire me, and take your fill of my fruits,
> For memories of me are sweeter than honey,
> Inheriting me is sweeter than the honeycomb.
> They who eat me will hunger for more.
> They who drink me will thirst for more.
>   (Ecclesiasticus 24:1, 13-14, 17-21)

Or consider this:

> I, Wisdom, am mistress of discretion,
> The inventor of the lucidity of thought.

Good advice and sound judgment belong to me,
Perception to me, strength to me.
I hate pride and arrogance, wicked behavior and a lying mouth.
I love those who love me, those who seek me eagerly shall find me.
By me monarchs rule and princes issue just laws; by me rulers govern
And the great impose justice on the world.
With me are riches and honor, lasting wealth and justice.
The fruit I give is better than gold, even the finest,
The return I make is better than pure silver.
I walk in the way of virtue, in the path of justice,
Enriching those who love me, filling their treasuries.
                    (Proverbs 8:12-21)

Like the widespread Isis cult and mythology, so also the variegated
Wisdom discourses of post-exilic Palestinian sages elaborate the image and
figure of Divine Chokmah-Wisdom as the "other name" of G*d. Her ways
are ways of justice and well-being. In the figure of Chokmah-Sophia-
Sapientia-Wisdom, ancient Jewish scriptures seek to hold together belief in
the "one" G*d of Israel and the language and metaphors of a female divine
being. Hence the texts struggle to subordinate Wisdom to YHWH:

From everlasting I was firmly set,
From the beginning before earth came into being.
The deep was not, when I came into existence,
There were no springs to gush with water. . . .
When G*d fixed the heavens firm, I was there. . . .
When G*d assigned the sea its boundaries
—and the waters will not invade the shore—
When G*d laid down the foundations of the earth,
I was by G*d's side, a master craftswoman,
Delighting G*d day after day,
Ever at play in G*d's presence, at play everywhere in the world,
Delighting to be with the children of humanity.
                    (Proverbs 8:23-24, 27, 29-31)

In recent years scholarship and texts about Divine Wisdom-Chokmah-
Sophia-Sapientia have received intensive feminist attention because of
the female gender of this figure. Feminists in the churches have translated
the results of biblical scholarship on early Jewish and Christian Wisdom
discourses into the idiom of song, poem, story, art, and ritual. This practical and creative feminist attention to the divine female figure of Wisdom
has brought the results of scholarship on biblical Wisdom literature to
public attention and has raised public objections.

For instance, in 1993 Protestant feminists sponsored a conference in Minneapolis that not only featured lectures on Divine Sophia but also invoked and celebrated her in prayer and liturgy. This Re-Imagining Conference was allegedly the most controversial ecumenical event in decades. Conservatives claimed that it challenged the very foundations of mainline Protestantism in the U.S. The reaction of the Christian Right to this conference was so violent that one high-ranking woman lost her church job and others have run into grave difficulties.[7] This struggle indicates the significance of Divine Chokmah-Sophia-Sapientia-Wisdom for contemporary Christian self-understanding.

Some European feminist theologians have raised serious historical and theological objections to attempts at recovering the earliest Sophia discourses in order to valorize "Lady Wisdom." They have argued that one must reject the figure of Divine Lady Wisdom as an elite male creation that serves both misogynist and elitist interests. According to them, the fascination of feminist theologians with Wisdom-Sophia is misplaced. Wisdom speculation is at home in Israel's elite male circles and bespeaks their interests. They also point to the possible theological dangers inherent in such biblical language and imagination.

The spirituality of the Divine Feminine that extols the ideal of the "Lady" has a long ideological tradition in biblical religions and is still pervasive in feminist spirituality. The Eternal Feminine or the Cult of True Womanhood which I have dubbed the discourse of the "White Lady" was developed in tandem with Western colonization and romanticism that celebrated Christian white elite European women/ladies as paradigms of civilized and cultured womanhood. This ideology served to legitimate the exclusion of elite wo/men from positions of power in society and church and at the same time made them colonial representatives who mediated European culture and civilization to the so-called savages.

This image of the Eternal Feminine or the cult of the "Lady" is a projection of elite, Western, educated "Gentlemen" and clergymen who stress that wo/men's nature is complementary to that of men in order to maintain a special sphere for upper-class white wo/men. This construct does not have the liberation of every wo/man as its goal but seeks to release the repressed feminine in order to make men whole. Associated with this cult of the "White Lady" was and is a spirituality of self-alienation, submission, service, self-abnegation, dependence, manipulating power, backbiting, powerlessness, beauty and body regimen, duplicity and helplessness— "feminine" behaviors which are inculcated in and through cultural socialization, spiritual direction, and ascetic disciplines such as dieting and cos-

---

[7]See Nancy J. Berneking and Pamela Carter Joern, eds., *Re-Membering and Re-Imaging* (Cleveland: Pilgrim Press, 1995).

metic surgery. In and through traditional biblical spirituality, wo/men either internalize that they are not made in the divine image because G*d is not She but He, Lord/Slave-master/Father/Male, or they are told that if they fulfill their religious and cultural calling to supplement and complement the Divine Other, they will embody the Divine Feminine. In both cases, cultural and religious structures of self-alienation and domination are kept in place in and through biblical Wisdom spirituality and the theological articulation of the Divine as Lord.

Feminists who object to the valorization of the biblical Wisdom tradition also point out that this tradition is permanently suspect not only as an elite male tradition but also as one that, in a dualistic fashion, plays the "good" woman against the "evil" woman.[8] Such a misogynist tradition cannot be concerned with justice at all. However, other scholars who specialize in Wisdom literature have rightly objected to such a negative evaluation of the Wisdom traditions. They not only have pointed out that Wisdom discourses are permeated with the teachings of justice[9] but also agree that in the first century, prophetic-apocalyptic and sapiential (Wisdom) traditions were intertwined, integrated, and changed. Wisdom traditions espouse a cosmopolitan ethos that can respect local particularities without giving up claims to universality.

In addition, the advocates of Wisdom argue that the Wisdom traditions had long been democratized and that many of the sapiential traditions of the gospels reflect folk wisdom which very well could have been articulated by and for wo/men. Finally, they point out that feminist exegetical-historical objections to the feminist regeneration of Divine Chokmah-Sophia-Sapientia-Wisdom may also be due to different confessional locations and indebtedness to Neo-orthodox theology.

Moreover, a closer look at the biblical Wisdom traditions reveals that these traditions do not so much portray Divine Wisdom in terms of the "Lady." Wisdom is a cosmic figure delighting in the dance of creation, a "master" craftswo/man and teacher of justice. She is the leader of Her people and accompanies them on their way through history. Very unladylike, she raises her voice in public places and calls everyone who will hear her. She transgresses boundaries, celebrates life, and nourishes those who will become her friends. Her cosmic house is without walls and her table is set for all.

Hence, I suggest that biblical discourses on Divine Wisdom are still significant today not only because they are a rich resource of female lan-

---

[8]However, in fairness to the Wisdom traditions, it must be pointed out that the prophetic or apocalyptic traditions are equally suspect because they are also permeated by kyriocentric bias.

[9]See also Claudia V. Camp, *Wisdom and the Feminine in the Book of Proverbs* (Bible and Literature 11; Sheffield: Almond, 1985).

guage for G*d but also because they provide a framework for developing a feminist ecological theology of creation and a biblical spirituality of nourishment and struggle. Moreover, they embody a religious ethos that is not exclusive of other religious visions but can be understood as a part of them, since wisdom/Wisdom is celebrated in all of them. The earliest Sophia-traditions that still can be traced in the margins of early Christian works intimate a perspective that combines Jewish prophetic, Wisdom, and *basileia* (which means the political realm of G*d or G*d's vision of a transformed creation and world) traditions as central to a political, open-ended, and cosmopolitan religious vision of struggle and well-being for everyone. In short, biblical wisdom/Wisdom spirituality is a spirituality of roads and journeys, public places and open borders, nourishment and celebration. It seeks for sustenance in the struggles for justice and cultivates creation and life in fullness.

The goal of Wisdom teaching is to impose a kind of order on the myriad experiences that determine a person and thus enable one to cope with life. Wisdom teaching is an orientation to proper action, to knowing when to do what. It means engaging in value judgments that urge a certain course of action. Truthfulness, fidelity, kindness, honesty, independence, self-control, doing justice—these are all means of walking in the way of Wisdom. In short, Wisdom holds out as a promise the fullness and possibility of the "good life"; it is a search for justice and order in the world that can be discerned by experience. Wisdom teaching does not keep faith and knowledge apart, it does not divide the world into religious and secular, but provides a model for living a "mysticism of everyday things."

The Radical Democratic Learning Space of Wisdom

To understand the bible in the paradigm of the open cosmopolitan house and spiraling dance of Divine Wisdom allows us to conceptualize Scripture as an open-ended prototype rather than as an archetype that has to be repeated in every generation. It requires us to understand the bible as a site of struggle over meaning and biblical interpretation as debate and argument rather than as transcript of the unchanging, inerrant Word of G*d. It requires that we rethink notions of struggle, debate, and argument that are usually understood in terms of battle, combat, and competition. Within the radical democratic space of Wisdom-Spirit, struggle can be recognized as turning conflict into opportunity and debate and argument as fostering difference and respect for a multiplicity of voices. If we do not view debate and argument as antagonistic-bellicose forms of communication, we can practice them as rhetorical means to clarify practical and theoretical differences and to respect different feminist voices and per-

spectives as strengthening rather than weakening the diverse struggles against kyriarchal relations of domination.

Moreover, to understand the bible as nourishing bread on the way and to conceptualize biblical inquiry as searching for Divine Wisdom in, between, and outside the words of the bible requires a different understanding of language and text. Scholars have pointed to two very different understandings of language, which they have dubbed the model of transmission and the dialogic model. A literalist understanding of the bible works with a transmission model of language and text that involves the translation (or "encoding") of an idea (the revelatory Word) into a signal (bible) by a sender (G*d), the transmission of this signal to a receiver (biblical readers and interpreters), and the decoding of the signal into a message (religion, dogma, history, ethics, etc.) by the receiver.

This transmission or conduit model determines for the most part our understanding of communication. Language functions like a conduit that transfers thought bodily from one person to another. Authoritative discourses such as those in and about the bible assume that utterances and their meanings are fixed once and for all and not modifiable as they come into contact with new voices and new situations. Instead of functioning as a generator of new meaning, an authoritative text such as the bible demands our unconditional allegiance.

In contrast to the univocal function of language and text, the second type of language theory conceives of language and text not as conduit but as dialogic. Language is not a passive link in transmitting some constant information or univocal message between sender and receiver. Rather, language has the function of generating new meanings. In this second understanding of language and text, the bible can be viewed as an "utterance" that reflects both the voice producing it and the voices to which it is addressed. To understand the bible and biblical interpretation not in terms of the conduit model but in terms of the dialogic model of language and text allows one to acknowledge the new meanings that are created by the multiplicity and heterogeneity of biblical voices and their "counter words" produced in biblical interpretation.

How, then, is one to go about learning to dance in the open space of Wisdom? There are different ways to learn the dance steps and movements of the hermeneutical circle dance. The following four pedagogical models are hegemonic models of instruction and learning. These four malestream modes of learning, I argue, need to be complemented and replaced by a radical democratic pedagogical model. Since feminist biblical studies have as their goal not just to produce specialists but to empower "citizens" for actively participating in biblical deliberation and self-determining decision-making processes, they seek to break down the walls between the biblical specialist and the common reader.

The **first model** of learning and acquiring knowledge is the traditional descriptive, factual "accumulation" and "absorption" model. In this educational-communicative model, authors/teachers are the experts who collect and deposit all the available knowledge and facts in the pages of their books or lectures. Readers/students absorb this knowledge by accepting and memorizing it. They repeat it when they want to prove their knowledge about something. The Brazilian educator Paulo Freire has dubbed this model the "banking" model because it treats knowledge like monetary funds. The author/teacher owns the assets and deposits knowledge in readers/students who are seen as passive receptacles. Like capital, knowledge can be owned, sold, or stored.

The author/teacher has the authority to guarantee the value of the knowledge that readers/students receive and bank in their memories. Examinations seek to ascertain whether readers/students can accurately repeat the knowledge stored in textbooks or lecture notes. Study plans and curricular requirements make sure that all the knowledge that is deemed essential and necessary is transmitted and memorized. If you assume that this book is a textbook and contains all that you need to know about feminist biblical hermeneutics, then your major concern is to take notes and to make sure that you cover all the main topics in order to be prepared for your next test or paper.

The **second model** of learning champions the master-apprentice method. In this model of learning/reading, the author/teacher is the expert who serves as a model for his readers/students. This model is common in graduate courses and seminars. Students will always insist, for instance, that I not just present the theoretical outline of issues but that I "apply" interpretive methods and theories by analyzing and exegeting a text. They believe that they will learn the skills of interpretation by imitating the "master."

In this model, students/readers do not focus so much on the content of a book or text, as in the first model. Rather, they are interested in the technologies of exegesis and explanation. These methods are seen as rules and norms, which if followed guarantee that the true meaning of a biblical text will be found. Students/readers believe that the truth can be nailed down if one knows the right methods and is trained to use them cleanly and skillfully. The author/teacher is the "master" or expert who controls the methods and knows the answers to questions. If you are working in this mode of learning, then you will expect that this book (or course) will teach you how to do feminist biblical interpretation in the correct way so that you will be able to determine the true meaning of the text.

The **third model** of learning is the consumer model, or smorgasbord approach. In this model, readers/students pick and choose what they think is

useful. They buy books or enroll in courses as they would buy cars or clothing, either for utility or entertainment. At Harvard Divinity School, for instance, we start every semester with a "shopping period" during which students move from class to class the way readers move from shelf to shelf in bookstores in order to select the most informative, the most cutting-edge, the easiest, or the most palatable fare.

In this model, authors/teachers must act not only as experts or masters but also as salespersons who are skilled in advertising their wares. Just as the semester begins with a shopping period, so it ends with students filling out (consumer) evaluation forms rating the teacher's performance, the quality of the reading material, and the fairness of the grading system. Just as books are judged on how much they have sold or how long they have been on the *New York Times* bestseller list, so also conferences and workshops or bible study groups are judged by the numbers they have attracted. If you are operating in this mode you might have purchased this book or enrolled in this class because for one reason or another you find it useful to know something about (feminist) biblical interpretation and will recommend it to friends if you are satisfied.

The **fourth model** or learning approach could be called the therapeutic model. In this model, books or workshops are selected and evaluated in terms of whether they make you "feel good." Books, courses, or workshops should not be too demanding but should satisfy the needs of their readers/participants. Religious books or events in particular are often judged solely with regard to whether they are spiritually edifying or aesthetically pleasing. Hence, books on all kinds of forms of spirituality abound.

Biblical readings must especially address individuals and gratify their spiritual wants and longings. The purpose of these texts is to provide security and certainty in an ever-changing world and alienating society. Books and courses on how to pray and meditate with the bible are much preferred to those that seek to foster a critical engagement with it. The bible becomes an oracle for spiritual guidance that helps its readers to accept and submit to the demands of everyday life. If you are interested in this book because you want to satisfy your emotional and spiritual needs, you may be disappointed in discussions of the bible that critically interrogate it rather than seek to persuade you to accept it.

All four malestream pedagogical models and learning approaches must also be analyzed in terms of gender. In the first two models, knowledge production is coded in culturally masculine terms insofar as they stress mastery, expertise, and control of knowledge. Both approaches are at home in the malestream academy and church that until very recently have excluded wo/men from authoritative knowledge production. These

first two learning models not only construct the author/master in masculine terms but also construe readers/students in culturally feminine terms.

In contrast, the last two pedagogical models, the consumer and therapeutic models, are coded in feminine terms. They construe agency in a culturally feminine code that privatizes and makes knowledge in general and biblical-theological knowledge in particular readily available commodities. These models construct readers/students as consumers or patients who purchase religious knowledge for their own private use, enjoyment, and edification. However, neither of these approaches qualifies as a feminist liberating educational experience.

While we all have engaged in these four learning approaches at one time or another, in this book I want to invite you to move to a different model of reading/learning that can integrate the positive aspects of all four of these models without falling victim to their self-alienating and distorting powers.

Instead of seeking to give the power of interpretation to so-called popular audiences or students, scholarship often denies them the tools for investigating the ideologies, discourses, and knowledge that shape their self-identity and determine their lives. Instead of empowering students/readers as critical thinkers, education/publication in general and biblical education in particular often contribute to their self-alienation and adaptation to the values and mores of hegemonic kyriarchal societies and religions.

Learning the Ways of Wisdom

A feminist emancipatory, radical democratic model of education is interested not so much in helping students/readers to internalize traditional biblical teachings and malestream scientific knowledge but in fostering our critical thinking and self-esteem. Its basic assumption is that knowledge is publicly available to all who can think and that everyone has something to contribute to knowledge. As Ralph Ellison has observed, a democracy requires not only democratic procedures and institutions but also a particular quality of vision and civic imagination.

One of the most important contributions of sixteenth-century Reformation theology was its insistence on a radical democratization of bible reading. The Reformers put the bible in the hands of everyone and insisted that one does not need advanced training to understand it. Similarly, feminist liberationist biblical study is best understood in such a radical democratic Wisdom key as insisting that all wo/men are competent biblical interpreters. It facilitates wo/men's critical reading by fostering examination of our own presuppositions and social locations. Feminist bible study searches for freedom from cultural bias and religious preju-

dice and seeks to replace them with critical arguments that appeal to reason and the emotions. It fosters self-scrutiny and the ability to imagine ourselves in someone else's shoes and to see the world from the point of view of an other who is both like and not like ourselves. It requires us to make sure that books—even the bible—and authors/teachers do not become unquestioned "authorities."

As Seneca, a Roman Stoic philosopher of the first century C.E., warned one of his students who relied on the authority of "great men" and "great books,"

> "This is what Zeno said." But what do you say? "This is Cleanthes' view." What is yours? How long will you march under another person's orders? Take command and say something memorable of your own.... It is one thing to remember, another to know. To remember is to safeguard something entrusted to the memory. But to know is to make each thing one's own, not to depend on the text and always to look back to the teacher. "Zeno said this, Cleanthes said this." Let there be a space between you and the book. (Seneca, *Letters*, 33)

Instead of looking to "great books" and "great men," a radical democratic model of biblical reading/learning in the open house of Wisdom engages in critical questioning and debate in order to be able to arrive at a deliberative judgment about the bible's contributions to the well-being of everyone, to democratic self-determination and self-esteem. It is about choice and deliberation and the power to take charge of our own life and thought, rather than about control, dependence, obedience, and passive reception. Its style of reasoning is not combative-competitive but deliberative, engaging in conversations about values and beliefs that are most important to us rather than retreating into positivism, dogmatism, or relativism to avoid engagement with differences.

In this Wisdom model of learning, thought and study are problem oriented rather than positivistic or dogmatic, perspectival rather than relativistic. They are contextual-collaborative, grounded in the recognition that our own perspective and knowledge are limited by our social-religious location and that differences enrich our thought and life. Truth and meaning are not a given fact or hidden revelation but are achieved in critical practices of deliberation. In short, to be able to achieve a constructive engagement with difference and diversity inscribed in the bible and in our contexts, we need to become aware of the pitfalls of one-dimensional thinking that strives to find in the bible definite answers and final solutions.

The ethos of a value-free scientific pedagogy, to the contrary, is articulated within the value-system of patriarchal authority where students/

readers silently absorb the materials on which the professor/author lectures. In contrast, a radical democratic feminist model of learning seeks to foster a style of biblical learning/reading that does not undermine democratic thinking. It supports and strengthens democratic modes of reasoning by recognizing the importance of experience, plural voices, emotions, and values in the educational process.

Page duBois has warned that traditional hegemonic modes of inquiry share in a form of reasoning that is competitive and combative. Their preferred mode of ascertaining truth is adversarial debate and the honing of arguments that can withstand the most acerbic assault. This form of reasoning and argument can be likened to the practice of forensic interrogation, to methods of arrest and discipline, to "police arts," to "a dividing, a splitting, a fracturing of the logical body, a process that resembles torture."[10]

The Platonic dialogue that is prevalent in biblical hermeneutics locates truth in the mind of the master who controls question and answer. The search for truth requires hard labor, hunting it down and coercing it through persistent questioning. However, this forensic-combative context of the Platonic dialogue is not intrinsic to it, as Martha Nussbaum has shown. If situated in a deliberative rhetorical context, such critical questioning and debate are oriented not toward "winning" the argument but toward weighing and evaluating arguments in order to be able to envision and articulate a biblical reading that serves the well-being of everyone. One of the major tasks of feminist bible study consists in making conscious the mechanisms and implications of oppressive modes of knowledge production. Wo/men and other theologically muted persons must learn to demystify the dominant structures of knowledge in order to find our own intellectual voices, exercise personal choice, and achieve satisfaction in our intellectual work.

Yet, wo/men will be able to achieve these goals only if we engage in the transformation of the present malestream paradigms of biblical knowledge production, making it into a *different,* co-intentional, radical democratic paradigm of biblical learning/reading that allows scholars/authors and students/readers to become collaborators in the creation as well as in the communication of the contents and methods of biblical knowledge. In such a political learning model situated in the *ekklesia of wo/men,* both teachers/authors and students/readers recognize that knowledge is power which can serve domination or liberation. As feminists, however, we construe power, not in malestream terms as control over, but in radical democratic terms, as energy that moves us and invigorates life. No longer subscribing to the ideal of a collectivist "leaderless" mode of interaction, feminist pedagogy has moved in the past decade to recognize energizing

---

[10]Page duBois, *Torture and Truth* (New York: Routledge, 2001), 13.

authority and to work for the articulation of a democratic understanding of power and alternating leadership.

An Italian feminist group in Milan,[11] for example, has articulated the concept of the "symbolic mother," a concept which recognizes that power differentials exist, for instance, between wo/men professors and wo/men students on grounds of experience, expertise, age, etc. Hence, feminist freedom is not to be construed in libertarian terms as freedom from all constraint. Rather, it entails a personal and social debt which is owed to other wo/men. The symbolic debt each wo/man has to other wo/men is figured, however, by this brand of feminism not in radical democratic terms but in the individualistic, culturally feminine-typed concept of the "symbolic mother."

Rather than placing the articulation of the "debt to other wo/men" into the gender-framework of an essential female difference, I have suggested that we should position it within the radical democratic space opened up by the liberation struggles of marginalized people for freedom and autonomy. Following the Indian American writer Paula Gunn Allen, I would prefer to situate such a symbolic mediation within the radical democratic tradition of the "friends of Wisdom," the tradition of the wo/men of wisdom and valor which Gunn Allen has named the "grandmother's tradition."[12]

Positioned in the radical democratic Wisdom "tradition of the grandmother's society," we can engage biblical texts and traditions as rhetorical discourses within the framework of a dialogic-democratic model of learning. Such a model integrates experience and imagination, emotion and feelings, valuation and vision with critical inquiry, scientific accuracy, intellectual clarity, and responsible persuasion in the process of interpretation.

Moreover, a feminist radical democratic approach is able to assert the subjectivity and agency of wo/men in kyriarchal texts, cultures, and religions. With Alicia Suskin Ostriker, who identifies herself as "critic and poet, as Jew, woman, and (dare I say) human being," I also would insist that such a radical democratic approach is

---

[11]Maria Cristina Marcuzzo and Anna Rossi-Doria, eds., *La ricerca delle donne: Studi feministi in Italia* (Turin: Rosenberg, 1987).

[12]Some of my readers have pointed out that "grandmother's" society also re-inscribes an essentialist gender framework. However, I do not think so, since our connection to our "grandmothers" is one of roots and history rather than one of immediate maternal dependency. Moreover, whereas motherhood has been culturally idealized and institutionalized in order to limit wo/men's identity and choices, this is not so in the case of "grandmother." Rather, in Western culture ageism is rampant and older wo/men are not respected and admired for the wisdom they have accumulated through living but are discriminated against and trivialized.

engaged both theoretically and practically in the question of what will happen when the spiritual imagination of women, women who may call themselves Jews or Christian, pagans or atheists, witches or worshippers of the Great Goddess, is released into language and into history. . . . I feel desperately fractured much of the time, as anyone in a pathological culture must. But I strive for healing. And so I must confront what is toxic—but I must do more than that.[13]

Suskin Ostriker goes on to argue for a revisionist reading of the bible that no longer posits a "simple adversarial relationship between male text and female writers," and points out that "woman's re-imaginings" of the bible are "both forbidden and invited by the very text and tradition she is challenging." In her view, such a revisionist reading consists of "three sometimes overlapping forms: a hermeneutics of suspicion, a hermeneutics of desire and a hermeneutics of indeterminacy." She reasons that a hermeneutics of desire, which she characterizes as "you see what you need to see," has always been practiced in traditional biblical exegesis and maintains that a hermeneutics of indeterminacy which fosters plural readings will be most significant for the future:

> Human civilization has a stake in plural readings. We've seen this at least since the eighteenth century when the notion of religious tolerance was invented to keep the Christian sects from killing each other. The notion of racial tolerance came later. . . . Most people need "right" answers, just as they need "superior" races. . . . At this particular moment it happens to be feminists and other socially marginal types who are battling for cultural pluralism. Still, this is an activity we're undertaking on behalf of humanity, all of whom would be the happier, I believe, were they to give up their addiction to final solutions.[14]

Because of the all-too-human need to use the bible for bolstering our identity over and against that of others, because of our need to use the bible as a security blanket, as an avenue for controlling the Divine, or as a means of possessing revelatory knowledge as an exclusive privilege, we are ever tempted to build up securing walls and to keep out those who are not like us. The Jewish feminist Asphodel Long has pointed to the poison within such walls by likening the bible

---

[13]Alicia Suskin Ostriker, *Feminist Revision and the Bible* (Cambridge: Blackwell, 1993), 30.

[14]Ostriker, 122–123.

to a magnificent garden of brilliant plants, some flowering, some fruiting, some in seed, some in bud, shaded by trees of age old, luxurious growth. Yet in the very soil which gives it life the poison has been inserted.... This poison is that of misogyny, the hatred of women, half the human race.[15]

Hence, feminist biblical inquiry not only celebrates multi-voiced texts and interpretations but also seeks to identify criteria for naming the "poison" of racism, misogyny, homophobia, poverty, and imperialism inscribed in biblical texts and their interpretations. It seeks to place on all biblical texts the label: "Caution! Could be dangerous to your health and survival!" Institutionalized religion as well as academic institutions have always been and still are constantly building high walls of exclusion and protection. They cultivate not only the beauty of the garden but also its poisonous fruits of misogyny and kyriarchy by turning living wisdom into kyriarchal authority that demands obedience and submission of will and intellect. Feminist biblical studies in turn seek to identify the killing potential of the bible; they attempt to scale down and to undo canonical or disciplinary walls in order to enjoy the freedom of the Spirit's breeze and the nourishment of wisdom/Wisdom words.

The Emancipatory Wisdom Paradigm of Biblical Interpretation

To engage in the spiraling Wisdom dance of biblical interpretation we need to pay attention not only to the language and pedagogical models of biblical studies but also to the ways in which we read and understand. Those of us who can read generally take reading skills for granted. We are not conscious that we have learned how to approach and how to read a text in order to achieve understanding. We are not aware that how we approach and read the bible is determined by institutions such as schools, the media, or churches, synagogues, and mosques.

Even those of us who do not read much or are not able to read at all are affected by cultural patterns of understanding and the "reading schools" that support them. Such "reading patterns" or "schools of understanding" have great impact on how we read the bible because the bible is not only Sacred Scripture for people in biblical religions but also a Western cultural classic. Hence, we have been trained to "make meaning" out of the most obtuse texts because they are found in the bible.

These "meaning-making" conventions and institutions that determine biblical readings, interpretations, hearing, and perceptions form para-

---

[15]Asphodel P. Long, *In a Chariot Drawn by Lions: The Search for the Female in Deity* (London: The Woman's Press, 1992), 195.

digms of approaches. In order to make it possible for wo/men to become conscious of the paradigms of biblical understanding that we have been taught and have internalized, I developed a method of paradigm-analysis or paradigm-criticism more than twenty years ago. Thomas Kuhn's categories of "scientific paradigm" and "heuristic model" provide a theoretical framework for comprehending how we read, hear, or understand the bible. According to Kuhn, a paradigm articulates a common ethos and constitutes a community of readers/listeners/viewers formed by common institutions and systems of knowledge.

Paradigm criticism works with a typology of shifting practices that shape and determine the discipline of biblical studies and biblical interpretation on the whole. Such paradigms or "schools" can exist alongside each other. They are not necessarily exclusive of each other but can work in corrective interaction with each other. Hence, Wisdom hermeneutics requires that we learn not only how to exegete texts but also how to chart, develop, and teach such interpretive paradigms. A shift in a research/reading/listening/viewing paradigm of interpretation can occur only if and when the institutional conditions of interpretation change and a different approach to biblical interpretation emerges. Such a paradigm shift in biblical interpretation takes place in people's minds, however, only when we become conscious of how we have been taught to read/listen/view/interpret. Whereas all of us have been taught and have internalized the reading conventions of one or more of the following interpretive paradigms, we have not learned to engage the emerging emancipatory paradigm if we are not feminists or liberationists.

The Doctrinal-Revelatory Paradigm

For centuries the prevalent paradigm of Christian biblical interpretation has been the doctrinal-revelatory paradigm, which understands the biblical record as Sacred Scripture and revealed Word of G*d. This paradigm of biblical interpretation is at home in biblical communities of faith. The bible is the holy book of Jews, Christians, and Muslims, albeit in very different forms and ways. Since I write from a Catholic Christian location, I will sketch the different approaches or models of interpretation which Christian bible study has developed over its long history.

In the doctrinal-revelatory paradigm, the bible fulfills a revelatory function. Throughout Scripture G*d has spoken to us for the purpose of leading us to the love of G*d and neighbor. Biblical interpretation has the task of decoding what the signs constituting the biblical texts are meant to say. In order to get at the revelatory meaning of biblical texts, two methods —that of typology and that of allegory—have been developed. The beginnings of both methods can be traced back to the bible.

The *typological* method reads biblical figures or events as types of Christ or the church and the believer. For instance, Paul understands

Christ as the New Adam or the New Moses. In such a typological interpretation, the Syrophoenician wo/man, for instance, becomes the prototype of the gentile church, and Mary, the mother of Jesus, becomes the
prototype of redeemed humanity.

The *allegorical* method does not so much look for the meaning under-
neath the text but seeks to establish the deeper spiritual sense to which the
text refers. For instance, it identifies "the holy hill" from which G*d speaks
in Psalm 3:4 with Christ or the church. Or, in the parable of the good
Samaritan, it likens the one fallen into the hands of robbers to the soul, the
priest and Levite who passed by to priests and bishops, the innkeeper to
Christ, and the inn to the church. Thus, every feature of a story receives a
deeper spiritual meaning. The allegorical method is concerned with pre-
serving the integrity and sacredness of the text, especially of those texts
that speak of G*d in a very anthropomorphic (human) manner.

This ancient and medieval method of interpretation seeks to establish a
fourfold sense of Scripture: the literal (historical), the tropological (moral),
the allegorical, and the anagogical (future oriented) meaning of a text.
Pope Gregory the Great likened the act of reading the bible to the building of a house: upon the historical foundation we erect the walls with the
help of our spiritual readings and we color them by the grace of moral
teaching. This method has been summed up in the following ditty:

> The letter shows us what G*d and our ancestors did,
> The allegory shows us where our faith is hid,
> The moral meaning gives rules of daily life,
> The anagogy shows us where we end our life.

Jewish hermeneutics developed a similar but distinctive method of
interpretation that was called *PaRDeS* (Paradise): *Peshat* seeks for the
plain sense of the text, *Remez* means the implied or allegorical sense,
Derush involves legal and narrative exegesis, comparing terms from different places, and *Sod* is the mystical sense of a text.

Beginning with Humanism and the Protestant Reformation, this open-
ended dynamic mode of medieval interpretation changed. The Reformation taught that "Scripture alone" (*sola scriptura*) is the foundation of
faith, that it is self-interpreting and can be understood by everyone.
Luther used the gospel as the "canon" by which to determine whether
biblical texts belonged to Sacred Scripture and he formulated the dogmatic principle "what brings forth Christ" as the measuring rod.

The orthodox successors of the Reformers went further by introducing
the dogma of "verbal inspiration" and the principle of biblical infallibility.
They insisted that the bible was identical with the Word of G*d. Thus, they
could use the bible as the infallible foundation and proof-text for a set of
dogmatic convictions. Interpretation was now a set of rules allowing us to

read the text in such a way as to confirm our dogmatic pre-understanding. The so-called pietistic movement, in turn, deplored such an objectivist reading, stressing the personal spiritual experience of interpreters.

Literalist fundamentalism in turn insists that the biblical message proclaims universal moral values and truth. Like modern orthodoxy and modern science, it claims that this truth can be positively established and proven. Thus, it stresses verbal inspiration and the bible as the direct, inerrant Word of G*d to be accepted by Christians without question. This emphasis on verbal inerrancy asserts that the bible and its interpretation transcend ideology and particularity. It obscures the interests at work in biblical texts and interpretations and reduces faith to intellectual assent rather than seeing it as a way of life. Such revelatory positivism promotes belief in the bible rather than faith in G*d.

Biblicist fundamentalism not only reads the bible through the theological lenses of individualized and privatized bourgeois religion, but also asserts militantly that its approach is the only legitimate Christian one. It thereby obscures the fact that different Christian communities and biblical religions use the bible differently; it ignores the reality that throughout the centuries different models of biblical interpretation have been and still are being developed. Although such dogmatic biblicism berates mainline religious groups for succumbing to modernity and secularization, it has itself adopted a particular modern rationalist understanding of religion and the bible as the only approach that is truly Christian. In spite of the fact that fundamentalism combats modern liberal religion and biblical criticism, it is itself a thoroughly modern mode of interpretation. Its ethos has been shaped in confrontation with modern science and critical thinking.

The "Scientific"-Positivist Paradigm

The second, or scientific-factual, paradigm of biblical studies was developed in the context of the European Enlightenment over and against the control and authority of the churches. Its social institutional location is the Enlightenment university. The scientific principle of the Enlightenment was institutionalized in the modern university as the empiricist paradigm of knowledge that gives primary import to evidence, data, and empirical inquiry, that is, to the "logic of facts." This modern logic relies on abstraction for the sake of rigor, evidence, and precision; it strives to establish a single true meaning of the text in order to claim universality for its interpretations. It does so, however, not on theological but on methodological scientific grounds.

Although the scientific paradigm demands objectivity, disinterestedness, and value-neutrality in order to control what constitutes the legitimate, scientifically established, true meaning of the text, it is patently Eurocentric. Just as European and American historiography as an academic

discipline sought in the last quarter of the nineteenth century to prove it-self an objective science analogous to the natural sciences, so also did biblical studies. Scientific historiography ostensibly sought to establish "facts" and "data" objectively, free from philosophical considerations or political interests. It was determined to hold strictly to facts and evidence, not to sermonize or to moralize but to tell the simple truth—in short, to narrate things as they really happened. Historical science is seen as a technique that applies critical methods to the evaluation of sources, which in turn are understood as data and evidence. The mandate to avoid theo-retical considerations and normative concepts in the immediate encounter with the text functions to ensure that the resulting historical accounts will be accurate and objective, free from any ideology.

Since biblical scholarship in the U.S. developed in the political con-text of several heresy trials at the turn to the twentieth century (for in-stance, the heresy trials of the Presbyterian David Swing in 1874, Charles A. Briggs in 1891, and Arthur Cushman McGiffert in 1900), its rhetoric of disinterested objectivity tends to reject all overt religious, socio-political, or theological engagement as "unscientific." The aspiration of biblical studies in particular and religious studies in general to "scientific" status in the academy and their claim to universal, unbiased modes of inquiry deny their hermeneutical-rhetorical character and mask their socio-historical lo-cation as well as their socio-political or ecclesiastical interests.

Insofar as biblical scientism insists that it is able to isolate the "facts" or the universal "truth" from the bible's multivalent and often contradic-tory meanings, it denies its own particular Eurocentric perspectives and kyriarchal rhetorical aims, which are indebted to the European Enlighten-ment. By objectifying, antiquating, reifying, and privatizing biblical scriptures it is in danger of playing into the hands of fundamentalist bibli-cism, which also claims that it can prove with certainty the univocal "word of G*d" in the bible as a "fact." Since this positivistic "mindset" of scientific biblical criticism is not just at home in the academy but has be-come popularized by literalist fundamentalism, it is especially important to explore how much we have internalized the presuppositions of the scien-tific-factual paradigm.

The Hermeneutic-Cultural Paradigm

The third, or hermeneutic-cultural, paradigm underscores the rhetorical character of biblical knowledge and acknowledges the symbolic, multi-dimensional power of biblical texts. It either ascribes personified status to the text in order to construe it as a dialogue partner or it sees the text as a multicolored tapestry of meaning. This paradigm likens the reading of the bible to the reading of the "great books" or classics of Western culture, whose greatness does not consist in their accuracy as records of facts, but

depends chiefly on their symbolic power to transfigure human experience
and symbolic systems of meaning.

The hermeneutic-cultural paradigm is not so much concerned with
proving dogmas or establishing "facts" as with understanding alien texts
and peoples. It does not assume that the text represents a given divine
revelation or a window to historical reality. It also does not understand
historical sources as data and evidence but sees them as perspectival discourses constructing a range of symbolic universes. Since alternative
symbolic universes engender competing definitions of the world, they
cannot be reduced to one single, definitive meaning. Competing interpretations are therefore not simply either right or wrong. Rather, they constitute different ways of reading and constructing historical and religious
meaning. Texts have a surplus of meaning that can never be fully mined.

A *postmodern* model of interpretation seeks to move beyond the
ethos and mindset of the modern hermeneutic model not in order to abolish the achievements of modernity but in order to deepen and enhance
them. Modernity—a deeply European event that took place at many levels from the mid-sixteenth century onward—questions all conventional
ways of doing things, substituting authorities of its own which are based
on science, economic growth, democracy, or law. It seeks to conquer the
world in the name of Reason, on which the social order is to be founded.

The scientific principle of modernity has engendered three major correctives that underscore the complexity, particularity, and political corrup-
tion of reality. The *aesthetic* corrective stresses experiential concreteness
and intuitive imagination over rationalist abstraction; the *cultural* corrective insists, over and against the universalizing tendencies of the Enlightenment, on cultural autonomy and on tradition as the wisdom and
heritage of a particular community; and the *political* corrective asserts
that there is no pure reason as instrument of knowledge that can lead to
a just society. In the beginning was not pure reason but power. The institutions of so-called pure reason—the sciences, scholarship, and the
university—hide from themselves their own complicity in societal agen-
das of power.

These three correctives seek to move scholarly discourses beyond
Western modernity without relinquishing its emancipatory achievements.
Most important, by critically demonstrating that the standard for the Enlightenment's claims about selfhood, reason, and universality was the
elite "Western Gentleman," feminist thinkers have shown that the rights
and knowledge of the modern elite male subject, the "man of reason"
(Genevieve Lloyd), were underwritten by the negation of such rights to
his devalued others, such as wives, children, slaves, aliens, natives, and
other disenfranchised wo/men. At this crossing point, postmodern
hermeneutic-cultural and emancipatory-postcolonial analyses meet in

their critique of modernity, whose achievements have been bought at the price of colonialism and slavery.

Like the modern "scientific"-positivist paradigm of biblical criticism, the hermeneutic-cultural approach to biblical interpretation is also located in universities, divinity schools, and other cultural institutions. Whereas a decade ago the historical-positivist and literary-formalist paradigms of scientific biblical interpretation reigned in the Anglo-American academy, today hermeneutical and postmodern epistemological discussions that are critical of the positivist-scientific ethos of biblical studies abound. Feminist and liberation theological interpretation have played a great part in the postmodern hermeneutical transformation of academic biblical scholarship.

While the postmodern hermeneutic-cultural paradigm has successfully destabilized the certitude of the scientific objectivist paradigm in biblical studies, it still asserts its own scientific value-neutral and a-theological character. Since it rejects any attempt to move from kyriocentric text to the socio-historical situation of struggle that either has generated the text or determines its function today, it tends to result in a playful proliferation of textual meanings that is not only pluralistic but also relativistic and seemingly eschews all truth claims. Hence, like the "scientific"-positivist paradigm, so also this postmodern hermeneutic-cultural paradigm of biblical studies is not capable of addressing the increasing insecurities of globalized inequality or of accepting the constraints that the ethical imperative of emancipatory movements places on the relativizing proliferation of meaning.

Moreover, it must not be overlooked that in modernity all three hegemonic paradigms of biblical studies have developed in conjunction not only with modern rationalism but also with European colonialism. The American Heritage Dictionary defines colonialism as a "policy by which a nation maintains or extends its control over foreign dependencies" that are called "colonies." Without question, the bible and biblical studies have worked hand in glove with Western colonialism. This is aptly expressed in the pithy saying ascribed to Bishop Tutu and others: "When the missionaries arrived they had the bible and we had the land. Now we have the bible and they have the land." Missionaries came to Asia or Africa not only in order to preach the gospel and to make converts but also in order to civilize and educate the heathens.

The Rhetorical-Emancipatory Paradigm

In the past two decades a new paradigm of interpretation has been evolving, one that inaugurates not just a hermeneutic-scientific but also an ethical-political turn. This paradigm of biblical interpretation is actually not new at all, but has a long history in political-radical democratic struggles for

emancipation. It is this paradigm that best embodies the "open house" or "school" of wisdom/Wisdom.

This fourth paradigm is not so much interested in dogmatic proof, spiritual edification, scientific facts, or cultural sublimation. Rather, it investigates the ways in which biblical texts exercise influence and power in social and religious life. Our commitment to change structures of domination and values of dehumanization compels us to explore how biblical texts function in specific social locations and religious contexts. Working within this paradigm we learn to investigate how the bible is used to inculcate mindsets and attitudes of submission and dependency as "obedience" to the will of G*d that dispose us to accept and internalize violence and prejudice.

In order to position ourselves theoretically and practically within this emerging critical emancipatory paradigm, we have to interrogate biblical texts, questions, methods, and strategies of interpretation as to their function in political and personal self-understandings and public convictions. To do so we need, first, to carefully analyze what stands emotionally, intellectually, or theologically in the way of our engaging in the paradigm shift from a kyriarchal Eurocentric to a radical egalitarian cosmopolitan model of biblical reading.

Although this paradigm shift has been under way for quite some time and has brought either ferment or upheaval—depending on one's political perspective—to the once stable field of biblical and religious studies, it has not been able to unseat the positivist-scientific or esthetic-cultural, disinterested, ethos of the discipline. Hence, it also has not yet been successful in fashioning a kind of biblical reading that no longer restricts its audience either to the academy or to organized religion but attempts to make available to a wider public research that is ethically accountable.

Since this fourth paradigm is still in the process of articulation and has not yet been able to create its own institutional structures, it has been difficult to give it its proper name. I have alternatively dubbed it the "pastoral-theological," the "liberationist-cultural," the "rhetorical-ethical," or the "rhetorical-political" paradigm. I have finally settled on the label "rhetorical-emancipatory" in order to articulate its method and goals which are to understand biblical texts not as scientific-descriptive but as rhetorical-political —that is, as texts addressed to an audience with whom they argue and whom they seek to persuade.

Although, just like the expression "feminist," the term "emancipation" is often used in a derogatory fashion—in German, for instance, feminists are often labeled negatively *Emanzen*—the word nevertheless recalls the process of liberation from slavery and tutelage. It is therefore an appropriate word for an interpretive approach that has as its goal the overcoming of structures of domination and the achieving of well-being

for everyone. Whatever its proper name will turn out to be, this fourth paradigm seeks to redefine the self-understanding of biblical interpretation in ethical, rhetorical, political, cultural, and emancipatory terms. It understands the biblical reader to be a "public," "transformative," "connected," or "integrated" subject who is able to communicate with variegated publics and seeks to achieve personal, social, and religious transformation for justice and well-being.

In contrast to postmodern criticism, the voices from the margins of biblical studies insist that the subjugated others cannot afford to abandon the notion of being subjects or agents, and the possibility of knowing the world differently. Rather, we insist that we who are the "subordinated others" must engage in a political and theoretical process of constituting ourselves as subjects of knowledge and history. We have to use what we know about the world and about wo/men's lives for critiquing the bible and biblical readings and for constructing a heterogeneous political biblical spirituality that allows for the recognition of particular voices and fosters appreciation of differences.

Studying the history of biblical interpretation from the perspective of emancipatory movements helps us realize that biblical interpretation has been articulated for the most part not only by elite, Western-educated clergymen but also in order to benefit Western culture and capitalist interests. A Western fundamentalist or scientific approach declares its own culturally particular readings as universal divine revelation or scientific facts that may not be questioned. In this model of reading, Scripture either becomes an absolute oracle of the will of G*d which cannot be questioned or challenged but must be obeyed or it becomes a storehouse of antiquity. Either the bible reveals timeless truth, universal principles, and definite answers to modern-day problems and questions, or it is a repository of historical and cultural facts. The form of biblical interpretation most closely associated with colonialism is manifested not only in otherworldly evangelicism and literalist fundamentalism, which are oriented toward the salvation of the soul and receiving Jesus in one's heart, but also in scientific-objectivist Eurocentric biblical scholarship.

Whenever we read/hear/interpret a biblical or any other text, we read/hear/interpret it by engaging one or more of these paradigms of interpretation. But whereas the three hegemonic malestream paradigms of interpretation do not call for a critical process of reading, the emancipatory paradigm makes explicit the hermeneutical lenses with which it approaches the text. While the others obfuscate the fact that they also operate within socio-political and religious analytic frameworks, the emancipatory paradigm openly confesses that it engages in biblical interpretation for the sake of conscientization. Hence, it spells out its analytic lenses or eyeglasses—that is, theoretical frameworks—which are deployed in the

process of reading. Such lenses are the analytical categories with which we approach the biblical text.

In short, if we want to become "liberated" from the interpretive conventions we have learned, we must become conscious of how such "regimes of truth"—to use a concept of Michel Foucault—affect our understanding of the bible and of ourselves. Biblical interpretation is not just something for the intellectual "ivory tower" or the clerical ghetto. Rather, biblical inquiry is important for all of us. In the open "school-house" of Wisdom we learn to ask: How has biblical interpretation been used and how is the bible still used either to protect powerful interests or to challenge them and engender socio-cultural, political, and religious change? How has the bible been used to define public discourse and groups of people? What are the mechanisms that obscure the cultural understanding of society and religion that is articulated in and through biblical texts?

Is—and how is—Scripture used to marginalize certain people, to legitimate racism and other languages of hate, or to intervene in discourses of injustice? Do I attempt to absolve the bible from such negative values and effects in order not to see how I have internalized them? Do I reject the bible and its prejudices in order to show that I am free from them? Do I think something is not true if it cannot be proven as a fact? Do I think that the bible should be read for edification and not be torn down by criticism? These and similar questions may help us to diagnose how one or more interpretive paradigms have affected not only how we "read" but also how we understand ourselves and others.

I would like to conclude by looking at a biblical text in order to elucidate the different questions being asked and approaches being taken in the space of each paradigm:

> As in all the churches [*ekklesiai* = assemblies] of the saints, the wo/men should be silent. For they are not permitted to speak but should be subordinate, as even the law says. If there is anything they desire to know, let them ask their husbands at home. For it is shameful for a woman to speak in church [*ekklesia* = assembly/congress]. What, did the word of G*d originate with you, or are you the only ones it has reached? (1 Corinthians 14:33b-36, RSV)

The dogmatic-literal interpretation of the first paradigm has used this text as a scriptural proof-text for the exclusion of wo/men from preaching, teaching, and public speaking. The doctrine that Scripture interprets Scripture has argued, for instance, that the equality referred to in Galatians 3:28 must be interpreted in light of this text as equality in heaven or as equality of souls but not as equality in the church. Those advocating wo/men's

emancipation in turn have insisted that this text must be understood in light of Galatians as a time-conditioned and culture-bound statement of Paul but not as divine revelation. Spiritual readings of this text in turn have exhorted wo/men to accept their secondary status as the will of G*d and to respect their husbands and/or fathers in Christ as spiritual directors.

Interpreters working within the framework of the second, scientific paradigm have argued that this text was not written by the Apostle Paul but that it was added later by one of his students. Historical reconstructive attempts have pointed out that the text tells us much about the agency of wo/men in the Corinthian church. Such an injunction would not have been necessary if wo/men had not been speaking and arguing in the assemblies. Others have pointed out that the Greek word for wo/man (γυνη) can also mean wife and that this meaning seems to be more adequate. Social-scientific exegesis in turn has looked at the social-cultural Mediterranean context and pointed out that this text fits perfectly into such a context.

The hermeneutical approach of the third paradigm exhorts us to become conscious of our presuppositions and life-relationship to the subject matter of the text. Hence, wo/men will read this text differently from churchmen if they read it in a feminist way, seeing themselves condemned to second-class citizenship by this text. Churchmen in turn will typically identify and side with Paul as a pastor who had to find a solution for a difficult situation. However, both are admonished that in the process of interpretation they should eliminate as far as possible their pre-understandings in order to achieve a true understanding of the text, figured as a "fusion of horizons." An empathic reading of the text seeks to respect and appropriate the meaning engendered by the text.

A postmodern approach in turn argues that meaning does not reside in the text but in the reader. In the process of reading 1 Corinthians 14 wo/men will produce a multiplicity of meanings that should not be reduced to a single "true" meaning. Rather, all readers deserve our respectful understanding. Both wo/men who value this text as spiritual guidance and wo/men who reject it produce "feminist" meanings.

Interpreting the text within the fourth—emancipatory—paradigm will first of all ask for the relations of power inscribed in the text and its functions in contemporary contexts. This approach locates the power of meaning-making both in the text and in the reader/listener/interpreter. It points out that 1 Corinthians 14 is a public political text that has served to legitimate and spiritually inculcate traditional kyriarchal gender relations not only in first-century Corinth but also throughout the centuries down to today. Hence, its critical analysis is important not only on theological-religious but also on cultural-societal grounds.

A feminist emancipatory approach seeks to lift into consciousness that this text advocates and inculcates relations of domination and sub-

mission. It warns interpreters not to read 1 Corinthians 14 as the expression of Paul's Jewish patriarchal mindset, which reinforces the "Law," because such a reading would perpetuate and re-inscribe Christian anti-Judaism. It also points out that the text does not speak about all wo/men but rather about wo/men who had elite status, either because they were married or because they were virgins. Such an interpretation makes connections with other scriptural texts of submission, not in order to establish this text as a secondary deutero-Pauline text but in order to point out how ideologies of subordination are interconnected. It indicates the differing effects of this text in the lives of wo/men who are different because of their race, culture, class, or colonial subjection. It urges readers to evaluate this text and to reject it as "divine revelation."

If, for example, within the doctrinal paradigm readers/listeners/viewers have learned to understand biblical authority in terms of kyriarchal obedience, they will accept this text as the revelatory and normative word of G*d, which does not allow for wo/men's ordination into positions of power. If readers operate within this paradigm but from a liberation theological perspective, they will try to find a way to argue that Paul's demand is not oppressive but liberating because it frees wo/men from the temptations of power. Within the historical and literary positivist paradigms, wo/men readers are socialized into seeking scientific "facticity." They have to prove their disinterestedness in the significance of Paul's statement and may only debate whether Paul actually wrote it. They are able, however, to produce such a reading only if they do not reflect on the kyriarchal tendencies of the scientific ethos that marginalizes and objectifies wo/men as the "others" of elite white Western "Gentlemen." The ethos of "scientific mastery and academic excellence" thereby prohibits not only a feminist but also an anti-imperialist reading, preventing readers/hearers/interpreters from asking, for instance, what role this text has played in the lives of wo/men colonialized by Christianity.

Equally, if a reading of 1 Corinthians 14 in the framework of the hermeneutical-cultural paradigm does not engage in an analysis of power relations but focuses on the skillful rhetoric of Paul that persuades readers to understand this injunction in light of the encomium on love in chapter 13, it will overlook how this rhetoric of love can turn into violence. If one reads this text primarily as a religious but not as a cultural text, one may indict and reject Christianity while overlooking how this text still determines cultural relations today. A critical emancipatory reading that focuses on the kyriarchal power relations inscribed in the text and its history of effects, in contrast, is able to critically assess the impact of such a biblical text on both religion and culture, church and society in the past and today.

If you have followed me and tried to identify the interpretive paradigm with which you or your teacher approach a text such as 1 Corinthians 14, you will have noticed that you generally operate out of a primary

paradigm of interpretation but that the other reading paradigms are not quite absent from your own engagement with the text. Paradigms are not totally exclusive of each other; they are overlapping and often share a common institutional basis. However, you also will have noticed that paradigm analysis helps you to locate the approach which you have internalized. Thus paradigm criticism is a critical tool or "spiritual practice" that allows us to identify and name the regimes of truth and hermeneutical frameworks that determine our biblical readings. In this section I have argued contrary to Pope Gregory the Great that our readings of the bible should not build up the walls of the house which we then "color by the grace of moral teaching." Rather, we need to tear down the disciplinary walls erected by dogmatic, scientific, and cultural interpretive paradigms so that the enlivening breath of Spirit-Wisdom can blow through it.

The open cosmic house of Divine Wisdom has no exclusive walls or boundaries, no fortifications or barricades to separate and shut up the insiders from the outsiders, the bible from its surrounding world. Wisdom imagination engenders a different understanding of the bible. To approach the bible as Wisdom's dwelling of cosmic dimensions means to acknowledge its multi-valence and its openness to change. It means giving up the attempt to use it as a "security blanket" and recognizing that the free spaces between its seven pillars invite the Spirit to blow where it wills.

> Wisdom has built Her house,
> She has set up Her seven pillars.
> She has slaughtered Her beasts,
> She has mixed Her wine,
> She also has set Her table.
> She has sent out Her wo/men ministers
> to call from the highest places in the town . . .
> "Come eat of my bread
> and drink of the wine I have mixed.
> Leave immaturity, and live,
> And walk in the way of Wisdom."
> (Proverbs 9:1-3, 5-6)

Wisdom's inviting biblical table with the bread of sustenance and the wine of celebration is set in a temple with seven pillars that allow the spirit of fresh air to blow through it. This image seeks to replace the understanding of canonical and scholarly authority as limiting, controlling, and exclusive authority. Instead, it understands the power of the bible in terms of the original Latin meaning of *augere/auctoritas* as enhancing, nurturing, and enriching creativity. Biblical authority and biblical interpretation in the paradigm of Wisdom foster creativity, strength, self-affirmation, and freedom, inviting spiraling movement and cosmic dance.

Deepening Movement

Elisabeth Schüssler Fiorenza, *Jesus: Miriam's Child and Sophia's Prophet* (New York: Continuum, 1994), 131–190.

Moving Steps[16]

- Do you feel excited, resistant, or anxious about engaging Wisdom Ways? In what way is this an empowering and liberating step? Would you say that there is a place for wisdom/Wisdom in your own life?

- Some of you may never have heard of Divine Wisdom-Sophia. Others may have a deep relationship with Her. Many of you might call Her by quite different names. No matter what your relation to Divine Wisdom, every reader will have a different understanding of who She is. How do you envision Sophia-Wisdom? What does She look like?

- How do you feel about envisioning the Divine as a wo/man? How does Wisdom's gender shape your own self-understanding? If you pray, are you able to pray to Divine Wisdom? Reflect on your emotional reactions to worshiping the Divine in the gestalt of a wo/man.

- Identify the four malestream pedagogical models and reflect on their relative drawbacks and bonuses. Which model of learning was predominant in your religious upbringing and education? Have you had any learning experiences within the radical democratic model of education? Do you enjoy debate and deliberation?

Movement Exercise

Use worksheet 2 to chart the four interpretive paradigms. Choose one of the quoted texts about Divine Wisdom and read it from the perspective of each of the paradigms discussed. Into which paradigm of interpretation have you been socialized? Are you working with one or more paradigms? Do you find thinking in paradigms threatening or empowering?

---

[16]I thank Kim Smiley, Gospel Stories of Wo/men, Fall 2000, for formulating most of these "exercises."

Paradigms of Biblical Interpretation

Paradigms and models are not exclusive of each other but are alternative reading strategies which are learned.

I. DOCTRINAL-REVELATORY PARADIGM

Magic/Mythic model: dictated word of G*d

Proof-text model: proofs for teachings of the church

Spiritual model: immediate relevance and instant edification

Moral model: rules or principles valid for all times
[Criterion: Augustine and Gregory—Throughout Scripture, G*d speaks to us for this purpose alone: to lead us to the love of G*d and neighbor; what is revealed *for the sake of our salvation*]

Medieval Method: CHRISTIAN—Classical model: fourfold sense of Scripture—literal; tropological (moral); allegorical (pertains to church); anagogical (eschatological). JEWISH—*PaRDeS* (Paradisical Garden): *Peshat* = plain sense of Tanakh; *Remez* = implied or allegorical sense; *Derush* = legal and narrative exegesis; *Sod* = mystical sense

Basic Assumption: divine revelation: Christian—Old and New Testament; Jewish—written and oral Torah

II. "SCIENTIFIC"-POSITIVIST PARADIGM

1. Historical Paradigm

Positivist Facticity model: sources provide scientific facts and accurate descriptions

History of Religions model: religious texts—cultural contexts

Tradition Historical model: form and redaction criticism—traces traditions back to origins

Social Historical model: description of social world

Method: historical-critical analysis—univocal understanding of language

Basic Assumption: chasm between the past and today—world behind the text

2. Literary-Anthropological-Sociological Paradigm

Literary-Formalist model: linguistic-structuralist analysis—text as given—only world of text

Anthropological-Sociological model: sociological-anthropological scientific models

Method: literary/sociological/anthropological, scientific analysis—univocal understanding of language

Basic Assumption: chasm between text and world / past and present societies

III. HERMENEUTIC-CULTURAL PARADIGM

Historical-Application model: separation of tasks—*meant:* scholar; *meaning today:* theologian

Historical-Dialogical model: fusion of horizons

Literary-Dialogical model: reader-response criticism

Theological-Address model: text always has meaning—text as language event—submission

Method: dialogue between text and context / text and reader

Basic Assumption: equivocal understanding of language; surplus of meaning—endless play of meaning

IV. RHETORICAL-EMANCIPATORY PARADIGM

Ideology Critical model: texts produce and are produced by interests and power relations; postmodern deconstruction and destabilization of texts—nothing outside text; self is constructed by reading

Liberationist Hermeneutical model: praxis of struggle, ideological suspicion; theological suspicion; exegetical suspicion; new interpretation and praxis [Segundo]

Multicultural Postcolonial model: different social-cultural-religious locations: pluralism of meanings

Critical Feminist Liberationist model: (1) socio-political analysis: experience-systemic analysis; (2) hermeneutical mediation: suspicion-reconstruction-evaluation-imagination; (3) goal: struggle, change, and transformation

Method: socio-political, symbolic-rhetorical analysis; meaning of texts is indeterminate but limited by contexts

Basic Assumption: texts have persuasive and performative power in particular situations—they function to legitimate or challenge the status quo

CHAPTER II

Roadblocks in Wisdom's Ways

To participate in the spiraling dance of Wisdom and to travel on the road to the open house of Justice we need first to remove some heavy stones that block our way and hinder our steps. *The Concise Oxford English Dictionary*[1] defines roadblock as "a barrier or barricade on a road, especially one set up by the authorities to stop and examine traffic." This dictionary definition emphasizes "the authorities" that have the power to erect roadblocks and to stop us from moving forward and from continuing on the ways to greater justice and invigorating wisdom.

Some of these roadblocks may just be obstacles on the way.[2] Others may block access to the road, or discourage us from pursuing our goal. Still others may just be pebbles in our shoes that make walking in the ways of Wisdom difficult. Such obstacles are usually unacknowledged assumptions and unconscious prejudices that need to become conscious if we are to fruitfully engage the ideas of this book and ponder Wisdom's multifaceted ways of justice. In this chapter we will examine these roadblocks and the authorities that keep them in place so that we may be able to move along Wisdom's liberating path of justice.

> To the saints she gave the wages of their labors;
> She led them by a marvelous road,
> She Herself was their shelter by day
> And their starlight through the night.
> (Wisdom 10:17)

---

[1] I owe this reference to Kim Smiley, Midterm Paper for Gospel Stories of Wo/men, Fall 2000.

[2] Some readers objected to the metaphor of roadblock because it suggests a unitary road for feminist biblical interpretation. Yet, on the contrary, the metaphor suggests that roadblocks and the "heaviness" of our assumptions and internalized "authorities" prevent us from seeing that there are many different paths to Wisdom's abode.

One of the first roadblocks that might have already hindered your forward movement and engagement with this book is the f-word, "feminism." Since the notion of feminism/feminist is hotly contested both in the general public and within the academy, many shy away from it. In her book *Feminism Is for Everybody,* the cultural critic and feminist theorist bell hooks notes that most people find it exciting to hear of her work as a cultural critic. Yet she says,

> Feminist theory—that's the place where the questions stop. Instead I tend to hear all about the evil of feminism and the bad feminists: how they "hate" men. How "they" want to go against nature and god; how "they" are all lesbians; how "they" are taking all the jobs and making the world hard for white men, who do not stand a chance.[3]

Hence, like bell hooks, I find it necessary to explain how I use the word. For many, feminism is still (or again) a "dirty word" associated with ideological bias and heresy. At a time when Rush Limbaugh has made "feminazi" a popular label, one needs to explicate the notion of "feminism" in order to address the emotional constraints which this term imposes on the intellectual understanding of academic and popular audiences.

U.S. polls have shown that about 70 percent of wo/men refuse to identify as feminists because to their mind this label characterizes a person as fanatic, biased, man-hating, and crazy. It is no wonder, then, that wo/men do not want to be tagged with the "feminist" label. Nevertheless, studies also have shown that the majority of wo/men subscribe to feminist political goals such as the following: an end to discrimination against wo/men; equal pay for equal work; sharing of both homemaking and child-rearing by married partners; non-criminalizing the termination of pregnancy; censure of violence against wo/men and sexual harassment; and the ordination of wo/men.

There are many different definitions and directions in feminism. If the f-word is used, the expression is generally understood in terms of gender dualism. Alice Duer Miller's witty jingle expresses this understanding well:

> Mother, what is a feminist?
> A feminist, my daughter
> Is any woman now who cares
> To think about her own affairs
> As men don't think she oughter.

---

[3]bell hooks, *Feminism Is for Everybody* (Boston: South End Press, 2000), vii.

The term has been reformulated by African-American ethicist Katie G. Cannon as *womanist*[4] and by Cuban-American ethicist Ada María Isasi-Díaz as *mujerista*.[5] Black feminists often prefer the term *womanist* which was defined by Alice Walker in a collection of essays entitled *In Search of Our Mothers' Gardens* as a feminist of color who is "committed to survival and wholeness of entire people, male and female."[6] According to the definition of Toinette Eugene,

> A womanist is an African American feminist who claims her roots in black history, religion and culture.... At issue in the appropriation of the term "womanist" as a descriptive genre for theology is the power of self-definition, of self-naming. "Womanist theology" is a signification for a theology that permits African American wo/men to define themselves, to embrace and intentionally affirm their cultural and religious traditions, and their embodiment. Thus, womanist theology taps directly into the roots of the historical liberation capability of black wo/men...[7]

Taking their cue from womanists, some Latina feminist theologians in the United States also looked for a name that would announce their cultural and religious distinctiveness. Hence, they accent the term *mujerista* for the purpose of naming themselves. According to Isasi-Díaz:

> A name is not just a word by which one is identified. A name also provides the conceptual framework, the point of reference, the mental constructs that are used in thinking, understanding and relating to a person, an idea, a movement.... Mujerista theology, which includes both ethics and theology, is a liberative praxis: reflective action that has as its goal liberation. As a liberative praxis, mujerista theology is a process of enablement for Latina wo/men, insisting on the development of a strong sense of moral agency, and clarifying the importance and value of who they are, what they think and what they do.[8]

---

[4]Katie Geneva Cannon, *Katie's Canon* (New York: Continuum, 1995).

[5]Ada María Isasi-Díaz, *Mujerista Theology* (Maryknoll, N.Y.: Orbis, 1996).

[6]Alice Walker, *In Search of Our Mothers' Gardens: Womanist Prose* (New York: Harcourt Brace & Co., 1983).

[7]Toinette M. Eugene, "Womanist Theology," in *An A to Z of Feminist Theology,* ed. Lisa Isherwood and Dorothea McEwan (Sheffield: Academic Press, 1996), 238.

[8]Ada María Isasi-Díaz, "Mujerista Theology," in *An A to Z of Feminist Theology,* ed. Lisa Isherwood and Dorothea McEwan (Sheffield: Academic Press, 1996), 153 and 154.

Other Latina feminist theologians, as, for instance, María Pilar Aquino, prefer to name themselves as "Latina or Chicana feminists" in order to express their solidarity and pride in a cultural Latina/Chicana feminist movement of which they are a part.[9]

My own preferred definition of feminism is a political definition. It is expressed by a well-known bumper sticker that asserts, tongue in cheek: "Feminism is the radical notion that wo/men are people." This definition accentuates the fact that feminism is a radical concept and at the same time ironically underscores that at the beginning of the twenty-first century, feminism should be a common-sense notion. Wo/men are not "ladies," wives, handmaids, seductresses, or beasts of burden, but wo/men of all colors, religions, and nations are without exception full self-determining citizens claiming equal rights, dignity, and power. This definition alludes to the radical democratic power of all people. It echoes the democratic motto "We, the people," and positions feminism within radical democratic discourses, which argue for the rights of all people who are wo/men. It evokes memories of struggles for dignity, full citizenship, and decision-making powers in society and religion not only in the U.S. but around the world. According to this political definition of feminism, men can advocate feminism just as wo/men can be anti-feminist.

Theologically, feminism understands wo/men as the people of G*d and indicts the death-dealing power of oppression as structural sin and life-destroying evil. Hence, feminist theologies and studies in religion have as a goal not only to fundamentally alter the nature of malestream knowledge about G*d, the self, and the world, but also to change institutionalized religion that has excluded wo/men from leadership positions. Feminism is thus best understood as a theoretical perspective and historical movement for changing socio-cultural and communal-religious structures of domination and exploitation.

In the past as in the present, feminist movements have emerged from the participation of wo/men in emancipatory struggles like those for full democratic citizenship, religious freedom, abolition of slavery, civil rights, national and cultural independence, as well as those of the ecological, labor, peace, and gay movements. In these struggles for religious, civil, and human rights, feminists have learned that words such as "human" or "worker" or "civil society" are gender-typed and often are not meant to include the rights and interests of wo/men. Therefore it becomes necessary to focus specifically on the struggle of wo/men for self-determination in society and religion which leads to a different self-understanding and vi-

---

[9]See the forthcoming reader edited by María Pilar Aquino, Daisy Machado, and Jeannette Rodriguez, *A Reader in Feminist Liberation Theology: Religion and Justice* (Austin: University of Texas Press, 2001).

sion of the world. To quote the African-American thinker Anna Julia Cooper:

> Woman...daring to think and move and speak—to undertake to help shape, mold and direct the thought of her age, is merely completing the circle of the world's vision. Hers is every interest that has lacked an interpreter and a defender. Her cause is linked with that of every agony that has been dumb—every wrong that needs a voice.... The world has had to limp along with the wobbling gait and one-sided hesitancy of a man with one eye. Suddenly the bandage is removed from the other eye and the whole body is filled with light. It sees a circle where before it saw a segment. The darkened eye restored, every member rejoices with it.[10]

The second roadblock that might prevent you from engaging with the ideas of this book may be the assumption that feminist interpretation is something just for wo/men. Since I address my text most often to wo/men, you may have concluded that I want to speak only to wo/men. Far from it. Rather than excluding men, I use the expression "wo/men" in an inclusive way and invite men to engage in a spiritual-intellectual exercise that reverses the usual linguistic practice. In an androcentric, grammatically male-determined language system such as English, masculine terms like "men," "he," and "mankind" are used as generic terms for human beings and are therefore presumed to include wo/men.

Simply by learning how to speak in an androcentric (i.e., male-centered) language system, men experience themselves as central and important whereas wo/men learn early on that they are not directly addressed but are subsumed under male terms. Religious and biblical language tells us that we are made in the image of G*d, who is generally understood as male. Wo/men thereby internalize that G*d has only beloved sons. Simply by learning to speak or to pray, wo/men learn that we are marginal, insignificant, "second-class citizens" in society and church. Reading the bible leads to wo/men's "immasculation," that is, internalization and identification with the male, to use an expression that Judith Fetterly coined a long time ago.[11]

In a grammatically androcentric language system, wo/men always have to think twice and to deliberate whether we are meant or not when we are told, for example, that "all men are created equal" or that Chris-

---

[10]Anna Julia Cooper, *A Voice from the South* (1892; republished in the Schomburg Library of Nineteenth Century Black Women Writers, New York: Oxford University Press, 1988).

[11]Judith Fetterly, *The Resisting Reader: A Feminist Approach to American Fiction* (Bloomington: Indiana University Press, 1978).

tians and Jews are "the sons of G*d." To lift these noxious language mechanisms into consciousness, I am using wo/men as inclusive of men, s/he as inclusive of he, and fe/male as inclusive of male. Thereby I invite male readers/students to deliberate and adjudicate whether they are meant when I speak about wo/men. At the same time, I want wo/men to pause and ask which wo/men are meant, since not all wo/men are the same and the differences between wo/men are as great or even greater than those between men. Since the limits of our language are the limits of our world, I recommend this "thinking twice" approach as a good spiritual exercise for the next hundred years or so.

By writing wo/men with a slash I want to make an additional point. I want to indicate that wo/men are not a unitary group and do not have a feminine nature and essence in common. Wo/men are not a different species from men nor are we all the same. Rather, wo/men come in all sizes, shapes, and colors. What it means to be a wo/man is different in Europe, Africa, or Asia. It means something different if you are black or white, young or old. It means something different if you have grown up in a pueblo or in an academic environment. It means something different if you are a beauty queen or differently abled, a girl or a mother, working at home or outside the home. It means something different if you are a student or a teacher, the lady of the house or a slave.

Wo/man or wo/men is an unstable, fragmented category and one cannot assume that all wo/men are similar in their hopes and desires. Hence, it becomes important to ask which wo/men come to mind when one speaks of wo/men's perspective. Are they right-wing or feminist, black or white, native or foreign? Wo/men as much as men are socialized into the mindsets and world-views of the dominant culture. We are not better human beings or able to envision a different future just because we are "wo/men." Changing language patterns is a very important step toward the realization of a new consciousness. Not femininity but diversity thus constitutes a "reading" from the perspective of wo/man. Finally, my writing of wo/men is meant to indicate that the oppression of wo/men also includes that of subaltern men (that is, men who do not share in elite male privilege). Hence I speak of "elite men" or "White Gentlemen" when I speak of men in power and refer to the discourse of the "White Lady" when I speak of elite wo/men's cultural-religious socialization and power.

Moreover, in the days of post-feminism it is often argued that wo/men are not discriminated against or oppressed, that feminist rhetorics and not discriminatory structures turn wo/men into victims. I am frequently told by young wo/men that they cannot connect with a critical feminist interpretation for liberation because they do not feel disadvantaged. If you feel this way, you will benefit little from working through this book, since the

method for reading the bible which is advocated here aims at enabling wo/men to become free from gender and other oppressions that they have internalized.

In general, my response to such interlocutors is that it is quite understandable that they have little experience of oppression or even discrimination if they come from an upper-class, white, racially and nationally privileged background. But a glance at statistical data on wo/men's situation in the U.S. and around the world gives clear evidence that wo/men as a group are still disadvantaged worldwide. Wo/men still earn only two-thirds of what men in similar situations earn; the majority of people living in poverty are wo/men; violence against wo/men and gynecide (the killing of wo/men) is on the increase; sexual trafficking, various forms of forced labor, illiteracy, migration, and refugee camps spell out wo/men's continuing oppression globally. The Human Rights Watch World Report 2000 extensively documents the systemic inequality, abuse, violence, discrimination, starvation, poverty, neglect, and denial of wo/men's rights that afflict the lives of wo/men around the globe. Hence, the experience of white middle- or upper-class U.S. wo/men is not typical and does not adequately reflect the extent of gender inequalities worldwide.

The third roadblock on the way to the freedom and nurture of Wisdom's open house is the assumption that not only all wo/men but also all feminists are alike, because allegedly feminism is a monolithic ideology that does not allow for any disagreement and debate. This objection does not recognize that the differences among various feminist theoretical frameworks and political goals are considerable and rich. Some of these feminist theories and practices seem exclusive of each other; others have great affinity, overlap, and flow into each other.

Since feminist biblical interpretation utilizes feminist theory as its frame of reference, it is important to distinguish between various feminist theoretical perspectives and political assumptions if one wants to understand the differences such frameworks make in feminist biblical interpretation. Needless to say, my enumeration of the following theoretical feminist frameworks does not pretend to be comprehensive nor does it propose definitions. Rather, by pointing out these different feminist directions I want to convince you that feminism speaks in many different voices and uses an array of intellectual, rhetorical, and emotional registers. Like all classifications and typologies, my circumscribing delineation of these perspectives is indicative rather than comprehensive and definitive. It is intended to be illustrative rather than exhaustive, cumulative rather than sequential. Since the borders of each perspective are unstable, porous, fluid, overlapping and extending beyond, individual inter-

preters are able to combine various feminist approaches to attack the many-headed monster of *kyriarchy*.[12]

- *Equal rights/liberal feminism* fights for the rights of wo/men in all societal, cultural, and religious institutions. It does not fight just for equal access to privilege and for the opportunity of wo/men to become like and the same as men, as is often alleged in postmodern discussions. Rather, it struggles to improve wo/men's present situation as much as possible while generally aware that finally equal rights and justice for wo/men cannot be won without the struggle to change sexist institutions and power relations.

- *Complementarity feminism* assumes that wo/men and men have essentially different natures. Like two halves of an apple, masculinity and femininity complement each other to make a whole in which the female is either the "deficient" or the "better" half. Masculine-feminine dualism is here seen not as oppositional but as corresponding and mutually balancing. This perspective is advocated, for instance, by Pope John Paul II. It re-inscribes not only heterosexism but also the discourse of the "White Lady," who has the task of mediating civilization to the uncivilized. Although in a theoretically and politically quite different way, the French feminist Luce Irigaray also seems to re-inscribe such complementarity by elaborating a sexual ethics and ontology of the "Divine Couple."

- *Gynecentric/radical feminism* believes that there are essential feminine modes of perception that create a special female culture. It often assumes that wo/men's special ways of knowing and experiencing the world make them naturally better, less corrupted human beings. This type of feminism focuses on the roots of wo/men's oppression primarily in male domination and claims that all other forms of oppression are engendered by male supremacy.

---

[12]Hence, I encourage you to explore these different feminist directions more fully and discuss how they determine the meaning and interpretation of androcentric biblical texts and language, for example,

> I was by his side, a master craftsman,
> delighting him day after day,
> ever at play in his presence,
> at play everywhere in his world,
> delighting to be with the sons of men.
> 'And now my sons, listen to me;
> listen to instruction and learn to be wise,
>   do not ignore it.
> Happy those who keep my ways!'
>   (Proverbs 8:30-33)

- *Lesbian feminism* has been one of the primary forces in radical wo/men's culture. The expression "Lesbian continuum" coined by Adrienne Rich in the 1980s has been a key political term that signifies a range of wo/men-identified experiences not limited to or necessarily including a wo/man's having genital contact with other wo/men. The opposite of Rich's term is "compulsory heterosexuality." The name "queer" or "lesbian-bisexual-gay-transexual-transgendered" (LBGT) captures more recent struggles over sexuality and the array of sexual alternatives.[13]

- *Gender feminism* (also sometimes called *difference feminism*) does not focus on wo/men but on cultural and social gender constructions. It does not assume that gender roles are based on natural differences rooted in biological sex but asserts that sex/gender is a culturally constructed system of domination. Because gender provides a functionalist dualistic framework, gender feminism requires that "both" genders and their cultural ideological reconstructions be studied.

- *Maternal feminism* promotes all the virtues of nurturing, preservation, growth, acceptance, and pacifism developed through child care and mothering. Maternal feminism seeks therefore to challenge autonomous individualism with a virtue ethics and politics based on the relational capacities cultivated and expressed in the private sphere. Maternal thinking is available to all wo/men whether they are mothers or not. It is a residual power accruing from women's capacity to bear and nurture children.

- *Relationality feminism* develops a philosophical and/or social ontology of the self, an ethics of mutuality and complementarity arguing that wo/men have been socially and discursively molded to perform the relational tasks that serve elite men. It is because of patriarchal sociopolitical power relations and not because of nature, i.e., their capacity to give birth and early empathy with their mothers, that wo/men are more likely to be sensitive to the ebb and flow of connections.

- *Marxist/Materialist feminism* seeks to describe the material bases of wo/men's subjugation and the relationship between the modes of production and wo/men's status. Materialist feminism abandons Marxist dual-system theory (class exploitation and patriarchy) and expands Marxist feminist theory to include other processes of domination that are absent from malestream Marxist theories of materialism. It argues that an analysis of wo/men's oppression must include both reproduction and production. The liberation of wo/men is possible only in and through an

---

[13]This was pointed out by Carolyn Stevenson in her Midterm Paper for Gospel Stories of Wo/men, Fall 2000.

egalitarian reordering of productive and reproductive labor in which economic and cultural structures of oppression are dismantled.

- *Ecofeminism* seeks to make connections between the destruction of the natural world and the oppression of wo/men. It stresses the notion that not just sentient life but all living things, present and future, form one sacred Body, and that in the evolutionary creative process we all become manifestations of it. The feminine is not strictly identified with the female but it is an energy or power in all living things.

- *Postmodern feminism* throws into radical doubt beliefs derived from the European Enlightenment. Feminist postmodern theories, like other forms of postmodernism, encourage us to tolerate ambivalence, ambiguity, multiplicity, instability, and complexity. They enable feminists to articulate the diversity and contradictions between and within various positions by denying that either the subject of discourse or the truth is singular. When combined with postcolonial feminism, postmodern feminism is sometimes theorized as postfeminism.

- *Third World/Differences feminism* recognizes not only gender *difference* but the *differences* of race, class, ethnicity, culture, sexuality, and religion. In contrast to postmodern feminist theory, however, it stresses not just the discursivity but also the materiality of such differences. It emphasizes that Eurocentric feminism has been mistaken in seeing the cultural and political experience of white middle-class wo/men as describing the experience and situation of all wo/men. Instead, it insists that a whole range of multiplicative structures of domination determine wo/men's lives differently.

- *Contextual feminism/Global feminism* emphasizes the liberationist adage that what we see depends on where we stand. Social-economic-cultural-religious location shapes not only our daily lives but also our theoretical perspectives and approaches. Knowledge is always situated, contextual, and unfinished. This theoretical perspective understands differences as produced in and through different locations within the structures of domination and not in and through an identity politics. For example, Euro-American or African feminism is not defined by an essentializing Euro-American or African identity politics but by one's primary formation and experiential rootedness in Euro-American or African socio-cultural contexts.

- *Postcolonial feminism* intensifies the arguments made by differences and contextual feminisms by pointing to the impact of Western imperialism and colonialism on wo/men's self-identity and social-cultural location. It investigates the interconnection between empire and the dis-

courses of empire and wrestles with the question of how to negotiate solidarity and alliances between different postcolonial social formations and interests. Like Marxist feminism, it tends to work with a dual-system analysis that uses patriarchy and imperialism as two parallel systems of oppression rather than constructing an integrated system of analysis such as that of a critical interpretation for liberation.

- *International feminism* is embodied by the four United Nations Conferences on Wo/men held in Mexico City (1975), Copenhagen (1980), Nairobi (1985), and Beijing (1995). These conferences together with the conference on population control in Cairo (1994) were important forums for grassroots and other non-governmental organizations (NGOs) to debate issues of wo/men's equality and well-being. In an era when globalization increases the exploitation of wo/men, such international movements for sharing and debating common problems and coalition building become more and more indispensable.

- *Religious feminism* (Jewish, Christian, Muslim, Goddess, Buddhist, American Indian, Hindu, Indigenous, Aboriginal, or Dalit religious feminisms) does not split the so-called secular from the religious feminist movement but seeks to comprehend the interaction between "secular" and "religious" feminists as one of different location rather than one of binary in-difference. It focuses feminist attention and inter-religious dialogue on the positive and negative presence of religion in wo/men's lives and argues that religion is not only a force for maintaining societal and cultural domination but also a resource in wo/men's struggles for survival and liberation.

- *Postbiblical feminism* rejects biblical religions as totally sexist and oppressive and points to their violent and dehumanizing impact in history. Positively, it has rediscovered the Goddess and Her spirituality that nourishes connectedness and ecological awareness. Whereas the Father G*d of Judaism and Christianity is seen as transcendent King of creation, the Goddess is imagined as birthing creation from Her body. Hence, creation is of the same substance as the Divine Mother and participates in Her divinity. Thus, Goddess religion and spirituality inspire a vision of life as organic and sacred wholeness where all living beings participate in their divine source and ground.

- *Critical liberationist feminism* is an offspring of the abolitionist movement in the nineteenth century as well as of the civil rights, radical gay, socialist student, and anti-colonialist movements of the 1960s. While it celebrates diversity and cultural particularity, it also insists that we forge alliances in the struggles for liberation until all wo/men have achieved their rights, recognition, well-being, and dignity as full

"citizens." Using this paradigmatic theoretical perspective, I have sought to develop the notion of the *ekklesia of wo/men* as an analytic category and instrument for conceptualizing the variegated struggles against the multiplicative and intersecting structures of domination such as class, race, gender, heterosexuality, and ethnic nationalism.

In conclusion, the point of this lengthy sketch of different feminist formations is not to give you complete and exact information such as you could find in feminist dictionaries and reference works. Rather, it is to argue that we must become conscious of the rich variety of feminisms and their different theoretical perspectives as well as their effects on the interpretation of biblical texts. Such differences in feminist interpretation are not "innocent" but always already predetermined and inundated with theoretical assumptions. This, however, is not only true for feminist interpretations but applies to all interpretation, biblical or otherwise.

The fourth roadblock or obstacle on the path to Wisdom is the conviction of many feminists that the bible and religion are anti-wo/men and hence must be rejected as hopelessly patriarchal. For them, biblical interpretation is the domain of believers, not the task of feminists. As early as the nineteenth century Elizabeth Cady Stanton pointed to the pitfalls of this feminist attitude. She maintained that feminists must concern themselves with the bible and religion because many wo/men still believe in them. She also pointed out that one cannot reform one segment of patriarchal society without reforming the whole. If feminists are concerned with the liberation of wo/men, then they must take account of the fact that many wo/men not only consult the bible as an inspiring authority but also value and transmit it as a source of strength and hope. Feminists, whether believers or not, must concern themselves with the bible and its interpretation because it still has great power in the lives of many wo/men.

In addition, feminists who have grown up in Western cultures have themselves internalized many biblical patterns and stereotypes. Western cultures are still permeated with the symbolism and values of the Scriptures. In order to understand Western art, music, and literature, one needs a certain amount of biblical literacy. Cultural ideologies and media stereotypes are still based on and derived from the bible. Biblical texts and images fund the cultural language of hate against wo/men, against blacks, against homosexuals, against Jews, and against pagans.

The fifth roadblock that may prevent you from engagement with feminist biblical interpretation is the conviction among many wo/men who read the bible and among many feminists that biblical interpretation and biblical studies are the domain of scholars and are useless in everyday

lives and struggles. Combined with this negative attitude toward biblical scholarship one often finds the assumption that the critical interpretation of the bible is restricted to the "ivory tower" of elite universities or denominational seminaries. This stumbling block overlooks the fact that all wo/men who read or hear the bible are always already interpreting it. Interpretation is not done by ivory tower academics only and it is not their prerogative. Moreover, such an assumption forgets the old adage that "knowledge is power."

Conversely, those who do not critically use scholarship but rely on their own "common-sense" understandings are in danger of uncritically repeating and reinscribing the doctrinal and theological assumptions and cultural-religious prejudices mediated to them through Sunday-school, sermons, televangelism, and "popular" books on the bible. That biblical knowledge still has great influence on public discourses and debates is evident, for instance, in the success of TV-evangelists and in the explosion of newspaper and magazine articles, TV shows, and popular and scientific books on the "historical Jesus." The bible and its interpretation have become a multi-million-dollar business and a worldwide consumer product. Hence, feminists and others concerned with the well-being of all world-citizens cannot leave the bible to the communications industries, whether scholarly or popular.

The sixth roadblock on the road to the open cosmic house of Divine Wisdom is the general conviction that we know what the bible is: it is "our" book—a classic of Western culture. Closely related to this is the notion that there is only one bible and that it belongs to Christians. These two misguided assumptions overlook the fact that the bible is not a book but a bookshelf or collection of works that span several thousands of years and several ancient cultures. The Greek word *biblia* (plural) which means *books* and not *book,* is the root of the English word "bible." The word "bible" thus signifies that it is a collection of *books* that were assembled and brought together in the process of canonization. This process preserved some books but eliminated others. For instance, the Acts of Thecla, which tell about a female disciple of Paul, were long considered to be part of Scripture whereas the Book of Revelation was not recognized by a large segment of the church for quite some time. Yet many of us know the Book of Revelation but not the Acts of Thecla because they are not in the canon.

The assumption that the bible is Western also overlooks the fact that the bible does not belong to the West. It originated and was nurtured in the cultural soil of the Middle East. True, the bible has been used as a tool of Western colonization and for inculcating European culture, but its origin and symbolic universe place it firmly within the context of the East

and the Mediterranean. In another way, one could say that the bible in its present form is a product of Western culture insofar as scholars pieced together the original text from numerous different manuscripts that are written not just in Hebrew or Greek but in various ancient languages such as Aramaic, Ethiopian, Coptic, Syriac, Abyssinian, and many more. When street preachers ring my doorbell to tell me "what the bible says," I usually reply, "Which bible?" and "In which language?" Most people have never heard of manuscript criticism and are unaware that their English translation is actually an interpretation and not a transcription. They don't realize that the biblical text is produced, translated, and interpreted by scholars today who are still mostly from the West and mostly elite white males.

Closely connected with the belief that the bible is a classic of Western culture is the assumption that the bible belongs to Christians and is a Christian book. This assumption fails to recognize that the bible is not just the Holy Book of Christians but also, in a different form, of Jews and Muslims. Jews and Christians, especially, share large parts of the bible though their canon is different. For the first followers of Jesus in the Greco-Roman world, the Tanakh was Holy Scripture, since many of them were Jews who used the Scriptures, especially the books of the prophets, as a quarry for proof-texts for their interpretation of the ministry and execution of Jesus as a criminal.

In the process of separation from Judaism, Christians appropriated the Jewish bible as the "Old Testament" and used it to show that all its promises had been transferred to them who were now the new (true) people of G*d. (This is traditionally called supersessionism.) Christians called their collection of scriptures the New Testament in distinction to the Old Testament, which is the other half of the Christian bible. Thus, the compositional framework of the Christian bible is suffused with anti-Judaism, since the New Testament is seen as the fulfillment of the promises given to G*d's people in the Old Testament, which the Jews are said to have refused.

In order to do away with this pejorative nomenclature, some have suggested renaming the two parts of the bible as the First and Second Testaments. Others have proposed renaming the so-called Old Testament as the Hebrew Scriptures, the bible of the Hebrews, although they are fully aware that the early Christians used the Septuagint, i.e., a Greek translation, as their scriptures. I have suggested that the second and latter part of the bible is best renamed the Christian Testament, since it contains the Christian writings. But whereas the designation Hebrew Scriptures or Hebrew Bible is widely accepted, that of Christian Testament, which together with the Hebrew Scriptures constitutes the Christian bible or Scriptures, has not caught on, probably because most bible scholars and readers cling to the

notion that the Hebrew Bible is "their" Old Testament. The Jewish bible or the Jewish Scriptures are not the same as the "Old Testament." Although the Hebrew Scriptures, the Torah, the Prophets, and the Writings are shared by Jews and Christians, they have a different sequence and have been transmitted, read, and interpreted in a different way.

Finally, the fact that there are several Christian bibles is often overlooked. Roman Catholics read in their bible writings that Protestants or Orthodox do not have in their bibles. Greek or Slavonic Orthodox Christians have books in their bibles, such as 3 Maccabees, that are not found in either the Protestant or the Catholic bible. Books not included in the Protestant bible variously are called apocryphal or deutero-canonical and are found in either the Catholic or the Greek or Slavonic Orthodox bible. For instance, several of the texts about Divine Wisdom are not found in the Protestant canon but are in the Roman Catholic canon and are read in the liturgy. Hence, many Protestant feminists feel uneasy with the revalorization of the divine figure of Sophia-Wisdom by Catholic feminists. I recall having been invited as a visiting scholar to preach in a Protestant church. When I suggested as the reading of the day a section from the book of Judith, I was told that I could not use this text because it was not canonical and therefore not to be read in a worship service. I ended up not preaching there, because I insisted on a text that was a part of "my" bible.

The seventh roadblock that could stand in the way of a fruitful feminist engagement with the bible is the supposition that Christians must believe in the bible as they believe in G*d. For many, the bible is to be believed as the direct word of G*d. The bible is like a fetish, an object seen as having magical power and deserving of extravagant trust, devotion, and reverence. Biblical interpretation becomes fetishism.

We are all familiar with the notion that the Holy Spirit in the form of a dove dictated the words into the ear of the evangelist who then wrote the words down as "G*d's word." This understanding of how the bible was written has its roots in the last book of the bible, the Apocalypse of John, as Catholics call it, or the Book of Revelation, as Protestants know it.

The Book of Revelation claims to be the "words of prophecy which were given to John through the mediation of angels." The introduction to Revelation thus establishes a chain of revelatory authority which resides with G*d and is communicated through Christ or the angelic interpreter to John and through him to the audience. Strictly speaking, the "words of prophecy" do not represent John's discourse but rather claim to be divine discourse. The *real* author of Revelation is not John, but G*d, the risen Jesus, and the Spirit. The One in Human Likeness and the Spirit "speak" to the *ekklesiai* and John merely transcribes their message (1:11, 19; 2:1–3:22). John's insistence on the divine authorship of Revelation has

decisively influenced theological understandings of canonical authority. If one accepts his portrayal of the revelatory process, one comes to an understanding of Scripture as the "dictated word of G*d" rather than as the inspired rhetorical responses of biblical writers to specific problems arising in particular socio-rhetorical locations.

Moreover, if the bible is the recorded direct word of G*d, then biblical criticism in general and feminist biblical criticism in particular are dangerous and come close to sacrilege. Such critical reflection raises many fears and anxieties in readers/students who have been socialized into trusting and obeying G*d's word rather than critically interrogating it. However, such a literalist understanding of the bible is a very modern, anti-rationalist assertion. Christian tradition and theology have always understood that the bible is not literally the word of G*d but that it mediates G*d's word. Not the individual words of the bible but the sacred authors and their readers are inspired. It is in the process of reading the bible under the guidance of the Holy Spirit or of hearing it preached that the Divine Presence, the Shekhinah, is experienced.

The early Christian insight that the Spirit must be discerned and the words and lifestyle of the prophets must be tested by the community has been too easily forgotten. The result is a lack of critical theological ability and spiritual practice to adjudicate scriptural texts. Theological education needs to train students in a critical stance toward all human words that claim the direct authority of G*d. What the Spirit says today to our own particular socio-political location and rhetorical situation must be assessed in a critical feminist practice of rhetorical analysis and ideology critique that can trace G*d's power for justice and well-being in today's political struggles against domination.

The eighth roadblock that I want to mention here is the assumption that texts, and especially sacred texts such as the bible, have a single, definite meaning and that this meaning can be established with proper methods. Such a literalist and positivist understanding of text and reading is naïve and outdated. The bible is not a unitary text, and it is also full of contradictions because, as we have seen, it is a collection of texts. For example, it is impossible to determine in many instances exactly what Jesus said and did because we have several versions of the same saying or story. Ancient Christians sought to establish a unitary text by telescoping all four gospels together into one single narrative that was called the Diatessaron. Rather than establishing the true meaning of the gospel text, however, this approach simply produces a new and different text. Moreover, there are many more gospels than we find in our canon. The gospel of Mary Magdalene is one such text that sheds a new light on the teachings of Jesus but is not known to many Christians because it did not make it into the

canon that, for Roman Catholics, was only finalized by the Council of Trent in the sixteenth century.

The problem of meaning posed by a multiplicity of sources also cannot be solved by applying the correct method of interpretation, because neither in the past nor today could scholars agree on such a "correct" method. Rather, there are a multiplicity of valid methods of exegeting and interpreting a biblical text that result in different, often contradictory meanings. Much ink has been spilled and much paper wasted because over and against other interpretations scholars try to show that their own interpretation is the only "correct" or at least the "best" one.

The discipline of hermeneutics in antiquity and today explores how the meaning of a text is produced and how it can be understood. The notion of hermeneutics derives from the Greek word *hermeneuein* and means to interpret, exegete, explain, or translate. It owes its name to Hermes, the messenger of the Gods, who has the task of mediating their announcements, declarations, and messages to mere mortals. His proclamations, however, are not a mere communication and mediation but are always also an explication of divine commands which he translates into human language so they can be comprehended and obeyed.

While hermeneutics can be understood as a matter of the free play of signs or as merely keeping the lines of communication open, according to the German philosopher Gadamer, hermeneutics has the task of translating meaning from one "world" into another. Like Hermes, the messenger of the Gods, hermeneutics not only communicates knowledge but also instructs, directs, and enjoins. Hermeneutics thus has affinities to manticism and prophecy. It conveys revelation and interprets signs and oracles. As a mode of understanding, it involves the Aristotelian virtue of *phronesis*—practical judgment and adjudication which is not secured by an a priori method but only in the process of understanding itself.

As a discipline, philosophical hermeneutics has its roots in biblical interpretation. It is best understood as a theory and practice of interpretation that explores the conditions and possibilities of understanding not just of texts but of other practices as well. As such, hermeneutics is not so much a disciplined scientific method and technique but rather an epistemological perspective and approach. Since Schleiermacher, Dilthey, and Gadamer, hermeneutics has maintained over and against scientific positivism that understanding takes place as a process of engagement in the hermeneutical circle or spiral, which is characterized by the part-whole relation. It stresses that understanding is not possible without pre-understandings or prejudices and therefore that understanding is always context-dependent.

Hermeneutics insists on the linguistic character of all knowledge, on its contextuality and its immersion in tradition. It stresses that human understanding can never take place without words and outside of time. Its key

concepts are *empathy, historicity, linguisticality, tradition, pre-understanding, fusion of horizons,* and *the classic* with its notion of *effective history* that is the impact interpretations of a text have had throughout the text's history. However, all seven aspects and theoretical emphases of hermeneutics are problematic from a critical feminist perspective because they do not take sufficiently into account relations of domination and power.

The ninth roadblock on Wisdom's path is the assumption that male-stream and feminist hermeneutics are not radically different but that they are the same. However, "hermeneutics" seems to be a misnomer for the method used to pursue feminist emancipatory research, since feminist biblical studies are primarily interested in a critical-emancipatory read-ing of the bible. Although I have named and developed biblical interpre-tation as "feminist hermeneutics," I would suggest that "feminist inter-pretation" goes beyond hermeneutics and is best understood in rhetorical terms.

Consequently, it is not the myth of Hermes but that of Metis and Athena that articulates the task of a critical feminist hermeneutic and rhetoric. Athena, the patron Goddess of the classical Athenian city-state, was not only the patron of the arts and technological and scientific knowledge but also a war goddess. According to Hesiod, she came fully grown and armored from the head of her father, Zeus. However, she only appears to be motherless. Her real mother is the Goddess Metis, the "most wise woman among Gods and humans."

According to the myth, Zeus, the father of the Gods, was in competi-tion with Metis, who is called in the bible Chokmah-Sophia-Wisdom. He duped her when she was pregnant with Athena because he feared that Metis, Divine Wisdom, would bear a child who would surpass him in wisdom and power. Hence, he changed Metis into a fly. But this was not enough! Zeus swallowed the fly Metis whole in order to have her always with him and to benefit from her wise counsel. This mythical story of Metis and Zeus reveals not only the Father of the Gods' fear that the child of Wisdom would surpass him in knowledge, but it also lays open the conditions under which wo/men in kyriarchal cultures and religions are able to exercise wisdom and produce knowledge.

Read with a hermeneutics of suspicion, the myth of Metis and Athena shows that kyriarchal systems of knowledge and power objectify wo/men and swallow them up in order to co-opt their wisdom and knowledge in the interests of domination. Women's studies remains therefore an am-biguous notion, since it has wo/men rather than structures of domination as objects of its research. Feminist studies, in contrast, seeks to empower wo/men by recognizing and changing such knowledges and structures of marginalization and oppression.

Since the goal of feminist hermeneutics is not simply to interpret biblical texts and communicate divine revelations but to undo kyriarchal mystification and dehumanization, it must derive its name and inspiration from Metis—from Divine Wisdom-Sophia—and not from Hermes, the trickster God. A feminist hermeneutic—or better, sophialogy—critically investigates malestream religious myths, texts, traditions, and practices for how much they marginalize, make invisible, or distort experience, tradition, language, knowledge, and wisdom to effect wo/men's elimination from cultural and religious consciousness and records. Positively, it seeks to produce not a knowledge divinely or naturally given which is hidden and must be unearthed, but a practical wisdom that must be lived and done.

I have developed, therefore, a complex hermeneutical approach for the critical process of a feminist interpretation for liberation, which I will develop more fully in chapter 6. Such a critical feminist hermeneutic-rhetorical method of interpretation does not subscribe to one single reading strategy but employs a variety of feminist theoretical insights and hermeneutical methods for articulating its own practices of interpretation. The seven hermeneutical strategies of interpretation which I have identified —a hermeneutics of *experience*, of *domination*, of *suspicion*, of *critical evaluation*, of *memory* and *re-membering*, of *imagination,* and of *transformation*—are constitutive for such a critical rhetorical praxis of interpretation for liberation and transformation.

The tenth and last roadblock is, in my experience, the most difficult to move out of the way because of its emotional "heaviness." To point separately to the emotional toil a critical approach to the bible has, does not mean to isolate it from other roadblocks that also are causing emotional turmoil. It only brings it into greater relief. Many wo/men have confessed that they suffer from anxiety attacks, break out in cold sweat, or shake and tremble when they engage in a critical reading and evaluation of the bible. Such uneasiness, fear, and apprehension are the instinctive and involuntary reactions to the taboo character of Sacred Scripture that we have internalized.

The bible is not just a book like any other book. It is sacred and holy! It is an icon that is venerated and worshiped. For instance, it is a great honor in Judaism to carry the Torah scroll and to read from it. In Catholic ritual, the priest carries the bible in procession, envelops it in incense, and lifts it up high proclaiming, "This is the Word of G*d." Many who have never read the whole bible have participated in rituals internalizing its mystical status. Others believe that the bible functions as Divine oracle and has a magical character. Those who have grown up in fundamentalist religious communities believing that the bible is the direct, in-

errant, and true Word of G*d will still have in mind the warnings and
curses of the Book of Revelation when they question the misogyny of
biblical texts:

> I warn everyone who hears the words of the prophecy of this
> book: if anyone adds to them, G*d will add to that person the
> plagues described in this book, and if anyone takes away from
> the words of the book of this prophecy, G*d will take away that
> person's share in the tree of life and in the holy city, which are
> described in this book. (Revelation 22:18-19)

The anxiety of others may be engendered by an overwhelming experience of loss. If the sacred story has given meaning to their life, the
recognition that it might be life-destroying can cause great sadness and
fear.[14] Tom Driver of Union Theological Seminary shares the following
experience of a session in his course "The Experiential Basis of Theological Thinking." After reading Phyllis Trible's book *Texts of Terror,* he introduced to his class a simple bible-study-group technique for reading the
story entitled in our bibles "The Levite's Concubine" (but which could be
more accurately entitled "The Rape and Dismemberment of a Wo/man
from Bethlehem" [Judges 19]), which is preceded by the story of the atro-
cious conquest of Laish by the Danites in Judges 18:27-31. Both stories
tell of unspeakable violence, one of the rape of wo/men, the other of the
rape of conquered lands.

In order to realize the full emotional impact of this violent text,
you need to read the story aloud in the fashion Driver describes:

> Readers sit in a circle, passing a Bible from hand to hand for
> each participant to read a verse or two of a chosen passage, then
> each one comments upon what she read before offering the text
> to the next person.[15]

When reading this violent biblical story, as well as Driver's narrative of
his class's response to the excruciating details, you need to be aware of
the violent experiences and fierce emotions that can be evoked:

---

[14]As Teresa Yi Suarez points out in her Midterm Paper for Gospel Stories of Wo/men,
Fall 2000: "There is a tremendous tragedy in how the bible has been used against wo/men,
a tragedy that in some sense cannot be redeemed or made right."

[15]Tom Driver, "Performance and Biblical Reading: Its Power and Hazard," in *Body
and Bible: Interpreting and Experiencing Biblical Narratives,* ed. Björn Krondorfer (Philadelphia: Trinity Press International, 1992), 159.

Reading this story aloud, using the method I have described, became terribly painful. The anguish could be felt in one's bones. It expressed itself in faltering, quavering voices. It could be seen in the twisting of bodies.... The reading seemed interminable. We went from one excruciating detail to another, and when the woman after her night's ordeal of rape has crawled back to the door of the house from which she had been turned out and put her dying hand upon the threshold, I heard moans. When the story was done, we looked at each other in silence.... We were a circle of refugees sitting in a broken landscape wondering where to go and what to do.[16]

But he goes on:

There was nothing to do but to keep going. Turning to one of the women who had spoken of being abused in childhood, I asked if she wished to tell us more about it. She did, and we began the difficult, pain-ridden work of sharing things long unspoken, comparing personal histories, seeing what they tell us of patriarchal society, and how they have influenced our understanding of God.[17]

Driver cautions, however, not to read the experience as a "success story," since there was no "recovery" from the anxiety, fear, and crisis engendered by the performative reading of this biblical story of terror. Hence, he concludes:

The power of the Bible to wound is very great—and so is that of the family. These two potentials came together in a way I had not anticipated—holy Scripture, holy family, and holy terror.... For those who have experienced the wounding power of Scripture and of the family, the structure of patriarchal theology cracks and crumbles.... To read the Bible with a strong sense of body presence is a challenge to the rule of the fathers. I see this more clearly since that day that my students and I passed a biblical text from hand to hand and came, to our dismay, upon the sickening reality of incest.[18]

Wrapping up my summary review of the kyriocentric roadblocks hindering our steps and movements on Wisdom's ways of justice, I hope you

---

[16]Driver, 171–172.
[17]Driver, 172.
[18]Driver, 173.

have caught sight of the "authorities" that engender the fear and anxiety that keep you from engaging in the movement for justice. If you have joined me in recognizing and naming the roadblocks that may be in the way of wisdom/Wisdom and that hinder fruitful engagement with feminist biblical interpretation, you may have discovered some stumbling blocks of your own which I did not mention or even think of.

The major point of this chapter is not to discourage you but rather to encourage you to become as conscious as you can of the roadblocks and prejudicial assumptions that may prevent deeper understanding and to move them out of the way or to circumvent them. If that is not possible, maybe you can learn how to use them as stepping stones on the muddy road or to take advantage of them as stone benches and resting places on your journey to Wisdom. For instance, you can either become overwhelmed by the sheer variety of feminist theoretical approaches or you may see such variety as a sign of vigor and life. Rather than bemoaning the confusion evoked by the multiplicity of interpretive practices and polyvalence of biblical texts, you may see them as stepping stones or building blocks for better understanding and transforming biblical texts and interpretations as well as the situation of wo/men today.

However, in order to do so you need first to become aware of and question the internalized authorities that keep the roadblocks in place. Since such internalized authorities are often unconscious and hard to discover, it is necessary not just to check whether you understand what has been said but also to keep in touch with your emotions and reactions. What keeps you from fully engaging in the hermeneutical spiraling dance of Wisdom-Spirit and from using the bible as inspiration for walking in Wisdom's ways of justice? If it is anxiety or fear, you may want to remember the promise of Divine Wisdom. As she has led the Israelites on their way to freedom, so she will accompany us on the road to justice:

> They journeyed through an unpopulated wilderness
> And pitched their tents in inaccessible places.
> They stood firm against their enemies, fought off their foes.
> On you they called when they were thirsty,
> And from the rocky cliff water was given them
> From hard stone their thirst was quenched.
>   (Wisdom 11:2-4)

Deepening Movement

Elisabeth Schüssler Fiorenza, *Jesus and the Politics of Interpretation* (New York: Continuum, 2000), 115–144.

Moving Steps

- What obstacles do you see ahead of you in your search for wisdom/ Wisdom and well-being? How will you deal with these obstacles and what stops you from dealing with them now?[19]

- Do you have any experience of oppression? Are you involved in a particular struggle against oppression? Do you think that focusing on the struggles against oppression promotes "victim feminism"?

- What does the bible mean to you? What problems do you have with the text or how the text has been interpreted and used by religious traditions and communities or by the public at large? If you have no problems with it, how do you feel about the goal of a critical feminist biblical interpretation?

- Carol Gilligan has argued that justice is a male concept. Do you agree with her? What justice issues are of utmost concern to you? Do you have a passion for justice? Share one experience of injustice that has marked your life.

- Imaginative exercise: Go on a quest for Thecla. Browse the World Wide Web or go to your local library to learn more about Thecla. Familiarize yourself with the Acts of Thecla and discuss why this text was not included in the canon. Imagine that you meet up with Thecla on the way to Wisdom's open house. What would you say to her and how might she respond? Imagine what she would say about wo/men in the early Christian movements.[20]

Movement Exercise

Name the roadblocks on your way to a fruitful engagement with feminist biblical interpretation.

---

[19]Thanks to Curtis Buddenhagen, Gospel Stories of Wo/men, Fall 2000, for suggesting this question.

[20]I am grateful to Kim Smiley for this suggestion.

Meeting Mary of Magdala on the Road

1. Imagine you have the opportunity to visit Galilee in the year
   _____ because you have heard that Mary of Magdala was
   _____ (fill in blanks).

2. Mary was among the wo/men who went to Jesus' tomb and
   wondered how they would remove the big stone blocking it. You
   plan to ask her about their anxiety as to who will remove the
   stone. How would you approach the question?

3. You have finally met Mary of Magdala. What is your first impres-
   sion of her? What does she look like?

4. What did she tell you about her relationship with Peter and her
   standing in the Jesus movement?

5. In your letter to Thecla you wrote about your visit:

6. Step back into the twenty-first century. Are you still asking "Who
   will remove the roadblocks?" or have you begun to do so?

CHAPTER III

Wo/men's Movements— Wisdom Struggles

In the preceding chapters I have argued that a feminist biblical Wisdom interpretation is best understood as a spiritual practice in the open space of Divine Wisdom through which, like the wind, the Spirit blows as it/s/he wills. In distinction to traditional spirituality, which is individualistic and privatized, the practice and space of wisdom/Wisdom spirituality are public. Wisdom's spiraling presence (Shekhinah) is global, embracing all of creation; Her voice is a public, radical democratic voice rather than a "feminine" privatized one:

> Wisdom calls aloud in the streets,
> She raises her voice in the public squares.
> She calls out at the street corners,
> She delivers her message at the city gates...
> > (Proverbs 1:20-21)

Like a prophet or street teacher, Wisdom is found where the economic, juridical public life of the city takes place:

> Does Wisdom not call meanwhile?
> Does Discernment not lift up her voice?
> On the hilltop, on the road, at the crossways
> She takes her stand;
> Beside the gates of the city, at the approaches to the gates
> She cries aloud:
> O people, I am calling to you;
> My cry goes out to all of humanity...
> > (Proverbs 8:1-4)

Her cosmic and creative presence is celebrated, for instance, in Proverbs 8:23-25:

> From everlasting I was firmly set,
> From the beginning before earth came into being.
> The deep was not, when I was born,
> There were no springs to gush with water.
> Before the mountains were settled,
> Before the hills, I came to birth.

Wisdom embraces the whole world and expresses all human capabilities:

> She deploys Her strength from one end of the earth to the other,
> Ordering all things for good....
> If in this life wealth is a desirable possession,
> What is more wealthy than Wisdom whose work is everywhere?
> Or, if it be the intellect that is at work,
> Where is there a greater intellect than Wisdom, designer of all?
> Or, if it be virtue you love, why virtues are the fruits of Her labors
> Since it is She who teaches temperance and prudence,
> Justice and fortitude;
> Nothing in life is more helpful to people than these.
> Or, if you are eager for wide experience,
> She knows the past, she forecasts the future;
> She knows how to turn maxims, and solve riddles,
> She has foreknowledge of signs and wonders,
> Of the unfolding of the ages and of times.
> ...immortality is found in being kin to Wisdom
> Pure contentment in Her friendship
> Inexhaustible riches in what She does,
> Intelligence in the cultivation of Her society
> And renown in the fellowship of Her conversation.
>   (Wisdom 8:1, 5-8, 17-18)

Hence, to walk in the ways of wisdom/Wisdom is to walk in the ways of insight and uprightness; it means to become one of Her justice-seeking friends. To re-imagine biblical interpretation as the spiraling circle dance of Wisdom is to imagine feminism as a Spirit/spiritual movement in the open space of wisdom/Wisdom who calls us out of isolation and invites us to join Her movements around the world. In short, this book does not seek to persuade you to read and accept the authority of the bible. Rather, it invites you to join a movement for change and transformation that is inspired by a vision of justice and human flourishing or well-being. For believers, such a vision is motivated and sustained by biblical readings.

Such a movement is best envisioned in the radical democratic space of wisdom/Wisdom.

The Public Radical Democratic Space of Wisdom's Movements

Such a *radical,* that is *grassroots* (from Latin *radix* = *roots*), democratic space is carved out today by social movements for change. Wo/men's grassroots movements around the globe have initiated processes of democratization that allow wo/men to determine their lives, participate in decision making, and contribute to the creation of a just civil society and religious community. When I use the word democracy, however, I do not mean representative formal democracy.

Three broad understandings of democracy and democratization can be distinguished: liberal democracy, Marxist/socialist democracy, and direct participatory democracy. *Liberal* democracy entails a shift from the direct rule of the people to representative government that protects individual rights, equal opportunity, constitutional government, and separation of powers. *Marxist/socialist* democracy argues that effective participation of citizens in the political process is prevented by class and other inequalities. Human emancipation is possible only with the overthrow of the capitalist system under the leadership of the Party. However, socialist democrats increasingly seek to incorporate pluralism and multiculturalism into the theory of democratization.

Participatory democracy insists on a literal understanding of democracy as "rule of and by the people." It distinguishes itself from other forms of democracy by the conviction that such a "people democracy" is actually realizable. It provides equal opportunities for all to take part in decision making in matters affecting not only the political realm but also the workplace, the community, and interpersonal relations. It encourages people to take control of the course of their lives and supports structural arrangements that encourage citizens to exercise self-determination, respect the rights of others, take part in debates about the "common good," and create new institutions that are truly participatory and egalitarian. Participatory democracy recognizes that

> Democracy needs to continue to undergo a process of re-creation and that a more active and substantial participation can only take place as a result of experimentation with new and different ways that seek to enhance citizen involvement and discussion. In a sense, democracy can never be achieved in any final form—it has to be continually re-created and renegotiated.[1]

---

[1]Jill M. Bystydzienski and Joti Sekhon, eds., *Democratization and Wo/men's Grassroots Movements* (Bloomington: Indiana University Press, 1999), 9. This book analyzes the

Grassroots movements are the embodiment of such ongoing democratization processes. They are community-based initiatives, base groups,
or people's organizations that address practical everyday problems, are
committed to improving living conditions in a particular location, and
promote values associated with local, decentralized democracy. They redefine the form and content of politics by seeking to create and to expand
spaces for democratic decision making, consciousness-raising, individual
self-development, group solidarity, and more effective public participation. Wo/men are and have been at the forefront in creating and shaping
such global processes of democratization.

In modernity most of the social movements for change have been inspired by the dream of radical democratic equality and equal human
rights. Since the Western democratic ideal has promised equal participation and equal rights to all but in actuality has restricted power and rights
to a small group of "Elite Gentlemen," those who have been deprived of
their human rights and dignity have struggled to transform their situations
of oppression and exclusion. However, such radical grassroots democratic
struggles are not just a product of modernity, nor is their ethos and vision
of radical democracy restricted to the West.

Since it is impossible to adequately represent these movements and
their struggles for changing structures of domination, I will just highlight
some of them by listing their names. My aim is not to be comprehensive
but to be illustrative. I invoke these struggles here because I want to con-
textualize feminist biblical interpretation within them.

 - Wo/men's struggle for democratic decision-making powers
 - Wo/men's struggle for the abolition of slavery
 - Wo/men's struggle for religious freedom
 - Wo/men's struggle for voting rights
 - Wo/men's struggle for education
 - Wo/men's struggle for workers' rights
 - Wo/men's struggle for human rights as wo/men's rights
 - Wo/men's struggle for access to the professions
 - Wo/men's struggle against colonialism and for national independence
 - Wo/men's struggle against sexual violence
 - Wo/men's struggle for reproductive rights
 - Wo/men's struggle for lesbian/gay/bisexual/transsexual rights
 - Wo/men's struggle against global capitalism
 - Wo/men's struggle for cultural preservation and artistic expression

---

variety of ways in which wo/men from sixteen different countries struggle "for more control over their daily lives while simultaneously creating and extending opportunities for
greater participation" (18).

- Wo/men's struggle for divorce as well as rights to their own names
- Wo/men's struggle for inheritance and property rights
- Wo/men's grassroots movements struggling for food, shelter, and resources
- Wo/men's struggle for the environment and against ecological devastation
- Wo/men's struggles against age, health-related, and disability discrimination
- Wo/men's struggles against debilitating beauty standards

All these struggles—and many more—have been struggles for wo/men's self-determination, rights, autonomy, dignity, and radical democratic equality. These and many others provide the context of a critical feminist interpretation for liberation. They do so not only by articulating ever-new sites of struggle but also by providing ever-more sophisticated categories of analysis of domination and visions of a radical democratic society.

The role and contributions of intellectuals in such social movements is greatly debated. Cornel West has called for intellectuals who understand themselves as cultural critics to become involved in a "cultural politics of difference."

> The new cultural politics of difference are neither simply oppositional in contesting the mainstream (or *malestream*) for inclusion, nor transgressive in the avant-gardist sense of shocking conventional bourgeois audiences. Rather, they are distinct articulations of talented (and usually privileged) contributors to culture who desire to align themselves with demoralized, demobilized, depoliticized, and disorganized people in order to empower and enable social action.... This perspective impels these cultural critics and artists to reveal, as an integral component of their production, the very operations of power within their immediate work contexts (i.e., academy, museums, gallery, mass media).[2]

Thus, cultural critics have the task of aligning themselves in solidarity with those who are dehumanized by the relations of domination and to spell out the operations of power in such relations. West acknowledges the feminist roots of the cultural politics of difference and observes that the decisive push toward it has come not from male intellectuals of the left but from black wo/men of the African diaspora. However, I wonder

---

[2]Cornel West, "The New Cultural Politics of Difference," in *The Cultural Studies Reader,* ed. S. During (New York: Routledge, 1993), 204.

whether the responsibility of such intellectuals is best characterized as "enabling and empowering social action." In my view, intellectuals will be able to articulate knowledges and visions that engender and empower socio-political action and a change in relations of domination only if and when we as participants in a socio-political movement for justice attempt to "hear into speech" the theoretical problems and challenges of a group of people involved in grassroots democratic struggles.

I do not want to be misunderstood. I do not propose an emphasis on theorizing and vision above social action. Rather, I want to shift attention from the question of the "role" of intellectuals in social movements for changing relations of domination to the question of the theoretical contributions of such movements to the articulation of what is considered knowledge. Such a shift stresses the significance of grassroots movements' creativity and initiative for articulating emancipatory knowledge and wisdom over and above that of the talented intellectual and privileged advocate. Seeking to empower and enable disorganized people, integrated or connected intellectuals must first be able to learn from the politics and values of such grassroots movements.

Since feminist theory and theology start with critically reflected experience, let me illustrate this point with reference to my own experience. When I wrote my first dissertation on "Ministries of Women in the Church" in the early 1960s,[3] I was very frustrated because I could not find any theological framework that corresponded to my experience, which questioned the hegemonic discourse of femininity, or, as I have dubbed it, that of the "White Lady." For whatever reasons—and I could mention many—I have never been successfully socialized into the cultural standards of femininity and therefore have never subscribed to them. However, most of the academic literature at the time[4] presupposed a cultural framework that insisted on feminine values and virtues culminating in either physical or spiritual motherhood.

During that time, the book by the German poet Gertrud von LeFort entitled *The Eternal Woman* was widely read in theology, and I could find only one work—that of Elisabeth Gössmann—which questioned the theological construct of the Eternal Woman. Gössmann's book, however, was not written as a scientific work. In order to find arguments and resources for critically deconstructing the hegemonic understanding of femininity and wo/men's place within religion, I looked desperately to political science, psychology, legal studies, literary studies, and sociology for a dif-

---

[3]See my book *Discipleship of Equals: A Critical Feminist Ekklesia-logy of Liberation* (New York: Crossroad, 1993), 13–22.

[4]Simone de Beauvoir's work *The Second Sex* was not considered academic at the time!

ferent theorization of wo/men's nature and role. However, just as the theologians did, the political scientists, sociologists, and anthropologists defined women's nature in terms of selfless motherhood and construed it either as inferior or as complementary to that of men.

Because of this frustrating experience of not being able to find within the academic literature of the day an alternative theoretical framework that would correspond to my own self-understanding as an intellectual wo/man, I was ripe for the wo/men's liberation movement. Finally I was able to find confirmation of my experience and critique of the hegemonic feminine in culture and religion after I came to the U.S. in 1970 and became part of the emerging women's liberation movement in the academy and in the churches.

The new and exciting experience of encountering for the first time a group of wo/men who claimed "doing theology" as their birthright, who reflected on their negative experiences of feminine socialization and role determination, and who set out to change their situations, made this different self-understanding possible. It was the experience of a wo/men's liberation movement that validated my own personal experience and perspective that sought to reject the ideology of the "White Lady." Because of it I was able to understand myself as a scholar "doing theology" with a focus on and in the interest of wo/men as my very own people. The criterion for evaluating such a different theology, which I early on named "a critical feminist theology of liberation," was not orthodoxy or doctrinal systematics but its ability to change religious structures of second-class citizenship in the academy and religion as well as its ability to transform theological and religious mindsets of self-alienation, low self-esteem, and subordination.

This experience of the wo/men's liberation movements in the States empowered me to re-conceptualize my own self-understanding as a theologian and biblical scholar. Although I had struggled to be admitted to my university as the first wo/man to study the full course of theology and to graduate with the equivalent of an M.Div. degree, I did not see myself as a theologian who would shape the discipline of theology and its study. Rather, I had studied theology in order to *mediate* the theology of the "White Fathers" in its liberal malestream form to "the people" either through pastoral work or through teaching. Yet, at that time I did (and could) not see myself as a creative theologian who would chart a different way of doing theology. Only after recognizing the injustice that wo/men as a group of people have been excluded by ecclesiastical law and academic custom from theological scholarship was I able to articulate theology in a different key.

It should be obvious by now that, in my understanding, *theology* is an umbrella term for all religious academic inquiry that is committed to a

group of people and not a dogmatic confessional enterprise. As a student in Germany I had experienced theological studies not as rigid and limiting, but rather as an opening of "windows" and perspectives that had not been accessible to me through religious instruction and catechism. Although I had problematized the exclusion of wo/men from ministry and the production of theology in my first dissertation on "Ministries of Women in the Church," I had not questioned the elite masculine genderization of theology (and religious studies) as a systemic feature that corrupts theological frameworks and theories of theology and religious studies. Only the emergence of the wo/men's liberation movement in society and church and its theoretical expression in feminist studies enabled me to articulate theology in a different key, as a critical feminist theology of liberation.

Historical Roots of Liberation Struggles

A liberationist Wisdom model of feminist theology is rooted in wo/men's grassroots struggles for justice and "the good life." The abolitionist movement of the nineteenth century and the liberation movements of the 1960s—the anti-slavery, workers', civil rights, anti-colonialist, gay, anti-war, and radical democratic student movements, and, last but not least, the wo/men's movement—constitute the social location of and have provided the language and discourses for a feminist Wisdom interpretation.

However, this liberationist heritage is often overlooked or repressed by the tendency to tell the history of feminism in progressivist terms. An evolutionist narrative of feminist theory conceptualizes the history of feminism as one of progressive development from theoretically unsophisticated beginnings to the intellectual heights of postmodern feminism. It distinguishes three stages in the development of the feminist movement: equal-rights feminism, radical wo/men-centered feminism, and difference feminism. Insofar as postmodern feminism—often identified with French feminism—is seen as the pinnacle of feminist theory, critical liberationist feminism is either completely eclipsed or relegated to the intellectually "primitive," not-so-sophisticated beginnings of the second wave of the women's movement.

Since my work has always been a part of the second wave of the wo/men's movement, which in its beginnings was called the Women's Liberation Movement (popularly called Women's Lib), I for one do not recognize my experience and history in this postmodern historiography of the wo/men's movement in the late 1960s and early 1970s. The early 1970s movement is generally depicted in contrast either to the more sophisticated ideas that have since developed, or to the later "feminism of difference." In this historical narrative of feminist postmodernism, the

wo/men's movement of the early 1970s becomes the "theoretical other" of an allegedly superior postmodern feminism. The analysis of "patriarchal" oppression that seeks to identify fundamental social causes of wo/men's second-class citizenship is rejected as "grand theory" in favor of an analysis of discursivity and representation. Such progressivist accounts of feminist history function to prevent the articulation of a feminist self-understanding that is able to value its beginnings as a significant part of the radical democratic liberation movements in the middle of the nineteenth and twentieth centuries.

This skewed history functions to effectively prohibit any positive feminist identification with the early wo/men's movement. No self-respecting feminist intellectual can afford to be associated with the early "feminism of sameness" and its struggles to have women become like men. By construing the second wave of the wo/men's movement in terms of the white middle-class feminism of Betty Friedan rather than in terms of the variegated liberation movements that flowered in the 1960s, such a re-construction of feminist history in terms of progress from naïve beginnings to postmodern sophistication represses the fact that, from the very beginning, the feminist movement and feminist thought were conceptualized in radical democratic, anti-racist, anti-homophobic, anti-imperialist, and anti-classist liberationist terms. To construe the beginnings of second-wave feminism as so-called equality/sameness feminism prevents a genuine feminist memory and history of the Women's Liberation Movement from emerging.

The theoretical sources of the Women's Liberation Movement, however, were not just Simone de Beauvoir and Betty Friedan but also Frantz Fanon, Paulo Freire, Martin Luther King, Angela Davis, and Rosa Luxemburg, among others. Liberation theory and theology came to Women's Liberation via socialist, Marxist, Black Power, gay, postcolonial, and indigenous liberation movements. The first U.S. publications in feminist theology, for example, were publications in feminist liberation theology that were developed parallel to Latin American liberation and Black theology. We did not seek to conceptualize feminist liberation theology in the interest of white middle-class wo/men but in the interest of oppressed wo/men. We struggled for a feminist theological voice in a field that throughout the centuries has excluded wo/men by law and custom from becoming theologians. We understood that the historical legacy of oppression was the reason why so very few white wo/men and almost no wo/men of other races could be found in theology and biblical studies in the 1960s and 1970s, and those few were often not interested in torpedoing their careers by doing feminist work.

However, it must be noted that the Women's Liberation Movement was not just a part of the radical democratic movements of the time but

was also in conflict with them. Many wo/men who were in the forefront of such movements soon experienced the reality that these movements were male centered and that wo/men were second-class citizens in them. They soon realized that they were "shit-workers" without much say or power. They were relegated to secretarial jobs, made sex objects, or seen as the muses of the "great men" of the movements.

Hence, wo/men in these movements began to form their own groups and task forces in an attempt to be heard and recognized. When they were rejected and ridiculed, they formed autonomous wo/men's groups, and the Women's Liberation Movement was born. However, the experience of exploitation in malestream social movements for change had important theoretical consequences. Because of this personal and collective negative experience and its historical context, feminist discourses have tended to be tinged with anti-male rhetoric and to see wo/men's oppression as the primordial form of oppression.

The experience of being marginalized and "used" by men committed to liberation struggles was exacerbated because it took place at a time when wo/men had become conscientized and the wo/men's liberation movements around the world had begun to advocate radical democratic and postcolonial theoretical frameworks. In reaction to marginalization and exclusion, feminists soon concentrated on articulating their own specific focus on wo/men, which such liberationist frameworks had neglected. They used as their basic analytic categories "patriarchy" and "woman" without fully recognizing that the category "woman" had been socially constructed in the interest of domination.

Feminists of different races and social locations soon objected correctly that a dualistic patriarchal gender analysis does not take the multiplicative structures of wo/men's oppression into account. However, rather than developing a comprehensive and complex systemic analytic, some have tended to put into effect a binary two-system analysis of patriarchal gender oppression on the one hand, and class, race, or colonial oppression on the other. Feminist theologians often adopt such a dual-system analysis (analysis of racism and patriarchy, colonialism and sexism, or a Marxist and a feminist analysis) and thereby also are in danger of re-inscribing in the antagonistic rhetoric of systemic dualism the hegemonic kyriarchal relations of domination that produce the intersection of gender, race, class, religion, and national domination.[5]

In the absence of a coherent and comprehensive systemic liberationist analysis that could articulate all the structures of wo/men's oppres-

---

[5]Over the years *The Journal of Feminist Studies in Religion* has sponsored intellectual "round tables" that seek to address and debate controverted and controversial issues in the articulation of feminist theology.

sion, feminist theorists and theologians have tended to enact the dualism of First World/Third World in their own discourses. Their rhetoric has turned more and more often against other feminists rather than against elite men who are still in charge and control. While feminist theologians, for instance, rightly denounce the failures of their Christian feminist colleagues, when solely directed against Christian feminists and not against *hegemonic* Christian theology this indictment leaves the structures of power unchanged.

An Emancipatory Grassroots Democratic Ethos

A critical feminist liberation theory and theology is so threatening to many, I suggest, because it not only focuses on the dehumanizing power of oppression and its effects as "power over," but also maintains the possibility of transformation. Far from re-inscribing the binary dualism between oppressor and oppressed, emancipatory discourses insist that the humanity of both oppressor and oppressed is severely deformed and damaged by the power of domination which liberation theologians have named structural sin. Emancipatory theory is an account of the oppressive workings of power whereby oppressive power or domination is seen as the ability of one person or group to dominate and exploit the other. Liberation theory and theology distinguish between two modalities of power: power as "power over," or as "domination," on the one hand, and power as "power for," or as energy and creativity, on the other hand. Hence, the transformation of oppressive experience is central for liberation theory and theology. It presupposes a principled opposition to domination and exploitation in the name of justice.

Liberation theory articulates feminism as an ethics or morality of radical equality and justice. With Simone Weil, it is adamant that "respect is due to the human being as such and it is not a matter of degree." With Hannah Arendt, it insists on the "equal dignity of the many." It is this ethic of the irreducible value of human beings who are wo/men that is the central moral truth in feminism. One's self-worth and dignity depend on oneself and are not derived in competition with others. There is something absolute about the value of human beings, who are all equal before G*d. This moral truth is completely at odds with the way our societies and communities are organized and structured, which is around marginal status and relations of domination. This moral stance rejects all arbitrary privilege and relations of dependence which generate all kinds of repression, equivocation, and uneasiness.

The discourses of domination engender an ethics of inequality that requires relations of superiority and inferiority between human beings who are wo/men and stresses the idea that some people are more impor-

tant and valuable than others. In the ethics of domination, one's sense of importance, goodness, and worth depends on the negation of those qualities in someone else, who must be in some way insignificant and inferior, if I am to be important and great. Discourses of domination not only socialize us into the ethos of superiority/inferiority but also pressure us into identifying and colluding with those who have status and power. They compel us to recognize their importance and to disassociate and distance ourselves from those who are "unacceptable" and without power. The economic, psychological, social, and political costs are high if one refuses to collude in this ethos of domination.

Insofar as human beings have the fundamental need to be recognized and respected by other human beings, domination psychologically and socially deforms people and these deformations in turn help to maintain dehumanizing power relations. The antagonism of oppressed people toward each other is the underside of this fundamental need for recognition. It keeps relations of domination in place by channeling aggression away from the powerful and onto the powerless. Competition and antagonism of the oppressed against each other, of wo/men against wo/men, are engendered by the discourses of domination. They are signs that even feminists have internalized the general cultural prejudice that considers wo/men to be "lesser" human beings. This ethos of superiority/inferiority is the psychological mechanism that sustains most relations of domination.

The fundamental need to be recognized as human is constitutive of what it means to be human. This definition of being human needs no specific content other than the satisfaction of the need itself. The need for unconditional recognition and respect as a human being is prior to any other need. The worth of human beings is considered by liberation theory and theology to be absolute, unchangeable, and not subject to comparison or competition. Such radical equality is not sameness but only the absence of any need to subordinate one person as inferior to the control of another who is more powerful.

Consequently, it is in the course of personal and political struggles and resistance against domination that the drive for respect and love becomes a drive for autonomy and self-determination. Resistance has two phases or moments that are interdependent: the abolition of relations of domination and the struggle for autonomy. The possibility of genuine human respect, love, and equality can be achieved only when relations of domination are resisted and transformed into relations of equality. The social character of being human requires that the liberation of one human being from domination is intrinsically dependent on all others attaining it too. This requires a transformation not only of oppressive structures but also of individual consciousness. In consequence, feminist biblical interpretation has focused from its inception on such a transformation of consciousness.

Feminist Biblical Studies as a Wisdom Movement
for Transformation

From the nineteenth into the twentieth and now twenty-first centuries, the bible has been used both as a weapon against wo/men's emancipation to equal citizenship in society and church and as a resource in their struggles for liberation. Feminist biblical interpretation, I propose, is best conceptualized as an integral part of wo/men's struggles for survival and well-being. If the bible has been used against and for wo/men in their diverse struggles, then the goal of biblical interpretation cannot be just *to understand* and *appropriate* biblical texts and traditions. Rather, feminist biblical hermeneutics has the task of *changing* biblical interpretation and its Western idealist hermeneutical frameworks, individualist practices, and socio-political relations of domination.

For that reason, liberation theologies of all colors take the experience and voices of the oppressed and marginalized, of those wo/men traditionally excluded from articulating theology and shaping communal life, as the starting point of biblical interpretation and theological reflection. In reclaiming the authority of wo/men as religious-theological subjects who must affirm their own spiritual authority for shaping and determining biblical religions, my own feminist work has attempted to re-conceptualize the act of biblical interpretation as a moment in the global struggles for liberation.

Feminist interpreters seek to develop new ways of reading the bible (and other culturally influential texts) in order to prevent biblical knowledge from continuing to be produced in the interest of domination and injustice. Usually it is assumed that biblical knowledges and reading practices are developed by academic or ecclesiastical leaders and then "translated" into the vernacular language of the "common reader," who is expected to appropriate and apply such knowledge to everyday life. I want to argue to the contrary, that wo/men struggling for change and recognition as full citizens in society, the academy, and churches articulate emancipatory knowledge and liberating insights.

Feminist scholars in turn have the task of "translating" these insights into academic and religious discourse so that they can become public knowledges and inspire research in the interest of wo/men. In other words, feminist interpreters have the task not so much of translating the methods and results of biblical scholarship to a wider audience, but rather of learning from and of "casting their lot" with wo/men struggling for survival and change in order to be able to "translate" wo/men's quest for self-esteem and justice into the language of the academy.

Long before postmodern theories, liberation theologies not only recognized the perspectival and contextual nature of knowledge and inter-

pretation but also asserted that biblical interpretation and theology are—knowingly or not—always engaged for or against the oppressed. Intellectual neutrality is not possible in a historical world of exploitation and oppression. However, such a position does not assume the innocence and purity of the oppressed. Neither does it see them just as victims incapable of being agents for change. Rather, a shift from a modern Western malestream to a critical liberation theological frame of reference engenders a fourfold change:

1. a change of interpretive assumptions and goals
2. a change of methodology and epistemology
3. a change of individual and collective consciousness, and
4. a change of social-ecclesial institutions and cultural-religious formations.

A critical interpretation for liberation does not begin with the text; it does not place the bible at the center of its attention. Rather, it begins with a reflection on one's experience and socio-political religious location. For such a reflection it utilizes a critical systemic analysis of the kyriarchal oppressive structures which shape our lives and are inscribed in biblical texts and interpretations. In reading biblical texts, I have consistently argued that we must take a "feminist stand" with wo/men who struggle at the bottom of the kyriarchal pyramid of domination and exploitation, because their struggles reveal both the fulcrum of dehumanizing oppression threatening every wo/man *and* the power of Divine Wisdom at work in our midst.

For this reason, a feminist critical interpretation for liberation insists on the hermeneutical priority of feminist struggles. It does so in order not only to disentangle the ideological (religious-theological) practices and functions of biblical texts for inculcating and legitimating the kyriarchal order, but also to identify the potential these texts have for fostering justice and liberation. Biblical readings that do not prioritize wo/men's struggles against multiplicative oppressions but privilege the biblical text itself as well as malestream doctrinal, theological, spiritual, or theoretical frameworks can only either be recuperative or deconstructive, but not liberating.

The challenge today is to open the hermeneutical conversation as widely as possible in the interest of struggles for justice, especially at a time when the discipline of feminist biblical studies is developing its own highly specialized vocabulary and allegiance to the academy or institutionalized religions. Feminist biblical studies are in danger of becoming "disciplined" and of deriving their theoretical frameworks or taking their measure from the discipline of biblical studies rather than from feminist movements for ending wo/men's second-class citizenship.

Again, I want to illustrate my point with an autobiographical reference. When I began working on what would later become *In Memory of Her,* I decided that I was not going to write another book *about women* in the bible. Rather, what I wanted to do was to engage the paradigm shift brought about by feminist theory and the movement for early Christian historiography. I sought to theorize the problems and issues raised by various groups of wo/men and to confront these feminist questions with the idiom and problematics of academic religious studies.

I remember quite distinctly one night when I was unable to bring together and integrate all the diverse information I had gathered. I suddenly realized what my problem was and why I could not merge the materials into a whole. It dawned on me that my problem stemmed from raising feminist issues and adopting feminist frameworks, but doing so in the language of the academy. Right then, I had an anxiety attack that the book would have no audience. I feared that feminists would not read the book because it was written in the "male" idiom of academic scholarship, while my colleagues in biblical studies and theology would not read it because it addressed feminist questions and operated within a feminist intellectual framework.

Fortunately, I was mistaken. While *In Memory of Her* did not achieve the same scholarly recognition as, for instance, the work of Wayne Meeks (which appeared in the same year), it was nevertheless read by many of my colleagues and used in many college and seminary courses. Most important, the book has been read and studied in many wo/men's groups, not only in the U.S. but around the world. In my experience, many wo/men who have little theological education and exegetical know-how have understood the book better than some of my colleagues who are steeped in historical or theological theoretical assumptions. Several years ago I received a letter from a wo/men's group in the interior of Australia. They wrote, "We are all not theologically trained. Some of us have not even a college degree, but we have read *In Memory of Her* for the last two years with the help of a dictionary. We feel we have received a good theological education in the process."

Grassroots feminists connect with the experience of struggle that underlies the book's conceptualization. Also important to them is the positive affirmation that wo/men as historical actors have shaped religious tradition and vision, even if hegemonic texts and traditions have eliminated them from the historical record. In contrast, many of my colleagues in biblical studies have not understood this basic framework, and still continue to misread the book as speaking about "golden origins" or as following the Protestant model of pristine beginnings that rapidly decayed into patriarchy. The reason for such a misreading is aptly expressed by Judith Plaskow.

I read this book excited and resisting every word. I made furious
notes in the margins asking, "How do you know women participated? Isn't it a large assumption, indeed an *a priori* commitment?" Forced to sort out my feelings for an American Academy
of Religion symposium on *In Memory of Her,* I realized that I
found the book deeply disturbing because it thrusts women into
an unaccustomed position of power. To take seriously the notion
that religious history is the history of women and men imposes
an enormous responsibility on women: It forces us to take on the
intellectual task of rewriting all of history. . . . It does these things,
moreover, without allowing us the luxury of nursing our anger
and waiting for the patriarchs to create change, for it reminds us
that we are part of a long line of women who were simultaneously victims of the tradition and historical agents struggling
within and against it.[6]

As a consequence, the understanding of a feminist text such as *In
Memory of Her* is not just an intellectual but also an emotional matter. To
engage in feminist biblical interpretation raises not just intellectual questions but also emotional ones. It asks for a commitment to the "preferen-
tial option for wo/men." Either one's overall theoretical practice is oriented to struggles for justice and to changing dehumanizing structures or
it is beholden to the academy or the church, which have consistently un-
dermined wo/men's intellectual and social powers.

A critical feminist interpretation for liberation that reads the bible
with the lens and in the context of wo/men struggling to change oppressive kyriarchal structures of religious, cultural, and societal texts and institutions, I continue to argue, must be distinguished both from Christian
"apologetic" biblical women's studies and from dualistic academic gender studies (i.e., studies that focus on the homogeneous categories of
male and female to address the problem of "women"). Popular and academic biblical readings *by women*, reading the bible as *a woman and from
the perspective of women*, as well as biblical interpretation in terms of
gender are not simply identical with a *critical feminist interpretation for
liberation*, insofar as these modes of reading do not question the religious
and cultural gender lens of interpretation.

In short, a critical feminist interpretation for liberation does not derive its lenses from the modern individualistic understanding of religion
and the bible. Rather, it seeks to shift attention to the politics of biblical

---

[6]Judith Plaskow, "Critique and Transformation: A Jewish Feminist History," in *Life-
cycles,* Vol. II, ed. Deborah Orenstein and Jane Rachel Litman (Woodstock, Vt.: Jewish
Lights Publishing House, 1997), 99.

studies and its socio-political contexts of struggle. It places wo/men as subjects and agents, as full decision-making citizens, at the center of attention. To that end, it develops and engages not only a de-constructive but also a (re)constructive approach to interpretation. It struggles to elucidate the ways in which religious doctrines, symbols, practices, and biblical texts function in the creation and maintenance of ideas about sex/gender, race, colonialism, class, and religion. It also examines how social constructions of sex/gender, race, colonialism, class, and religion have influenced and shaped theoretical frameworks, theological formulations, and biblical interpretations. It understands the bible and its own work of interpretation as a site of struggle over meaning making, authorization, and symbolic power. I invite you to join others and myself in the struggles on the road to the cosmopolitan house of Divine Wisdom.

Such a feminist rhetorical model of reading "in the way of Wisdom" is not an individualistic accomplishment. Rather, it must be situated in its own context of origin. This model owes its articulation to the feminist liberation movements within biblical religions and society at large as well as to its engagement with feminist critical theory in general, and with alternative strategies of feminist biblical interpretations in particular. In this emancipatory Wisdom paradigm, the goal of biblical interpretation is not just explanation and understanding but conscientization.

Feminist Biblical Interpretation as a Process of Conscientization

The method to achieve the cultural and religious transformation of relations of domination into relations of radical equality that was developed by the Women's Liberation Movement is consciousness-raising, a process through which wo/men grow in feminist awareness. Feminist consciousness insists on wo/men's full humanness and their freedom for self-definition, self-determination, self-respect, self-esteem, and self-affirmation. Feminist awareness begins with the recognition by wo/men that their "lesser" being, inferiority, and oppression are structural and not their personal fault. It is the discovery of structures of socio-economic domination and the recognition that one belongs to an exploited and oppressed group even if one is individually privileged and well-off. It is the discovery that the personal is political.

In an interview added as a postscript to her international bestseller *Hanna's Daughters,* Marianne Fredrickson addresses the problem of why wo/men in Western societies are not able to realize and live the rights they have received in the last century. Although most wo/men today have rights and opportunities, have the same educational opportunities as men, have their own jobs, have legal rights and make money—rights their grandmothers could not have dreamed of—most of them continue the tra-

dition of self-negation and service: needing to be married, putting their children first, tending to their homes, loving their husbands, taking care of everyone and everything. This raises the question of where the line between real love and self-obliteration[7] begins. *Hanna's Daughters* explores this pattern of self-sacrificing love and suggests it is a social inheritance that is passed on from generation to generation. Thus, the book is an excellent literary exploration of "feminine" consciousness.

Consciousness-raising or conscientization is a term derived from the Portuguese *conscientização*. It was introduced by Brazilian educator Paulo Freire to designate a learning process in which groups become skilled at recognizing forms and experiences of social, political, cultural, religious, and economic oppression and dehumanization. Such a consciousness-raising process was first used in literacy training among poor Brazilian peasants in order to teach them how, with the help of systemic analysis, to "decode" their situation of poverty and exploitation.

According to Freire, conscientization means learning to *name* and *change* oneself and one's situation. In *Pedagogy of the Oppressed* Freire asserts that humans *"are* because they *are* in a situation, and they will be *more* the more they not only critically reflect upon their existence but critically act upon it."[8] Those who become conscientized see through the socio-cultural myth of superiority/inferiority that keeps them in situations of oppression. When people recognize and acknowledge that they are exploited and oppressed, they are empowered to achieve liberation. They do so by becoming committed to their own liberation as well as to that of others and by transforming themselves and their oppressive situation. Conscientization is a critical process, a spiraling dance that is never ending. A critical feminist liberationist interpretation engages the bible for such conscientization.

In contrast, the scientific ethos of biblical studies insists that we as readers must silence our interests and abstract from our socio-political situation in order to respect the "alien" character of the biblical text and the historical chasm that exists between it and ourselves. This rhetoric of disinterestedness and presupposition-free exegesis silences reflection on the political interests and functions of biblical scholarship. Its claim to public scientific status suppresses the rhetorical character of biblical texts and readings and obscures the power relations through which they are constituted and kept in place.

---

[7]Several of my student readers objected to this paragraph and asked me to eliminate it because it suggests that "wo/men should not be wives and mothers." However, my point is not a critique of egalitarian marriage and motherhood but of wo/men's socialization to become *self-negating and self-sacrificing* wives and mothers.

[8]Paulo Freire, *Pedagogy of the Oppressed* (New York: Seabury Press, 1970), 100.

Such a suppression of present-day theological socio-ecclesial locations and religious-theological interests is due largely to the prevailing assumption that the form of exegetical commentary demands scientific objectivity and disinterestedness rather than a self-conscious reading/hearing that is engaged and perspectival. In order to respect the rights of the text, we as interpreters have to suppress our own questions. Biblical interpretation is here construed in kyriarchal terms insofar as readers have to *submit* themselves to the unequivocal meaning of the text that is established by biblical scholars or religious authorities. Moreover, this scientific model of biblical studies shares in the pathology of modernity, which, according to Jürgen Habermas, splits off expert cultures from everyday cultural practices and life. Finally, by understanding the "first" or historical meaning of the biblical text as a deposit of the definitive meaning of the author, historical biblical interpretation runs the risk of "shutting up" the "meaning" of the text in the past and turning it into an artifact of antiquity that is accessible only to the expert in biblical history or philology.

Theologians and ministers in turn are interested in the religious, "spiritualized" meaning of biblical texts for today. Through "application" they seek to liberate the text from its "historical captivity" in order to rescue the message of the bible for contemporary Christians. One form of this rescue and liberation of the text is accomplished by "updating and actualizing" aspects of it: by "translating" and rendering its mythic images into contemporary frameworks of meaning, by selecting those passages that still speak to us and illumine our own questions, by reducing its world of vision to theological or ethical principles and themes.

Another form of theological "application" of biblical texts is achieved by correlating the text's discursive situation with present-day religious-problem situations. Whereas theological liberals frustrated by the mythological content or outdated injunctions of the bible look for commentaries that enable them to "squeeze" the living water of revelation and theological truth out of the hard stone of ancient biblical facts, biblical fundamentalists insist on the inerrant literal sense of the text as a "given fact."

Insofar as scientific exegesis tends to foreclose the text's multivalent meanings and does not acknowledge that we always interpret texts from a particular socio-theological location, it is contrary to the practice of conscientization. It overlooks the fact that the practice of interpretation does not simply understand and comprehend texts and symbols (hermeneutic); it also produces new meanings speaking from different socio-political locations and from changed rhetorical situations (rhetoric). A rhetorical conceptualization of text and interpretation situates biblical scholarship in such a way that its public character and political responsibility become an integral part of our literary readings and historical re-

constructions of the biblical world. Hence, it can function as a practice of conscientization.

This understanding of rhetoric/rhetorical as a communicative practice that involves interests, values, and visions must be carefully distinguished from the popular use of the expression. Popular parlance often labels as "rhetoric/rhetorical" those statements which it believes to be "mere talk," stylistic figure, deceptive propaganda—any clever form of speech that is not true and honest, that lacks substance. Rhetoric is often misunderstood as "mere" rhetoric, as stylistic ornament, technical device, or linguistic manipulation, as discourse utilizing irrational, emotional devices that are contrary to critical thinking and reasoning.

When I reclaim the term "rhetoric" for a critical feminist interpretation of liberation as a practice of conscientization, I do not use it in this colloquial sense. Indeed, I seek to utilize rhetorical analysis not as one more way of doing literary or structural analysis, but rather as a means to analyze how biblical texts and interpretations participate in creating or sustaining oppressive or liberating theo-ethical values, socio-political practices, and worlds of vision for their respective audiences.

Biblical interpretation understood as a rhetorical or communicative practice lends itself to conscientization insofar as it seeks to display how biblical texts and their contemporary interpretations are political and religious discursive practices. Authorial aims, point of view, narrative strategies, persuasive means, and authorial closure, as well as audience perceptions and constructions, are rhetorical practices which have determined not only the production of the bible but also its subsequent interpretations.

Moreover, a critical feminist rhetoric of conscientization insists that context is as important as text. What we see depends on where we stand. Our social location or rhetorical context is decisive for how we see the world, construct reality, or interpret biblical texts. For instance, I recall that as a teenager I agonized over the decision as to whether to go to university or to learn a trade that would allow me to earn money and become independent. Reading the parable of the talents, I was persuaded that I should use my intellectual talents and go on to higher education. However, I then came across Paul's statement in 1 Corinthians that G*d will destroy the "wisdom of the wise" and choose what is foolish and weak in the eyes of the world. This deepened my predicament. Accepting Paul's advice would mean not bothering with higher studies, but following the spirit of Jesus' parable would mean deciding to develop my intellectual talents rather than squandering them. Luckily, my pastor supported the "talents" interpretation and the rest is history!

Studying theology I soon learned that my readings both of the parable and 1 Corinthians were "naïve" and unscientific. I could have saved myself a lot of agonizing deliberation if I had known that Paul does not

mean higher education when he writes of the "wisdom of the wise." However, such a historically oriented explanation overlooks the social context and location in which I was reading the biblical text for help with making a decision. Since I was not only a wo/man, traditionally barred from biblical studies, but also came from a rural and working-class background, the decision not to go to university would have conformed to the socio-cultural standards of hegemonic culture. Paul's injunction received its power not so much from its "original" meaning but from its resonance with my socio-cultural context, which reserved higher education for middle- and upper-class "cultured" people and university positions in theology for ordained males only.

However, if I, for instance, had been reading this text from the position of an elite educated German male, the warning of Paul may have had a quite different resonance. Or if I had read the story of the talents, let's say, as a neo-capitalist international banker, I might have been inspired to justify increasing exploitation of the "have-nots." In short, if context is as important as text for meaning making, then we need not only to look at texts and their literary-historical contexts but also to analyze our own socio-cultural and political contexts, with which a biblical reading will resonate or which it will challenge.

Insofar as feminist conscientization seeks to transform academic as well as ecclesial biblical interpretation, it must always have both a theoretical *and* a practical goal. This praxis-orientation locates a feminist biblical interpretation for liberation in the context of emancipatory movements in society and religion as well as at the intersection of feminist critical theories and liberation theologies. Since feminist studies, in distinction to gender studies, are explicitly committed to the struggle for changing kyriarchal structures of oppression in religious, cultural, and societal institutions, they must disentangle the ideological (religious-theological) functions of biblical texts for inculcating and legitimating relations of domination.

In short, the transformation of the scientific-positivist ethos of biblical studies into a rhetorical-ethical one creates a grassroots democratic space in which feminist and other readers/hearers can participate in defining and debating the meaning and significance of a biblical text in contemporary social-political locations and cultural-religious rhetorical situations. Such democratizing deliberations from within particular struggles and political coalitions acknowledge the multiple locations of feminist voices manifesting themselves in a diversity of intellectual constructs and competing interest groups.

To the extent that different liberationist publics articulate feminist analyses, proposals, and strategies differently, it becomes necessary to adjudicate not only between different interpretations of a biblical text but

also between competing feminist definitions of the world and alternative constructions of symbolic universes. Such competing feminist analyses and divergent articulations of feminist visions are not simply right or wrong; they are not to be construed as dogmatic positions but to be understood as strategic practices of conscientization and deliberation.

By constantly engendering critique, dispute, and debate, feminist biblical practices of democratization and conscientization seek out more adequate strategies and visions for constructing a different understanding of reality. In so doing, we always have to privilege those theories and strategies of feminists who speak from within the experience of multiplicative kyriarchal oppressions. By clarifying and adjudicating contested concepts and proposals, critical feminist biblical studies engender biblical interpretation as a process of grassroots democratization, moral deliberation, and practical solidarity in the midst of diverse and often competing emancipatory struggles.

To read the bible "in the way of Wisdom" has as its goal to engender grassroots democratization, to become fully aware of the powers of domination and to discover the possibilities for achieving justice and the "good life." It requires a decision for *metanoia*—a turning around—from the ways of injustice to walking in the ways of Wisdom's justice and wellbeing. It requires us to join in Wisdom's grassroots democratic movements for justice and self-determination around the globe. Such a turning around also requires the articulation of a systemic analysis that can identify the roadblocks as well as the radical democratic visions that either hinder or inspire wo/men to walk in the ways of Wisdom. Feminist biblical interpretation understood in the paradigm of Wisdom's ever-spiraling dance, public call, and inviting table can provide insight, courage, and sustenance on the journey to the *ekklesia of wo/men* as the spiritual vision and practice of a radical democratic society and religious community.

Deepening Movement

Elisabeth Schüssler Fiorenza, *Sharing Her Word: Feminist Biblical Interpretation in Context* (Boston: Beacon Press, 1998), 50–74, 137–159.

Moving Steps

- Imagine Wisdom calling in the streets and public places of Washington, Los Angeles, New York, Chicago, or your own town. How would she be perceived? What is your emotional reaction to wo/men raising their voice in public? Do you have anxiety attacks when called on to speak in public?

- What do you know about the nineteenth-century suffrage movements? Were they part of your study of history? What do you know about Matilda Jocelyn Gage, the Grimké Sisters, or Anna Julia Cooper?

- What is your understanding of democracy? Draw a circle and fill in the structures and values that determine a radical democratic space. What would radical democracy look like in the areas of economics, education, politics, religion, biblical interpretation? (See worksheet 5.)

- Explore your own experience with femininity. List the values and virtues that are necessary to be considered "feminine." How have you been socalized into femininity? Do you have any experience with opposing or rejecting feminine behavior? Does femininity play a role in biblical interpretation? If so, how?

- Imagine you meet Mary of Magdala on the road. What do you ask her? What does she tell you about herself? Does she like or is she angry about her depiction in the gospels, in the tradition, in commentaries, in popular imagination, in novels, in the musical "Jesus Christ Superstar"? Share your imaginings with your study partner or group and analyze how much your understanding of femininity shapes it.

- What is the difference in method between a scientific and a liberationist understanding of biblical interpretation? Explain what conscientization means and how you will practice it.

Movement Exercise

Use worksheet 4 to look more closely at your own socio-religious location.

Socio-Religious Location Self-Inventory

1. The values and biases into which we have been socialized remain
    generally unconscious but nevertheless determine our hermeneu-
    tical perspective and view of the world. Please reflect on and
    explore each of the following areas:

ETHNICITY	RACE
NATION	SEXUALITY
GENDER	CLASS
SOCIAL STATUS	AGE
HEALTH	EDUCATION
CULTURE	RELIGION
GEOGRAPHICAL LOCATION	COLONIALISM

    in terms of *values/visions of the world, biases/prejudices,* as well
    as *areas of resistance* and *struggles for change* in which you are
    involved and/or of which you know.

2. Describe the type of homes your family of origin occupied, their
    geographical locations, the work your parents did, your family's
    access to and attitude toward money, education, and religion.

3. Look at patterns of gender, race, class, and national relations in
    your family, your church/religious community, or among your
    friends.

4. Identify your struggles and the positive values that inspire you to
    claim your own ethical or theological voice and vision (see work-
    sheet 5).

Ekklesia of Wo/men

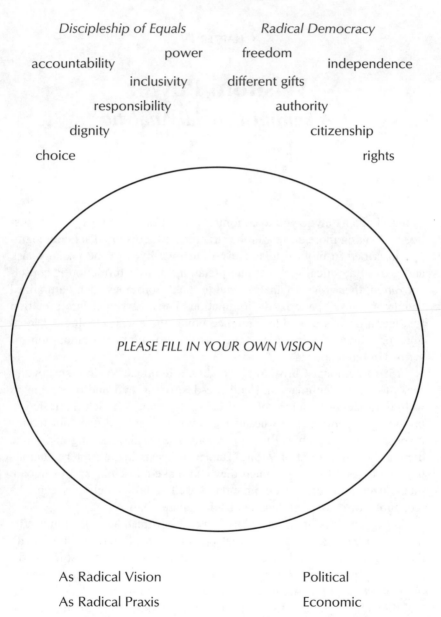

Discipleship of Equals   *Radical Democracy*

power   freedom

accountability   independence

inclusivity   different gifts

responsibility   authority

dignity   citizenship

choice   rights

PLEASE FILL IN YOUR OWN VISION

As Radical Vision   Political

As Radical Praxis   Economic

As Radical Process   Social

As Radical Justice   Religious Equality

CHAPTER IV

Wisdom Power

A Feminist Social Analytic

In this chapter I invite you to continue with me on Wisdom's ways of justice by looking more closely at the structural patterns or social choreography inscribed in biblical texts and in our own lives. If the primary task and goal of a critical feminist interpretation for transformation is conscientization, then it has to analyze and to make conscious such naturalized "common-sense" patterns of domination. Thus, a critical interpretation for liberation has a double reference point: the social-ideological locations of biblical interpreters as well as the structures of domination inscribed in biblical texts.

Like traditional Christian spirituality, a feminist Wisdom spirituality seeks to name dehumanizing and life-destroying evil and deception as well as to identify sources of well-being. It is not so much interested in providing the correct and true interpretation of a text. It does not reduce divergent feminist biblical interpretations to a single meaning and judge them to be either right or wrong. Rather, it insists that all interpretations must be assessed for how much they can make conscious and overcome internalized structures of domination as well as how much they can correct public discourses of dehumanization and prejudice.

Such practices of critical reflection and informed adjudication can be likened to the traditional "spiritual practice" of "discerning the Spirit" that requires prayer and meditation as well as obedience to "spiritual direction." It presupposes that we cannot see reality and ourselves clearly but that we need the "light and guidance of the Holy Spirit" and a spiritual director or "father" to escape self-deception and the "snares" of the evil one. Feminist spirituality also does not eschew centering prayer and meditation but replaces the kyriarchal discipline of "spiritual direction" with the practice of systemic analysis.

Whether we are able to recognize the structural patterns and mechanisms of domination and dehumanization depends on the lenses or analytic categories we use. Social analytic categories offer "lenses" with which we can approach both the biblical text in its own historical context *and* the socio-historical rhetorical situations and contexts of our own lives. Such lenses of interpretation illuminate the bible and its many contexts in the past and in the present as sites of emancipatory struggles. Thus, biblical interpretation in the "open house" of Wisdom seeks to tear down the walls and patterns that dehumanize and divide us from creation and from each other.

To return to the metaphor of the dance, the patterns of domination can be seen as functioning like the choreographic design that determines the steps and movements of the dance, although often such designs are not conscious to the dancers. Similarly, some kind of a socio-political and religious "choreography" of domination is always at work, not only in biblical texts and interpretations but also in our own experience and rhetorical situation, even though such patterns are often not consciously identified or critically reflected.

In order to make conscious the "choreography" of domination, we need a feminist social analytic that also can identify an alternative "choreography." Such an analytic is an assembly of critical concepts and categories that are necessary for critically naming the "choreography" or patterns of domination. It must also be an assembly of the practices of liberation inscribed in biblical texts and their contexts, because, like any other texts, biblical texts are not reflections or mirrors of reality nor are they the direct unfettered Word of G*d. Rather, they communicate divine revelation in and through historical kyriocentric language that rhetorically constructs reality from a socio-political and religious kyriarchal perspective.

Feminist theory, for instance, has made plain that "what it means to be a man or a wo/man" is not a "naturally given" or "divinely ordained" fact but is socially and historically constructed and activated or "performed" in and through the technologies of gender. Equally, race, class, sexual, or ethnic identities are not simply "biologically" given or divinely designed, but are social-historical constructs that have become naturalized as cultural "common sense." Finally, if we always produce or read texts from a certain location and within a certain perspective, then it is important to explore this location and to ask how much it determines not only the reading of biblical texts but also our own self-understanding and view of the world.

The following moving incident, shared by the Jewish theologian Arthur Waskow, speaks powerfully to both the constructedness of text and its construction of oppression in particular discourses and biblical texts. In a National Havurah Summer Institute, Waskow explains,

The passage addressed was Genesis 34, the rape of Dinah....
A silence gathered in the room, and finally one woman took a
deep breath, rose, shut her eyes, and said:
"Raped.
I have been raped three times in the story.
Once. I was raped by Sh'chem.
Twice. I was raped when my brothers ignored me, refused to ask
me what I wanted—
And murdered all the men of Sh'chem.
Three times. The Torah itself is raping me. Still raping me.
Because it does not speak my voice."
Then she sat down in tears. The room was deathly silent.[1]

Waskow goes on to say that afterwards no other wo/man wanted to
speak because all participants agreed that "there are no other words they
want Dinah to say." This is one of the biblical "texts of terror" that derives its rhetorical power from its systemic "resonances" with oppressive
power and wo/men's subjugated knowledges. In contrast to malestream
Jewish interpretation, this interpretation figures the Torah as of "masculine" gender, perpetrating violence and rape.

In light of the great honor the Torah is accorded and the extensive rit-
ualizations of the Torah scroll in Jewish liturgy and of the bible in
Christian liturgy, such an interpretation elicits stark emotions and calls for
great courage. It has become possible because of the consciousness-raising processes engendered by Jewish feminist theology. Since this reading
shares in the consciousness of a feminist movement for justice, it is able
to name the dehumanizing powers of domination and their often unconscious inscriptions in sacred texts.

Accordingly, a critical feminist exploration of context and voice requires us to develop a social analytic that can investigate the political-
cultural "resonances" and "choreography of domination" inscribed in
religious locations of biblical texts and their interpreters. A feminist
socio-cultural analytic attempts to explain not only what the world looks
like but also why it is the way it is. At the same time, it seeks to show that
neither the "world" of Scripture nor the present social order is G*d-given,
natural, and biologically preordained, but rather that it is the outcome and
manifestation of relations of domination.

Different socio-cultural analytics have been developed by liberalism,
Marxism, colonialism, socialism, fascism, capitalism, feminism, post-

---

[1]Arthur Waskow, "God's Body: The Midrashic Process, and the Embodiment of
Torah," in *Body and Bible: Interpreting and Experiencing Biblical Narratives,* ed. Björn
Krondorfer (Philadelphia: Trinity Press International, 1992), 136.

modernism, and other socio-political theories. Since malestream theories, however, generally do not focus on the situation of wo/men but take elite men—or better "Gentlemen"—as the paradigm for being human, feminists seek to develop a socio-cultural analytic that can provide an interpretation of ourselves and the world in which wo/men are no longer marginal and subordinate. In order to be able to adequately "decode" situations of wo/men's oppression and to engage in the ongoing process of transformation, wo/men need categories of analysis that can help us to recognize malestream socio-political and religious-cultural kyriarchal identity formations and discourses of dehumanization.

The preconditions for the articulation of an emancipatory social analytic, I have argued in chapter 1, are social-political movements for change. The emergence of such movements is necessary because subversive practices never automatically follow from the simple fact of exploitation and oppression that generally has been internalized as a "personal problem." As I have pointed out previously, I understand the wo/men's movement as just such a socio-political movement that engages in radical grassroots democratic struggles for justice around the globe. The ability of subordinated and oppressed people to imagine a complete overthrow of relations of domination and situations of injustice depends on the articulation, circulation, radicalization, and institutionalization of grassroots movements and radical egalitarian democratic discourses. As de Tocqueville pointed out a long time ago, once people have cultivated the spirit and legitimacy of the principle of justice and equality they will seek to extend it to all spheres of life.

A radical egalitarian democratic Wisdom movement for justice and the well-being of everyone without exception, consequently, must evolve a theory that can articulate such a radical democratic horizon. For developing a social analytic of domination and liberation I prefer a *status* (rather than an *identity*) model of social organization that is able to examine the institutionalized structures and value patterns of domination for their effects on the relative status of social actors both in a given society and in a text. If such status inscriptions constitute persons as peers, capable of participating on a par with each other, then we can speak of status equality or grassroots democracy. If they do not do so, then we speak of domination. Wo/men's struggles for radical democratic equality seek to abolish relations of domination and to establish those of subordinated status as full partners and peers.

In and through cultural, political, and religious discourses, the social structures in which we are positioned are interpreted. Since we cannot stand outside of the interpretive frameworks available in our society and time, we "make sense" out of life with their help. For instance, one wo/man might be influenced by neo-conservatism and believe that her so-

cial position results from the fact that she worked harder in life than the
wo/man on welfare who lives down the street. Another wo/man influenced by right-wing religious fundamentalism might explain her situation
by the fact that she is blessed by G*d because of her virtuous life,
whereas the unmarried mother on welfare has gravely sinned and therefore is punished. Again, another wo/man might believe that her success as
a wife and mother is due to her feminine attractiveness and selfless dedication to her husband and children, and that the fate of the wo/man on
welfare is due to her lack thereof.

If we always have to resort to existing interpretive discourses for
making sense of our lives or of biblical texts, then the importance of social movements for justice becomes obvious. Since malestream hegemonic discourses provide the frameworks in which we "make meaning"
in oppressive situations, feminist discourses must provide frameworks
that illuminate not only the choreography of oppression but also the possibilities for a radical democratic society and religion. We are able to articulate an emancipatory self- and world-understanding only within the
context of radical democratic movements, which shape theories that help
us to exploit the contradictions existing between diverse socio-hegemonic
discourses.

Here the distinction between a person's *structural position* and her
subject position becomes important. Every individual is *structurally* positioned within social, cultural, economic, political, and religious systems
by virtue of birth. No one chooses to be born white, black, Asian,
European, mixed race, poor, healthy, male, or female. We always find
ourselves already positioned by and within structures of domination and
the chances we get in life are limited by them. For example, wo/men are
not poor or homeless because we have low motivation, faulty self-esteem,
or poor work habits. Rather wo/men are poor or homeless because of our
structural position within relations of domination.

Unlike a *structural position,* a *subject position* is variable, open to in-
tervention and changeable, but also limited by hegemonic structures of
domination. According to the theorists Ernest Laclau and Chantal Mouffe,

> A "subject position" refers to the ensemble of beliefs through
> which an individual interprets and responds to her structural po-
> sitions within a social formation. In this sense an individual be-
> comes a social agent insofar as she lives her structural positions
> through an ensemble of subject positions.[2]

---

[2]Anna Marie Smith, *Laclau and Mouffe: The Radical Democratic Imagination* (New
York: London, 1998), 58–59.

The relationship between a *structural position* and a *subject position* is quite complex, since our self-understandings are always already determined by our *structural position* with its rewards and pressures. Thus, a person might be theoretically able to live her structural positions through a wide range of subject positions, but practically restricted to a rigidly defined and closed set of available interpretive frameworks. Hence, emancipatory movements and the different interpretive frameworks they articulate are important.

Feminist theory has made a range of such interpretive frameworks and categories available for shaping wo/men's subject positions. It has provided various social analytics for diagnosing and changing wo/men's structural positions in and through the articulation of different subject positions. Key analytic concepts and categories for reading in a feminist fashion have been developed either as reverse discourse to the binary intellectual framework of systemic dualisms or in a critical liberationist frame. Such key categories of feminist deconstructive analysis are, I suggest, on the one hand wo/men and oppression, as well as gender, androcentrism, and patriarchy and on the other hand kyriarchy and kyriocentrism. Androgyny, gynecentrism/gynaikocentrism, matriarchy, relationality, and the *ekklesia of wo/men,* in turn, are categories that seek to provide an alternative theoretical space from which to interpret.

Primary Categories of Analysis

Woman/Women

Feminist movements have crystallized around the category of "woman" and feminist analysis has used "woman" or "women" as its primary category of analysis. In feminist biblical studies, "wo/man" has been understood both as the object and as the subject of interpretation. Wo/men have claimed the authority to interpret the bible and have identified with wo/men of the bible and placed them in the center of attention. By focusing their studies on "women in the bible," they have at the same time continued the malestream discourses that have turned "woman" or "women" but not men into objects of study.

Hence, critical postmodern feminist studies have rendered problematic the function of the signifier "woman/feminine" and have suggested doing away with the concept "woman" altogether. They have done so because the unitary category "woman" not only serves to classify persons in dualistic naturalized sex-gender terms but also characterizes us as belonging to an inferior class of being human. Discourses on "woman/women" have naturalized gender difference as primary difference.

Critical liberationist studies, moreover, have pointed out that frequently wo/men have more in common with men of their own class, race,

age, culture, and religion than with females of other races, classes, ages, cultures, and religions. The differences between wo/men are often greater than those between wo/men and men of the same race, class, age, culture, and religion. Finally, there are also considerable differences within wo/men themselves. Thus, the meaning of "woman" is unstable and ever shifting; it depends not so much on its sex/gender relation but on its socio-systemic contextualization.

The category "woman" today is used interchangeably with female/feminine and thus has become a "naturalized" generic sex-based term, although until very recently it was utilized as an appellation for lower-class females only. One can perceive the slippage, cultural constructedness, and historical ambiguity of the term "woman" much more easily in the term "lady" [Greek *kyria*], because this discursive appellation readily "reveals" its race, class, and colonial bias. Until very recently, the term "Lady" has been restricted to wo/men of higher status or educational refinement. It also has functioned to symbolize "true womanhood" and femininity.

For instance, Elizabeth Spelman has shown that the notion of "natural" gender differences applies in classical Platonic and Aristotelian philosophy only to freeborn elite males and females, to gentlemen and ladies. Strictly speaking, slave wo/men and alien resident wo/men were not considered to be wo/men. They were "gendered" not with respect to slave or alien resident men but with respect to their masters. They were subordinated to and therefore different in "nature" from not only elite men but also from elite wo/men. As a result, the relations of domination and subordination have produced not only male-female and male-male but also female-female "natural" differences.

A statement such as "slaves were not women" offends our "commonsense" understanding, whereas a statement such as "slaves were not ladies" makes perfect sense. In the Western androcentric language system, the lady/mistress/mother is the other of the lord/master/father. All other wo/men are marked as "inferior" on grounds of race, class, religion, or culture. They are seen as the others of the feminine other, the "Lady." Hence, they are not mentioned in historical records at all.

Such a rendering of the basic category of feminist analysis (i.e., "woman") as problematic has introduced a crisis into the self-understandings and practices of feminist liberation theory. I have sought to mark this crisis by writing *wo/men* in a broken form in order to complicate the category of "woman" as a social construct and also to indicate that wo/men are not a unitary social group but are fragmented by structures of race, class, ethnicity, religion, heterosexuality, colonialism, and age.

I have introduced this writing of wo/men in the interest of liberationist feminism because I do not think that we can relinquish the analytic

category "wo/man" entirely and replace it with that of gender if we do not
want to continue marginalizing and erasing the presence of wo/men in
and through our own feminist discourses. Dropping "woman" as the
name for the liberationist subject would eradicate actual wo/men again
from historical, cultural-religious kyriocentric records. Hence, it is necessary to construct a theoretical framework that is able to articulate wo/men
as subjects of struggle for change and at the same time does not re-
inscribe the hegemonic cultural-symbolic, social-political feminine structure of the sex/gender framework that solidifies wo/men's inferiority,
marginality, and oppression as "common sense" and "natural."

Wo/men's Oppression

How much we are implicated in structures of domination can be assessed
by analyzing social location, positionality, or status within structures of
domination. The feminist political scientist Iris Marion Young has developed seven diagnostic criteria for recognizing the choreography of oppression, and I have expanded her criteria to include cultural-religious oppression. The following criteria indicate whether it is justified to speak of
oppression with reference to individuals or groups.

- Exploitation: Statistics show that in all countries of the world
  wo/men are exploited economically, culturally, politically, and religiously. Although their status as second-class citizen seems to be
  universal, their economic exploitation is quite different and hence
  creates structural inequalities between wo/men. For instance, in the
  U.S. the median income for black wo/men in 1993 was $18,820 as
  compared to $22,020 for white wo/men, $23,020 for black men,
  and $31,090 for white men. Forty-four percent of single mothers
  remain below the poverty line and two out of three adults living in
  poverty are wo/men.[3]
- Marginalization: Wo/men are under-represented in all social, cultural, scientific, and religious institutions. Either wo/men are not
  present in leadership positions at all or, if they are, their authority
  is less than that of men. Moreover, wo/men's contributions are
  often not recognized or are seen as peripheral.
- Powerlessness: Although wo/men have achieved the right to vote in
  almost all countries of the world, they are rarely found in decision-
  making positions. Wo/men's interests are not seen as public-political
  interests and their influence is often relegated to private life.
- Cultural imperialism: Oppressed people are marked through prejudicial stereotypes that make them at one and the same time in-

---

[3]M. Parenti, *Democracy for the Few* (New York: St. Martin's Press, 1995), 27–29.

visible. Wo/men are never seen first as human beings or citizens with individual characteristics and gifts but are always seen as females. At the same time, wo/men are made invisible through androcentric language and science, insofar as Western culture understands white elite man as the paradigm of being human and being citizen.

- Systemic violence: Violence against wo/men is often not seen as a violation of basic human rights but as brought about by wo/men's own fault and weakness. Wo/men are maltreated physically, psychologically, sexually, and religiously. They are sexually violated, starved, tortured, beaten, and killed only because they are wo/men.

- Silencing: Wo/men have been prohibited from speaking in public and have been relegated to the private sphere. Until very recently they have been excluded from academic study and knowledge production. Being humble, silent, and unassuming has been extolled throughout the centuries as a feminine virtue. The cultural injunction "Wo/men should be seen but not heard" has biblical roots and still discourages wo/men from speaking in public.

- Deprecation and vilification: Wo/men who do not adapt to the kyriarchal ethos of malestream society are vilified, maligned, and slandered as "bad" women. Wo/men have been seen as the devil's gateway, portrayed as temptresses and heretics, as prone to evil, and as unfit to represent the Divine. The cultural pattern that pits the "good woman" and the "bad woman" against each other is also found, for instance, in biblical Wisdom literature where Wisdom, the desirable woman, is played out against the "bad woman" who is characterized as a treacherous foreigner.

Theologically speaking, the choreography of oppression must be named as structural sin. Liberation theology understands sin not primarily as personal, individual failure or guilt but as the institutional and structural embodiment and realization of evil. Sexism, racism, colonialism, and imperialism are theologically best understood as just such structural sin and evil that implicate everyone in different degrees and ways. Individuals can either resist or collaborate with such structural sin but they are never free and innocent of it.

Structural sin has the following characteristics:

- Structural sin is realized and practiced through institutional injustices, collective discrimination, and dehumanizing ideologies and prejudices.
- Structural sin is not recognized and acknowledged as injustice and wrongdoing because it is legitimated, naturalized, and presented as

common sense again and again through cultural ideologies, religious symbols, ethical systems, and public educational discourses.

- Structural sin produces an individual and collective consciousness that is self-alienated. This self-alienated consciousness is accepted because it is seen as natural and common sense. It convinces people that situations of oppression and dehumanization are normal or divinely ordained. It sees these situations as evidence of individual failure and weakness.
- Alienated consciousness compels people to accept their own exploitation and dehumanization as natural, normal, and willed by G*d, and therefore to internalize and to make their own the values and mindsets of oppression. Education, the media, public and scientific discourses, as well as cultural and religious socialization, are the public means for internalizing structural sin.
- Self-alienated consciousness also compels wo/men to collaborate with our own kyriarchal exploitation and oppression insofar as we do not resist our own dehumanization in and through discourses of femininity, race, class, or nationalist consciousness and even participate as teachers, pastors, or mothers in their re-inscription.

This liberation theological notion of structural sin, however, must be distinguished from the concept of sin that is prevalent in malestream theology. As Judith Plaskow noted a long time ago, the understanding of sin and grace in modern malestream theology is formulated in individualistic masculine terms. For instance, one of the most discussed and condemned sins is pride and self-aggrandizement. However, while pride may be a great temptation for educated men, Plaskow points out that wo/men lack self-esteem and a sense of accomplishment. Hence, pride should not be considered a sin but a virtue that needs to be cultivated as a spiritual practice by wo/men.

But this interpretation of sin is not the primary reason why feminist theology has been reluctant to use the notion of sin as an analytic category. The main reason has been the assertion by biblical tradition and malestream theology that "woman" brought sin into the world and that she is the source of all evil. 1 Timothy 2:12-15, for instance, clearly teaches that sin was brought into the world by a "woman." The biblical theology of sin thus appears to be a theology of "blaming the victim," which makes the victims of domination responsible and accountable for their own exploitation and oppression.

A genderized malestream theology of sin is not able to articulate the evil, life-destroying power of structural sin and to speak about emancipation in theological terms. Such an articulation of structural sin in theological terms is, however, necessary if biblical interpretation is to serve as a

tool of conscientization rather than one of further self-alienation. Since not only religious but also cultural readers of the bible have internalized socio-cultural values that promote oppression and unjust and life-destroying structures of domination, such a process of conscientization is not just a religious but also a spiritual radical democratic practice.

Dualistic Categories of Analysis

Gender
According to Webster's Dictionary, "gender" derives from the Latin *gener-, genus,* birth, race, kind, gender. It refers to (1) Sex, and (2) "A subclass within a grammatical class (as noun, pronoun, adjective, or verb) of a language that is partly arbitrary but also partly based on distinguishable characteristics (such as shape, social rank, manner of existence, or sex) and that determines agreement with and selection of other words or grammatical forms." In English, gender is a classificatory dualistic system distinguishing the sexes as male and female, masculine and feminine, man and woman. Already before birth we are indexed either as girls or boys. Countless questionnaires continue to re-inscribe this classification when they invite us to identify either as male (m) or as female (f).

In Western societies there are only two genders and they are understood as at worst mutually exclusive and at best complementary: one is either a woman or a man but not both. Rather than stressing the common traits shared by wo/men and men in distinction to, for instance, mice or rocks, Western intellectual systems construct gender dichotomies and naturalize them with reference to biological sex. The cultural construction of male and female/masculine and feminine as both complementary and mutually exclusive categories constitutes the Western sex/gender system that correlates sex to cultural contents according to social hierarchies and values.

Gender has become a key analytical category in feminist analysis. Feminist theorists have elaborated on Simone de Beauvoir's dictum "wo/men are not born but made" and argued that gender is not a natural given but a societal construct, a socio-cultural principle of classification that imposes psychological, social, cultural, religious, and political meaning upon biological sexual identity. The category of gender questions seemingly universal beliefs about wo/men and men and unmasks their cultural-societal roots. However, whereas at first women's studies distinguished social gender roles from biological sex, in the mid-1980s gender studies emerged as a distinct field of inquiry within feminist criticism. In the last decade feminist theory has elaborated on both sex and gender as socio-cultural constructs which together constitute the Western sex/gender system.

Feminist theories first sought to show that one must distinguish between sex as a physical given and gender as a cultural construct. More recent work has gone further, arguing that both sex and gender are social constructs. If one does not distinguish between sex as a biological given and gender as a cultural construct, but sees both sex and gender as socio-cultural constructions, one can understand the Western sex/gender system as an economic and cultural-symbolic structure of representation and exploitation that has become naturalized and "common sense." As an ideological structure, gender is active through grammar, language, biology, economics, politics, and culture, making its constructions of difference "common sense" and natural.

Feminist anthropologists have pointed out that not all cultures and languages know of only two sexes/genders, and historians of gender have argued that even in Western cultures the dual sex/gender system is of modern origins. Thomas Laqueur, for instance, has shown that a decisive shift took place in modernity from the ancient one-sex model to the present dichotomous two-sex model. For thousands of years it was held as commonplace that wo/men had the same sex and genitals as men except that they were inside their bodies whereas men's were outside. The vagina was understood as an interior penis, the labia as foreskin, the uterus as scrotum, and the ovaries as testicles.

What it meant to be a "man" or a "woman" was determined by social rank and by one's place in society, not by sexual organs. Whether a "man" or a "woman," one had to perform a cultural role according to one's *social status* and not as organically one of two incommensurable biological sexes. Not sex but the social status of the elite, propertied, male head of household and his subordinates determined gender status. The ancients did not need the facts of sexual difference to support the claim that wo/men were inferior to men and therefore subordinate beings.

Beginning with the European Enlightenment, the two-sex model, the notion that there are two stable, incommensurable, opposite biological sexes, emerges. Now it is held that the economic, political, and cultural lives of wo/men and men, their gender roles, are based on these two incommensurable, biologically given sexes. Just as in antiquity the body was seen as reflecting the cosmic socio-political order, so in modernity the body and sexuality are seen as representing and legitimating the social-political-individual order. Social and political changes wrought by the European Enlightenment produced the change from the one-sex to the two-sex model. Since the universalistic claims for human liberty and equality included freeborn wo/men, arguments had to be fashioned if elite men were to justify their dominance of the public domain whose difference from the private world of wo/men was figured in terms of sexual difference.

The assumption of "natural" sex/gender differences informs everyday experience and turns it into "common-sense" knowledge in such a way that gender difference appears natural, "commonplace," and divinely bestowed. This naturalized understanding of gender serves as a "given" frame of meaning for individual wo/men and cultural institutions. By presenting the sex/gender system of male/female or masculine/feminine as natural, universal, and "common sense," this gender frame of meaning obscures and mystifies the reality that the very notion of two sexes is a socio-cultural construct. This linguistic-cultural gender framework hides the fact that not so long ago racial and national differences also were, and still are, considered by some to be natural biological facts or to be ordained by G*d.

Androcentrism

While gender is a functionalist category that construes male-female relationships in a dualistic fashion, it does not recognize that generally wo/men and not men are seen as gendered. The category of androcentrism (which is derived from the Greek word *aner*) means literally "male-centeredness." Like the category of gender, it marks the socially constructed differences between the sexes. However, unlike gender, androcentrism does not just construct dualistic sex-differences but also articulates the power relation between the sexes. "Man" is the paradigmatic human being who is the center of androcentric societies, cultures, and religions; "woman" is the other. The ideology of androcentrism is so pervasive because it is inculcated in and through the grammatical structures of ancient and modern Western languages such as Hebrew, Greek, Latin, or English.

Grammarians use masculine/feminine gender as a classification system and distinguish between the so-called "natural" gender and the grammatical gender of a word. For instance, in Latin and English the moon is grammatically feminine whereas in German it is masculine. The distinction between natural and grammatical gender, however, hides the fact that all linguistic gender classifications are grammatical. It obscures the fact that such gender classifications constitute a linguistic-symbolic process of "naturalizing" grammatical gender into "biological fact."

This linguistically and socially produced gender system does not just divide humans into two equal, separate groups that exclude each other. It also ranks them in an asymmetric fashion, placing the "masculine" in the center and making it the standard while making the "feminine" the exception. In so doing, it ranks and valorizes the masculine gender. The English language commonly gives the masculine gender to nouns that are active as well as strong and efficacious. It gives the feminine gender to words that are particularly beautiful or amiable. In English the sun, for instance,

is masculine, and the moon is feminine, because it is the receptacle of the sun's light. The earth, a ship, a country, a city are also feminine in English, because they are seen as receivers or containers.

Moreover, in an androcentric language system, masculine terms such as slaves, Americans, professors, Christians, Jews, etc. function as "generic" inclusive terms. Man/male/masculine/he stands for human *and* male whereas woman/female/feminine/she connotes only femaleness. Grammatically androcentric, so-called "generic" Western languages explicitly mention wo/men only as the exception to the rule, as problematic, or in order to specify them as particular individuals. In all other cases, one has to adjudicate in light of contextual linguistic markers whether wo/men are meant or not. In addition, Western androcentric languages and discourses do not just marginalize wo/men or eliminate them from historical cultural-religious records. They also construct the meaning of being "wo/men" or being "men" differently.

One can illustrate how such supposedly generic masculine language is read with reference to the famous text of Galatians 3:28 which states that in Christ there is "neither Jew nor Greek, slave nor free, male and female." Generally this passage is understood as referring to three different groups: Jew and Greek as religious ethnic characterizations, slave and free as socio-political determinations, and male and female as biological sex/gender differences. However, this understanding of the text tacitly substitutes a gender-specific reading for a generic one when it infers on the one hand that Jew, Greek, slave, and free are terms pertaining solely to men, and on the other hand that only the third pair—"male and female"—refers to wo/men.

Patriarchy

Whereas androcentrism functions as a linguistic-ideological explanation of the world, patriarchy articulates structural and institutional relations of domination. Patriarchy literally means the power of the father over his children and other members of the clan or household. In feminist theory, the meaning of patriarchy is generally no longer restricted to the power of the father over his kinship group, as is the case in social anthropology. Rather, the concept is developed as a means for identifying and challenging the social structures and ideologies that have enabled men to dominate and exploit wo/men throughout recorded history. In this feminist understanding, all men have power over wo/men to exploit and use them. If the notion of patriarchy is defined in terms of male-female gender dualism, then exploitation and victimization on the basis of gender and sex become the primary oppression.

While some feminist theorists reject patriarchy as an a-historical, universalizing, and totalizing concept, most utilize it as a key theoretical

notion for explaining the creation and maintenance of men's sexual, social, political, and ideological power over wo/men. The difference between male and female is believed to be the most basic and *essential* difference of humanity: the division and power relations between men and wo/men are the origin and basis of all other divisions and structures of domination—of economic class, culture, race, religion, nationality, and age. In this view, the system of patriarchy understood as men's domination over wo/men, as well as wo/men's exclusion from politics, culture, history, and religion, has been total across time and space. Wo/men were not only the objects and victims of male rule but also compliant agents who according to nature or according to the will of G*d have desired to live for men's well-being.

Feminist liberationist theory also understands "patriarchy" as referring to the subordination of wo/men to men. However, it understands the power relations between wo/men and men as "structural," i.e., as existing in the institutions and social practices of society rather than as "natural" or divinely instituted. Patriarchal structures *pre-exist* individual men and wo/men. Since all meaning is constituted in language, and since systems of meaning precede individual wo/men, our subjectivity, the sense of who we are and the ways we relate to the world, is not a fixed and coherent essence, but the product of patriarchal society, culture, and religion as well as of our own meaning-making practices. Therefore, wo/men are always the site of conflicting discourses. Biological sex differences do not have an "inherent" meaning but are negotiated and produced within a range of conflicting legal, medical, religious, and cultural patriarchal discourses.

However, this understanding of systemic oppression as patriarchy in the sense of father-domination is problematic for the following reasons:

- It understands wo/men as helpless victims, and it absolutizes the power of men over wo/men. It is true that men have greater access to power than wo/men, but this access is lessened and fractured because of other status markers and privileges that men have or do not have on grounds of race, class, age, or nationalism. It thereby overlooks that men also inhabit unequal positions of domination.
- Conversely, wo/men are never totally helpless and powerless but also participate in "power over." Elite wo/men always have exercised power not only over wo/men but also over subordinated men although they may not have had political power and cultural-religious authority. For instance, elite freeborn wo/men have had power over slave men throughout the centuries.
- A bi-polar analysis of patriarchy assumes absolute gender domination and sexism, although sex/gender represents only one dimension of a complex system of domination. Gender analysis that is

not at one and the same time also a race, class, and imperialism analysis does not suffice. A complex analysis of the intersection of structures of domination is necessary. Hence, it would be wrong to assume that only one form of racism (classism, heterosexism, etc.) exists for all wo/men. The various forms of racism have had different shapes and effects historically and culturally.

- A bi-polar dualistic analysis of patriarchy also neglects the power of wo/men over other wo/men. Wo/men have participated in promoting and inflicting many atrocities, such as those of colonialism, slavery, anti-Semitism, and prejudice against foreigners. Especially elite, educated wo/men have mediated and supported prejudices and structures of domination in and through education and "missionary" work, albeit generally in a lesser degree than men of their own race, class, and nation.

A Complex Systemic Analysis

Consequently, the interpretation of wo/men's oppression solely in terms of gender dualism has been problematized for years by socialist-Marxist feminists, as well as by Third World feminists. They have pointed out, on the one hand, that wo/men are oppressed not only by hetero-sexism but also by racism, classism, and colonialism. On the other hand, they have rejected the mainstream feminist definition of patriarchy which holds that men are the oppressors and wo/men the victims, as well as the tenet that culture, history, and religion are man-made.

Instead, these theorists have argued consistently that wo/men of subordinated races, nations, and classes are often more oppressed by elite white wo/men than by the men of their own class, race, culture, or religion. As a result of this contradiction in wo/men's lives, neither the interconnection between the exclusion of Euro-American wo/men and the exclusion of all other "subordinates" from citizenship nor its ideological justification in terms of reified "natural" sexual/racial/class/cultural differences has been given sufficient attention.

If and whenever mainline liberal, radical, or socialist-Marxist feminists have paid attention to the objections of Third World feminists, they have tended to adopt an "adding on" approach of listing oppressions. This "add and stir" procedure ignores the fact that structures of oppression criss-cross and feed upon each other in wo/men's lives. Such an "adding on" method conceptualizes the oppression of wo/men not as an interlocking, multiplicative, and overarching system of domination, but as parallel discrete structures of domination. To list parallel oppressions, or to speak of "dual-system oppression" (patriarchy and capitalism or patriarchy and colonialism), obscures the multiplicative pyramidal inter-structuring of

the relations of domination which positions wo/men of different social status differently.

Indeed, such an "adding up" feminist approach disregards the historical inter-structuring of race, class, gender, age, and nation as forms of stratification which develop together out of the same set of dominations and which therefore need to be changed simultaneously. Structures of wo/men's oppression are not just multiple but multiplicative: racism is multiplied by sexism multiplied by ageism, multiplied by classism multiplied by colonial exploitation. Hence, feminist theory and practice need to be (re-)conceptualized as practices of struggle against intersecting oppressions; it must make wo/men's *differing* experiences of multiplicative oppressions central to all feminist discourses. In order to articulate and make visible the complex interstructuring of the conflicting oppressions of different groups of wo/men, I have argued that patriarchy must be re-conceptualized as *kyriarchy*, a neologism which is derived from the Greek *kyrios* (lord, master, father, husband) and the verb *archein* (to rule, dominate).

Kyriarchy

Kyriarchy in classical antiquity was the rule of the lord, slave master, husband, elite freeborn, propertied, educated gentleman to whom disenfranchised men and all wo/men were subordinated. In antiquity, kyriarchy was institutionalized either as a monarchical or as a democratic political form of ruling. Kyriarchy is best theorized as a complex pyramidal system of intersecting multiplicative social structures of superordination and subordination, of ruling and oppression. Kyriarchal relations of domination are built on elite male property rights as well as on the exploitation, dependency, inferiority, and obedience of wo/men.[4]

Kyriarchy as a socio-cultural and religious system of domination is constituted by intersecting multiplicative structures of oppression. The different sets of relations of domination shift historically and produce different constellations of oppression in different times and cultures. The structural positions of subordination which have been fashioned by kyriarchal relations of domination and subordination stand in tension with those required by democracy. Hence, in the context of Greek democracy Western political philosophy has engaged in discourses and debates to justify such structures of domination. These political discourses of subordination that shape the subject positions of domination have been mediated by Christian Scriptures and have decisively determined modern forms of democracy.

---

[4]In order to continue in the process of consciousness-raising and becoming aware of how language functions, you might want to list all people who are meant here by the expression "wo/men."

Rather than identifying kyriarchy with binary male-over-female domination, it is best to understand the political system denoted by the term in antiquity. Modern democracies are still structured as complex pyramidal political systems of superiority and inferiority, of dominance and subordination. As kyriarchal democracies, they are stratified by gender, race, class, religion, heterosexuality, and age—*structural positions* which are assigned to us more or less by birth. However, the way we live these structural kyriarchal positions and respond to them is conditioned not simply by the mere fact of the structural positions themselves but also by the subject positions through which we live our structural kyriarchal positions. Whereas an essentialist approach assigns to us an "authentic" identity, let's say of gender, that is derived from our structural position, our subject position becomes coherent and compelling through a certain political discourse, interpretive framework, and theoretical horizon, which I have termed kyriocentrism.

Thus, a critical feminist analytic does not understand kyriarchy as an essentialist a-historical system. Instead, it articulates kyriarchy as a heuristic (derived from the Greek and meaning "to find") concept, or as a diagnostic, analytic instrument that allows us to investigate the multiplicative interdependence of gender, race, and class stratifications as well as their discursive inscriptions and ideological reproductions. Moreover, it helps us understand that we inhabit structural positions of race, gender, class, and ethnicity, but that one of them might become privileged so that it constitutes a nodal point. While in any particular historical moment class may be the primary modality through which I experience gender and race, in other circumstances gender may be the privileged position through which I experience race and class.

Rather than trace the different historical formations of kyriarchy in Western societies and biblical religions, I direct attention here to the classic and modern forms of democratic kyriarchy and its legitimating discourses. Greek kyriarchal democracy constituted itself by the exclusion of the "others" who did not have a share in the land but whose labor sustained society. Freedom and citizenship not only were measured over and against slavery but also were restricted in terms of gender. Moreover, the socio-economic realities in the Greek city-state were such that only a few select freeborn, propertied, elite, male heads of households could actually exercise democratic government. According to the theoretical vision, but not the historical realization, of democracy, all those living in the *polis*, the city-state, should be equal citizens, able to participate in government. In theory, all citizens are equal in rights, speech, and power. As the assembly or congress (in Greek *ekklesia*) of free citizens, they came together in order to deliberate and decide the best course of action for pursuing their own well-being and for securing the welfare of all citizens. In

practice, however, most of the inhabitants of the city-state were excluded from democratic government.

This classic Greek form of kyriarchal democracy was both kyriocentric and ethnocentric. It drew its boundaries in terms of dualistic polarities and analogies between gods/humans, Greeks/Barbarians, male/female, human/beast, culture/nature, the civilized and the uncivilized world. The boundaries of citizenship were constituted through civilization, war, and marriage. The structuring dividing lines ran between those men who owned property and those who were owned, between those who were rulers and those who were ruled, between those who as superiors commanded and those who as subordinates had to obey, between those who were free from manual labor and had leisure for philosophical and political activity and those who were economically dependent and whose labor was exploited. This mapping of kyriarchy as an overarching system of domination, however, must not be misconstrued as a universal a-historical "master paradigm." Rather, it is best understood as a particular concrete reflection of the socio-political situation of the Athenian city-state.

The Roman imperial form of kyriarchy was exemplified by a monarchical pyramid of "interlocking structures of domination" (bell hooks) that incorporated elements of traditional democratic practices (such as the Senate). At its apex stood the emperor, who was called *pater patrum*, that is, the Father of all fathers. Roman imperial power was seen as *Pax Romana*, as a beneficial system for all the conquered peoples. Its harsh ways of ruling and exploitation are symbolically indicted in the Book of Revelation.

However, the Roman kyriarchal model of imperial power was legitimated by Neo-Aristotelian philosophy, which found its way into the Christian Scriptures in the form of the patriarchal injunctions to submission. The first epistle of Peter, for instance, admonishes Christians who are servants to be submissive even to brutal masters (2:18-25) and instructs freeborn wives to subordinate themselves to their husbands, even to those who are not Christians (3:1-6). It also entreats Christians to be subject and give honor to the emperor as supreme, as well as to his governors (2:13-17). The post-Constantinian ancient church most closely resembles this Roman imperial pyramid in Christian terms.

At first, the modern Western form of democratic kyriarchy or kyriarchal democracy excluded propertied and all other freeborn wo/men, as well as immigrant, poor, and slave wo/men from the democratic right to elect those who govern them. "Property" and elite male status by birth and education, not simply biological-cultural masculinity, entitled men to participate in the government of the few over the many. Hence, modern political philosophy continues to assume that propertied, educated, elite Western Man is defined by reason, self-determination, and full citizen-

ship, whereas wo/men and other subordinated peoples are characterized by emotion, service, and dependence. They are seen not as rational and responsible adult subjects but as emotional, helpless, and child-like, available to be exploited.

Modern political thought elaborates two aspects of kyriarchal power: one seeking to secure species reproduction, the other sexual gratification. The first one sustains the kyriarchal order by wielding control over wives, children, servants, and wealth. The second one articulates kyriarchal power as masculine-phallic power that wields control over those it desires. Whereas in modern capitalist societies "father-right" operates primarily on an institutional structural level, "masculine" or phallic power operates primarily but not exclusively on a linguistic-ideological level. The "politics" of domination fashions ideological subject positions that form the foundations on which notions of domination are constructed.

Since there are not many cross-cultural studies of non-Western patriarchy/kyriarchy, I am especially grateful to Hisako Kinukawa for pointing to the "emperor system" of Japan as an example of such a form of kyriarchal relations of domination. The Japanese emperor system consisted of the emperor standing at the apex of the imperial pyramid, and his various agents who came from the nobility and ruled the country socially, culturally, and politically. The emperor system was supported by state Shintoism and consisted of a pyramid of domination with the emperor on top and the people divided into four descending classes of samurai, farmers, craftsmen, and merchants, and, at the very bottom, the poor and despised outcast class. Although the nationalist Japanese "emperor system" was replaced by democracy in 1945, its shame culture, values, and politics are still perpetuated today, especially in and through the patriarchal family, which is a small-scale model of the "emperor system."[5]

In conclusion, I want to stress the following structural aspects of kyriarchy:

- Kyriarchy is not simply the domination of men over wo/men. Rather, it is a complex pyramidal system of domination that works through the violence of economic exploitation and lived subordination. The kyriarchal pyramid of gradated dominations must not be seen as static but as an always changing net of relations of domination.
- Kyriarchy must not be understood as a-historical or monolithic but must be seen as realized differently in different historical contexts. Democratic kyriarchy or kyriarchal democracy was articulated dif-

---

[5]Hisako Kinukawa, *Women and Jesus in Mark: A Japanese Feminist Perspective* (Maryknoll, N.Y.: Orbis Books, 1994), 15–22.

ferently in antiquity and modernity. It is different in Greece, Rome, Asia Minor, Europe, America, Japan, or India; it is different in Judaism, Hellenism, Islam, or Catholicism.

- Not only the gender system but also the stratification systems of race, class, colonialism, and heterosexism structure and determine a kyriarchal system. Wo/men not only live in pluralistic societies and religions but are also separated into social groups with unequal status, unequal power, and unequal access to resources. Structures of domination—racism, heterosexism, classism, and colonialism—are not parallel but multiplicative. The full power of kyriarchal oppression comes to the fore in the lives of wo/men living on the bottom of the kyriarchal pyramid.

- Kyriarchal societies and cultures need for their functioning a servant class, a servant race, a servant gender, and a servant religion of people. The existence of a servant class is maintained through law, education, socialization, and brute violence. It is sustained by the belief that members of a servant class of people are by nature or by divine decree inferior to those whom they are destined to serve.

- Both in Western modernity and in Greco-Roman antiquity kyriarchy has been in tension with a democratic ethos and system of equality and freedom. In a radical democratic system, power is not exercised through "power over" or through violence and subordination, but through the human capacity for respect, responsibility, self-determination, and self-esteem. This radical democratic ethos has again and again engendered emancipatory movements that insist on the equal freedom, dignity, and equal rights of all.

Kyriocentrism

Feminist political theorists have shown that the classical Greek philosophers Aristotle and Plato articulated in different ways a theory of kyriarchal democracy in order to justify the incapacity of certain groups of people, such as freeborn wo/men or slave wo/men and men, to participate in democratic government. These groups of people were not fit to rule or to govern, the philosophers argued, because of their deficient natural powers of reasoning. Such an explicit ideological justification and kyriocentric theory needed to be developed at a point in history when it became increasingly obvious that those who were excluded from the political life of the *polis* (the city-state), such as freeborn wo/men, educated slaves, wealthy *metics* (alien residents), and traveling mercenaries, were actually indispensable to it. Philosophical rationalizations of the exclusion of diverse people from citizenship and government are engendered by the contradiction between the democratic vision of the city-state and its actual kyriarchal socio-economic and political practices.

In short, the contradiction between the logic of democracy and historical socio-political kyriarchal practices has produced the kyriocentric (master-centered) logic of identity as the assertion of "natural differences" between elite men and wo/men, freeborn and slaves, property owners and farmers or artisans, Athenian-born citizens and other residents, Greeks and Barbarians, the civilized and uncivilized world. A similar process of ideological kyriocentrism is inscribed in Christian Scriptures in and through the so-called (household) codes of submission.

Since modern liberal democracies are modeled after the classical ideal of kyriarchal democracy, they continue the contradiction between kyriarchal practices and democratic self-understandings inscribed in the discourses of democracy in antiquity. It must not be overlooked, however, that this institutionalized contradiction between the ideals of radical democracy and their historical kyriarchal actualizations has also engendered movements for emancipation seeking full self-determining citizenship. In the past two centuries the emancipatory struggles for equal rights have gained voting and civil rights for all adult citizens. Since these movements, however, could not completely overcome the kyriarchal stratifications that continue to determine modern liberal representative democracies, they seem to have made the democratic circle merely coextensive with the kyriarchal pyramid, thus reinscribing the contradiction between democratic vision and political kyriarchal practice and thereby spawning new movements of emancipation.

To sum up my argument, modern liberal democracy perpetrates many of the ideological practices found in ancient democratic kyriarchy, insofar as it claims that its citizens "are created equal" and are entitled to "liberty and the pursuit of happiness," while at the same time retaining "natural" kyriarchal, economic, and socio-political stratifications. Kyriarchal power operates not only along the axis of the gender system but also along those of race, class, heterosexual culture, and religion. These axes of power structure the more general system of domination in a matrix—or, better, patrix-like—fashion.

In light of this analysis, it becomes clear that the universalist kyriocentric rhetoric of Euro-American elite men does not simply reinforce the dominance of the male sex, but legitimates the "White Father" or, in black idiom, the "Boss-Man," as the universal subject. By implication, European American feminist theory and theology that articulate gender difference as primary mask more than the complex interstructuring of kyriarchal dominations inscribed *within* wo/men and in the relationships of dominance and subordination *between* wo/men. They also mask the participation of white elite wo/men or ladies and of Christian religion in kyriarchal oppression, insofar as both have served as the civilizing colonialist conduits of kyriarchal knowledge, values, religion, and culture.

The Western kyriocentric symbolic order not only defines "woman" as "the other" of the Western Man of Reason but also maps the systems of oppression in opposition to the democratic logic of radical equality for everyone.

In short, as an ideology or subject position, kyriocentrism, like androcentrism, operates on four levels:

- On the grammatical-linguistic level: Language is not just androcentric but it places elite men in the center, marginalizes elite wo/men and other men, and makes slave wo/men or poor wo/men doubly invisible.
- On the symbolic-cultural level: Kyriocentrism constructs and naturalizes gender, race, class, and colonial relations as essentialist differences.
- On the ideological-cultural level: Kyriocentrism makes gender, racial, class, and colonial prejudice look normal and hides the fact that such differences are socially constructed. It constructs these differences as relations of domination.
- On the social-institutional level: Kyriocentrism maintains the second-class citizenship of all the others of elite men. It does so through economic and legal-political means and especially through socialization, education, and internalization.

Feminist Reconstructive Frameworks

A radical democratic "politics of interpretation" cannot restrict itself to deconstructing kyriarchal structural positions of domination but also must positively articulate alternative subject positions for liberation. Yet, whereas feminists generally agree on the deconstructive move in sociocultural biblical analysis, they part company on whether the articulation of a positive alternative social and ideological position from which to speak is possible. Nevertheless, as a political movement, feminism has provided several heuristic concepts for articulating an alternative position to the structural and subject positions of domination.

Androgyny – Gynecentrism – Maternal Feminism
Within the dualistic framework of the androcentric gender system, the notion of androgyny is one such alternative concept; gynecentrism and matriarchy are others. Androgyny is a synthetic term consisting of the Greek words for man (*aner*) and woman (*gyne*), that combines the two, strictly separate genders. Hence, the term has served for some feminists as an expression of the ideal of true humanity. It is used to characterize an individual who has successfully integrated traditionally masculine and femi-

nine qualities and virtues. However, other feminists object to "androg-yny" because it ostensibly claims to eliminate sexual division, yet its conceptual framework gives priority to the masculine and re-inscribes the dualism of masculinity and femininity.

Again, other feminists seek to replace androcentrism with gynecentrism or gynaikocentrism (from Greek *gyne* = woman) and patriarchy with matriarchy, i.e., the rule of the mother in prehistoric societies, as feminist utopian alternatives, although matriarchy is envisioned as quite a different form of socio-political organization than that of patriarchal domination. They believe that if wo/men were socially dominant they would create a social order that is in harmony with nature and hence qualitatively different from androcentric patriarchy. Such feminists argue that wo/men are, in essence, the better human beings, since their nature has not been corrupted by patriarchal power drives. Whereas the masculine self is impersonal, violent, abstract, striving for conflict and domination, wo/men's true essence is nurturant, intuitive, receptive, organic, and sensuous.

Such an essentialist position can take a constructivist turn when it argues that binary masculine/feminine gender polarity is not biologically innate or divinely ordained but socially constructed. Yet there are still others who reassert some form of biological determinism to being female, or a philosophical essentialism of the feminine, or both when they assume that femininity and woman are less corrupted by patriarchy than masculinity and man.

Four basic strategic positions with respect to the feminine as alternative ideal and theoretical space have been developed in Euro-American feminist philosophical-psychoanalytic discourses. The *first* strategic position involves a feminist appropriation and critical reformulation of Jungian psychoanalytic theory that revalorizes the repressed feminine archetype in order to achieve androgyny. The *second* position, most brilliantly articulated by Mary Daly, uses an ontological-linguistic strategy for articulating an understanding of feminism as a process of becoming the Wild, Original, Self-actualizing Wo/man who has made the leap from "phallocracy" into freedom, into the Other-world of Be-ing. This strategy is actualized by the "metamorphosizing" woman, by the Crone and the Original Witch, by the Archaic, Elemental, "metapatriarchally" moving Woman. She is the one who represents a new species, an Original Race.

The *third* strategy for revalorizing Woman and the feminine is the theory of the maternal-feminine, which is an import from what is usually called "French feminism," but generally refers only to the work of Kristeva, Cixous, and Irigaray. Although American work on the "maternal" has on the whole concentrated on the socio-historical critique of motherhood as an institution, more recent multi-disciplinary studies on Maternal Thinking "repeatedly extol pre-oedipal unboundedness, related-

ness, plurality, fecundity, tenderness, and nurturance in the name of the difference of female identity."[6]

Feminist scholars are careful to emphasize that the theory of the maternal-feminine seeks to subvert the patriarchal feminine. Nevertheless, with the popular reception of so-called French feminist theory, which is concerned with the feminine and maternal as metaphor and construct, this approach tends to re-inscribe the cultural feminine: fluidity, softness, plurality, sea, nature, peacefulness, nurturance, body, life, and Mother-Goddess as antithetical to the cultural masculine, defined by solidity, hardness, rigidity, aggressiveness, reason, control, death, Father-God.

As a result, such theories of the feminine sometimes come dangerously close to reproducing traditional cultural-religious ascriptions of femininity and motherhood, all too familiar from papal pronouncements —ascriptions which have now become feminist norms. In addition, the alignment of the masculine with rationality and of the feminine with the language of poetry, mysticism, magic, and religion re-inscribes not only Western theories and theologies of the feminine, that is, the ideology of the "White Lady," but also colonialist constructions of the "Native," the "Noble Savage," or "the Mystical Oriental."

A *fourth* strategy of valorizing (feminine) relationality has become central to feminist theology. Inspired by the organic relational process thought of Alfred North Whitehead, leading feminist theologians such as Valerie Saving, Penelope Washburn, Marjorie Suchocki, Carter Heyward, Katherine Keller, Rita Nakashima Brock, Beverly Harrison, Mary Grey, Nancy Howell, and many more have articulated the social ontology of relational feminism, which according to Katherine Keller allows us to acknowledge "the potent influences of our own sexual self-formation, while acknowledging the maternal itself as the effect of multiply layered social formations."[7] Over and against those who understand maternal feminism in essentialist terms, Keller insists that wo/men are "not necessarily more nurturant by nature," but that "we have been socially and discursively molded to perform the intimately and consciously relational task which men of power always would abdicate."[8]

Without question, we are all born into relationships, and wo/men have been socialized into performing relational tasks. However, the relations into which we are born are relations of domination that not only position the self structurally but also shape and define it. The cultural and

[6]See Elisabeth Schüssler Fiorenza, *But She Said: Feminist Practices of Interpretation* (Boston: Beacon Press, 1992), 103–104

[7]Katherine Keller, "Seeking and Sucking: On Relations and Essence in Feminist Theology," in *Horizons in Feminist Theology: Identity, Tradition, and Norms,* ed. Rebecca S. Chopp and Sheila Greeve Davaney (Minneapolis: Fortress Press, 1997), 75.

[8]Keller, 76.

religious discourses of femininity fashion gendered subject positions of kyriarchal relationality by inculcating it either as "romantic love" or as wo/men's personal responsibility on grounds of their maternal qualities for maintaining right relations.

The Ekklesia of Wo/men

If it is true that hegemonic cultural discourses no longer construct sex/gender subject positions as relations of domination and subordination, but either as romantic heterosexual love relations—men are to be educated for themselves, whereas wo/men are to be socialized for men (Rousseau)—or as self-sacrificing maternal relationships, I argue, then, that feminists must fashion political discourses that do not re-inscribe but provide alternatives to those of the maternal-feminine. Friendship and Sisterhood have been suggested as such alternative discourses.

A growing body of feminist literature, therefore, does not suggest the maternal-feminine but female friendship as paradigm for relations and relationality. For instance, Mary Hunt understands friendship as a personal and a political activity characterized by love, power, embodiment, and spirituality. Friendship is the expression of "voluntary human relationships that are entered into by people who intend one another's well-being and who intend that their love relationship is part of a justice-seeking community."[9] This last qualification indicates that friendship is a personal-relational concept that presupposes intersubjective sympathy and trust but that must become part of a "justice-seeking community" in order to be political.

More recently, bell hooks has attempted in *Feminism Is for Everybody* to valorize sisterhood again. "Sisterhood is powerful" was the motto of the wo/men's movement in the 1970s and 1980s. However, it soon fell into disrepute because of "its elevation as a universal descriptive category deduced from essentialist notions of female oppression, without regard to economic and other differences between and among wo/men" (Joan Martin).[10] While I agree with bell hooks that "we must continue the work of bonding across race and class,"[11] I do not think that the naturalized concept of sisterhood, which not only advocates solidarity but also re-inscribes kyriarchal family relations and sibling rivalry, provides the horizon and discourse for "making feminist political solidarity between women an ongoing reality."

Instead of the feminist discourses of androgyny, matriarchy, the feminine, friendship, and sisterhood, I have suggested *ekklesia* = democratic assembly/congress that must be qualified with wo/men if it is to function

---

[9]Mary E. Hunt, *Fierce Tenderness: A Feminist Theology of Friendship* (New York: Crossroad, 1991), 8.

[10]Letty M. Russell and J. S. Shannon Clarkson, eds., *Dictionary of Feminist Theologies* (Louisville: Westminster John Knox Press, 1996), 262.

[11]bell hooks, *Feminism Is for Everybody* (Boston: South End Press, 2000), 17.

as a radical democratic alternative discourse to kyriarchy. Historically and politically the *ekklesia of wo/men*, in the sense of the democratic assembly or the people's congress, is an *oxymoron*, a combination of contradictory terms for the purpose of articulating a feminist political discursive space and horizon.

With *ekklesia of wo/men* I have a heuristic construct in mind that is similar to what Chandra Talpade Mohanti has called the "imagined community of Third World oppositional struggles." She envisions it as the kind of space that provides a political rather than biological or cultural basis for alliances between wo/men of all colors and moves away from essentialist notions of Third World feminisms. Within the context of social movements for change, one can theorize the *ekklesia of wo/men* not only as a virtual, utopian space but also as an already partially realized space of radical equality and as a site of feminist struggles for transforming societal and religious institutions.

Emancipatory movements, including the Women's Liberation Movement, do not struggle for equal rights in order to become masculine and the same as men. They struggle in order to achieve the rights, benefits, and privileges of equal authority and citizenship which are legitimately theirs but which are denied to them by the kyriarchal regimes of most societies and the major world religions. They respect particular struggles while at the same time forging complex solidarities in the global struggles against interlocking systems of domination.

In the past three decades the feminist movement in society in general and biblical religions in particular has offered one of the most dynamic examples of such a counter-discourse and practice. It has constituted an oppositional public arena or forum in which to generate critical analysis of kyriarchal oppression and to articulate feminist interests and visions. The theoretical framework of the *ekklesia of wo/men,* I suggest, is able to displace the social constructs *Woman* and *The Feminine* as the theoretical space from whence to struggle and to speak, with a radical democratic construct that is at once a historical and an imagined political-cultural-religious reality, already partially realized but still to be struggled for.

Situating feminist theorizing and theologizing within the logic of equality rather than within that of feminine identity allows one to understand so-called natural binary gender arrangements together with those of race, ethnicity, or class as socio-political ideological constructions. In addition to living in pluralistic structures, wo/men are stratified, differentiated into social groups traversed by pervasive axes of inequality along lines of class, gender, race, ethnicity, and age. Consequently, we must take care not to re-inscribe such kyriarchal status *divisions* as positive pluralistic *differences* among wo/men, but to "denaturalize" patriarchal racial, gender, cultural, and other status inscriptions.

The notion of the *ekklesia of wo/men* conceptualized as radical democratic horizon also seeks to overcome the division between the societal, or so-called secular, and religious social movements. Translating the term as "wo/men-church" is in danger of losing the radical democratic meaning of the expression. Since in Latin languages the word "ecclesia" means church, *ekklesia of wo/men* is seen as a Christian religious community rather than as a radical democratic movement. This reduction of *ekklesia* to church overlooks the fact that the linguistic roots of church are not *ekklesia* but *kyriake,* which means belonging to the lord, slave-master, father, gentleman. The reduction of the meaning of *ekklesia* to church also introduces the opposition between church and synagogue which is traditionally represented by two female figures.

Finally, the radical democratic horizon of the *ekklesia of wo/men,* I suggest, promotes a culture of debate and discussion for better detecting the hidden "choreography" of domination. Since the "feminine" conceptualization of an alternative space to domination stresses wo/men's caring relationality and loving friendship or sisterhood, it tends to suppress conflict and debate.[12] Wo/men's "feminine" socialization has made us fearful of conflict and taught us to "patch over" differences. Hence, we have not cultivated intellectual debate that is inspired by the horizon of radical equality.

For instance, last summer I was involved in planning an international symposium on feminist biblical interpretation in Switzerland. The conflicts before the conference had to do with how to develop a program for a feminist international discussion of feminist biblical studies. Since we could not convince the organizers to create a programmatic platform of radical democratic exchange and debate, they scheduled prominent speakers from different continents alongside each other on different days without giving them the opportunity to engage in a substantive discussion with each other. Consequently, the "particular" voices of speakers from Africa, Latin America, Asia, or Eastern Europe were ghettoized and frequently romanticized, thus prohibiting the speakers from discussing with each other important differences in theoretical conceptualization, from celebrating the "common ground" that came to the fore in their work, and from forging strategies for an international biblical Wisdom movement of justice. An important moment for building solidarity and forging alliances was lost.

In conclusion, as a site of contested socio-political contradictions, feminist alternatives, and unrealized possibilities at the intersection of a multiplicity of public feminist discourses, the *ekklesia of wo/men* requires

---

[12]For instance, many of my student readers have suggested that I should stress dialogue and conversation rather than debate and conflict.

a rhetorical rather than a scientific conceptualization of feminist biblical interpretation. Feminist biblical discourses, then, are best understood in the classical sense of deliberative rhetoric that seeks to persuade the democratic assembly and to adjudicate arguments in order to make decisions for the sake of the welfare of everyone.

In this chapter I have invited you to "dance" with me in the horizon of the *ekklesia of wo/men* and to engage in the movements of Divine Wisdom today. Naming the global Wisdom movements for justice *"ekklesia of wo/men"* seeks to break down the modern split between so-called secular and religious wo/men's movements by identifying Christian community and biblical interpretation as important sites of feminist political-intellectual struggles to transform kyriarchal relations of domination. Feminist theology and biblical interpretation, I have argued, derive their criteria for "discerning the spirits" not from appeals to the universal Divine Feminine, to wo/men's female nature, or to saving sisterhood, but from the radical egalitarian vision of *ekklesia*. For such a process of discernment, we can utilize insights derived from wo/men's specific historical-political-religious struggles against the systems of oppression operating on the axes of class, race, gender, ethnicity, sexual preference, and so on.

In the wisdom/Wisdom space of the *ekklesia of wo/men,* I have proposed, we can reclaim the power of the Word. Feminist biblical interpretation can either re-inscribe kyriarchal subject positions or fashion emancipatory Wisdom spaces for feminist biblical "meaning making." To become critically aware of the mechanisms of oppression and alienation does not turn us into victims but empowers us to continue the Wisdom struggles around the globe for justice and the well-being of all.

Deepening Movement

Elisabeth Schüssler Fiorenza, *Rhetoric and Ethic: The Politics of Biblical Studies* (Minneapolis: Fortress Press, 1999), 149–173 and/or Elisabeth Schüssler Fiorenza, *But She Said: Feminist Practices of Biblical Interpretation* (Boston: Beacon Press, 1992), 195–217.

Moving Steps

- So far, how have the reflections on feminist biblical interpretation advocated in this book related to your own experience and to the concerns of your group? Do you agree or disagree that the task of feminist biblical interpretation is conscientization? Do you believe feminists can use the notion of sin? Why is it important to distinguish structural from personal sin? When does collaboration with oppressive structures turn into personal sin?

- What is the difference between patriarchy and kyriarchy? Are kyriarchal relations of domination only a Western phenomenon? Do they apply only to gender relations? Why is it necessary to distinguish between kyriarchy and kyriocentrism? How do you decide whether texts are kyriocentric/kyriarchal?

- Draw or visualize the Greek or the Roman kyriarchal pyramid. Draw the kyriarchal pyramid of your own church polity and religious community and compare it with the forms of ancient kyriarchy. Draw the kyriarchal pyramid of your own country and society. What are the defining structures of domination?

- What do you understand your social location to be within the kyriarchal pyramid? How is it determined also by the circle of *ekklesia?* Have you experienced the contradictions and struggles between kyriarchal mindsets and perspectives and those of *ekklesia?* Do you find *ekklesia* to be a helpful category for analysis, imagination, organization, and envisioning the world and your life?

Movement Exercise

1. Use the worksheets for visualizing kyriarchy and *ekklesia.*

2. Read 1 Peter 2:5–3:7. Are the recipients Jewish or Gentile Christians? Can you detect values and visions of *ekklesia* and/or of kyriarchal structures? Imagine yourself a member of the community to whom 1 Peter is addressed. How would you seek to persuade your friends to write a response to the authors of the letter? Draw a diagram of the community to whom the letter is addressed.

Kyriarchal Household as Model of Kyriarchal State

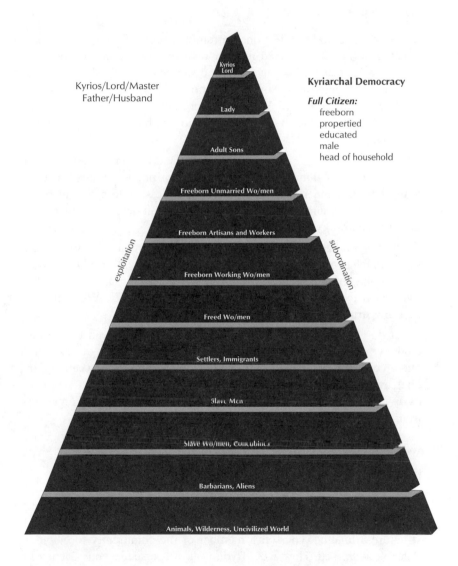

Kyrios/Lord/Master
Father/Husband

Kyriarchal Democracy

Full Citizen:
freeborn
propertied
educated
male
head of household

Kyrios
Lord

Lady

Adult Sons

Freeborn Unmarried Wo/men

Freeborn Artisans and Workers

Freeborn Working Wo/men

Freed Wo/men

Settlers, Immigrants

Slave Men

Slave Wo/men, Concubines

Barbarians, Aliens

Animals, Wilderness, Uncivilized World

exploitation

subordination

"Constantinian" Roman Patriarchal Model of Church*

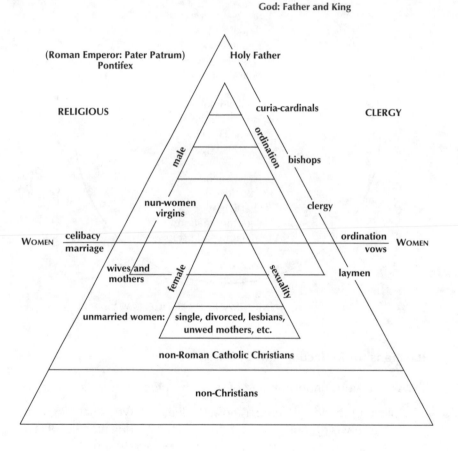

*See my book *Discipleship of Equals,* 226.

Radical Democracy – *Ekklesia* – Discipleship of Equals

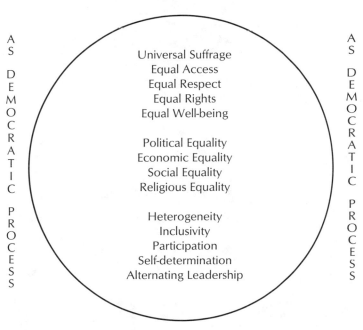

AS DEMOCRATIC VISION*

A S D E M O C R A T I C   P R O C E S S

Universal Suffrage
Equal Access
Equal Respect
Equal Rights
Equal Well-being

Political Equality
Economic Equality
Social Equality
Religious Equality

Heterogeneity
Inclusivity
Participation
Self-determination
Alternating Leadership

A S D E M O C R A T I C   P R O C E S S

AS DEMOCRATIC PRACTICE

Questions for Reflection and Discussion

1. What is your understanding of equality? Does it mean sameness?

2. Utilizing the radical democratic as well as the kyriarchal diagrams, seek to envision political, economic, familial, educational, social, legal, theological, religious, or cultural democratic structures. Share any experience of such structures which you might have had. What makes it difficult to envision such structures?

3. Draw a symbol of your vision of church as a discipleship of equals and share it with the group. What makes it difficult to realize such a vision?

*See my book *But She Said,* 119.

CHAPTER V

Wisdom Steps
Feminist Methods of Interpretation

Dancing in the ways of Wisdom requires dancing shoes and the ability to move; it calls for vigor and determination. Struggling for justice demands dedication and strength. Searching the bible for the power of Wisdom is one way of strengthening our spirit and keeping alive our commitments. Hence, in this chapter I invite you to learn about various feminist critical "reading" approaches and interpretive methods for undoing the mechanisms of domination and alienation inscribed in biblical texts and for reading "otherwise."

Since no fool-proof recipe for how to go about producing a feminist reading is available, feminist interpreters do not subscribe to one single reading strategy and interpretive method but employ a variety of exegetical and interpretive methods for understanding the bible as public discourse. Whereas exegetical-historical methods are often restricted to the experts and not accessible to a general readership, a critical, rhetorical feminist interpretation is to be accessible to everyone. Hence, I suggest that feminist interpretive methods are best understood as ways of engaging in the process and movement of conscientization.

I assume that if you are a student of religion or a minister, you have learned standard methods of interpretation that are used in the field of biblical studies, such as philology, textual criticism, style criticism, archeology, history of religions, form criticism, source criticism, redaction criticism, narrative criticism, structuralism, and composition criticism. If you are not familiar with such technical tools, you might want to read an introduction to standard exegetical methods or you might do without them, since such methods are helpful but not necessary for a feminist process of interpretation.

In any case, I hope you will focus on the methods or "dance steps" that feminists have assembled for such a task. In some cases it is helpful

135

to learn how others have executed them; in other instances you might just want to go with the flow of the music. It might be helpful not to read through the chapter but to practice the different methodological steps. Whichever way you learn such methodological steps for a feminist process or dance of interpretation, you will always need to use them in conjunction with the critical liberationist analytic that we have discussed in the preceding chapter.

To enter the process of biblical interpretation does not mean, however, to use methods as rules or techniques that guarantee the outcome. Rather, it means to use methods as dance steps in such a way that the moving powers of biblical texts that have been frozen or fossilized by the regimes of domination are released and can become effective. It also means to identify the poisons and eliminate the roadblocks that hinder the movement of wisdom/Wisdom. Finally, it means to understand kyriocentric language as rhetorical and prescriptive rather than as descriptive and documentary. As language reflective of and shaping reality in the interest of domination, however, such language is not completely fictive or innocent.

Feminist biblical studies have pointed to a basic contradiction in how the bible is to be understood. On the one hand, the feminist recognition that the bible is G*d's word in male words, that it is written in kyriocentric language, came into existence in kyriarchal societies and cultures, and has served throughout the centuries to inculcate and sustain relations of domination changes malestream biblical assumptions. On the other hand, the recognition that the bible has functioned to inspire and empower movements for radical equality, human rights, and the well-being of all without exception is equally basic for feminist biblical studies. In one way or another, all feminist approaches and methods of interpretation are engaged by both facets of this contradiction. They are not exclusive of each other but must be braided together in the process of interpretation.

Since a critical liberationist interpretation understands kyriarchy/ kyriocentrism as an institutional and ideological system of domination, it must focus especially on the problem of how to read andro-kyriocentric language and texts in such a way that their poisonous powers and choreography of negative world-construction, self-alienation, and damaging persuasion can be undone. Hence, feminist liberationist interpretation concentrates especially on the ideological inscriptions of kyriocentric texts. Malestream interpretations, on the other hand, are either positioned within the historical paradigm of interpretation and tend to be caught up in the factual, objectivist, and antiquarian framework of biblical studies or they are at home in a literary formalist paradigm of biblical studies and insist that we are not able to move beyond the kyriocentric text to the historical reality of wo/men. They rightly reject the understanding of the biblical text as a transparent medium and favor the understanding of biblical

texts as ideological constructions that naturalize and legitimate kyriarchal relations of domination, although both scientific paradigms, the historical and the literary one, tend to overlook that kyriocentric texts construct the reality of domination as well as produce it as "common-sense"
knowledge.

Corrective Methods of Interpretation

The oldest methodological step in feminist biblical interpretation has both
a remedial and a revisionist aim. Such a revisionist approach was articulated and adopted in the nineteenth century and has strongly influenced
subsequent feminist interpretations. In response to those who quote the
bible for supporting the socio-symbolic kyriarchal order, such a feminist
remedial or corrective approach asserts that the bible does not prohibit
but rather authorizes the equal rights and liberation of wo/men *if it is understood correctly*.

• Critical biblical studies began with *textual* criticism. In the nineteenth
century, as today, feminists learned Greek and Hebrew in order to understand the true and uncontaminated meaning of the text and to correct
false translations and commentaries. Sarah Moore Grimké, for instance,
protested not only against the false translation of some passages but also
"against the perverted interpretations of the MEN who undertook to
write commentaries." She expressed her conviction that when they were
admitted "to the honor of studying Greek and Hebrew," wo/men would
produce readings of the bible quite different from those of men. In a similar vein, Lucretia Mott argued that wo/men ought to examine and compare biblical texts with other biblical passages so that a different reading
becomes possible.

   However, not enough critical analysis has been devoted to the actual
functioning of kyriocentric language that purports to be generic language.
Greek, like German, possesses what is called grammatical gender, which is
a three-way (masculine/feminine/neuter) classification system. According
to this grammatical system, nouns do not have to correspond with "nature"
but can behave in three different ways when it comes to the agreement
with an adjective, the choice of article, replacement by a pronoun, and in-
flectional patterns or word endings. For instance, in Romans 16:1-2 a
wo/man by the name of Phoebe is given the title *diakonos*, a title that has a
grammatically masculine form although it refers to a wo/man.

• A second step pays attention to how "generic" language is translated and
explores how translation depends on the *intellectual frameworks* and
socio-political location of the translator and interpreter. Grammatically

masculine language generally subsumes wo/men under generic terms such as man, mankind, brotherhood, etc. and mentions them explicitly only as a special case—either as the exception to the rule or as a problem.

Whereas grammatically masculine language is presumed to include both wo/men and men, this is not the case for language and images referring to wo/men, because common gender exhibits a sexual asymmetry. For instance, although most schoolteachers are actually wo/men, we do not say the "teacher and her class" but "the teacher and his class" when referring in a generalized way to teachers.

To illustrate my point: the word for the Holy Spirit in Hebrew is grammatically feminine, in Greek grammatically neuter, and in Latin grammatically masculine. Yet there seems to be no doubt regarding the Spirit's masculine gender among Christians, since almost all translations of the Greek word *to pneuma* render it as masculine. In doing so they seem still to depend either on the Roman Catholic doctrine that the Vulgate, the Latin translation of the bible, represents the inspired word of G*d, or on the fact that the doctrine of the Trinity is generally understood in kyriocentric masculinist terms despite the fact that Christians and Jews believe that the Divine is beyond gender. The masculine gendering of the Holy Spirit is thus not due to the original Hebrew or Greek biblical text. This example demonstrates how grammatically feminine or neutral language becomes masculinized and then naturalized and made "common sense."

• *Feminist textual criticism* shows that the kyriocentric tendencies which marginalize wo/men can be detected not only in subsequent translations and editions but also in the selection and redaction of traditional materials by the biblical writers themselves, including the selective canonization of early Christian texts. Most people do not read the bible in the original languages nor are they aware that the original text is not dictated by G*d but has been pieced together by scholars from various manuscript traditions. They frequently are not aware that biblical criticism began with textual criticism, which pointed out that we no longer have the "pristine original" of the verbally inspired text, but only its subsequent diverging manuscript forms. Scholars not only have to adjudicate between various manuscript versions in order to establish the "original" text; they also then translate this text into English from the vantage point of their own kyriocentric-kyriarchal knowledge of the world.

Studies of the transmission of Christian Testament texts and their variant readings indicate that an active elimination of texts speaking about wo/men's leadership actually has been at work in and through canon formation. The example of Colossians 4:15 is well known. Here the author extends greetings to the community of Laodicea and then to a person by

the name of *Nympha(s)* and the church in her/his/their house. The accusative form *Nymphan* can refer to a man named Nymphas or to a wo/man named Nympha. If one accepts the variant reading of Codex Vaticanus, some Minuscles, and the Syriac translation which reads "and the church in her [*autes*] house," then the greeting in Colossians refers to a wo/man as the leader of a house church. If one reads, with the Egyptian text, "their [*autōn*] house," then the author greets either Nympha(s) and her/his family or Nympha(s) and her/his friends. The Western and Byzantine textual variants, however, leave no doubt that the person in question is a man when they stress that the church met in "his [*autou*] house." Until very recently, most bible editions have chosen "his house" as the most original reading. However, according to general methodological rules of textual criticism, scholars have to prefer the more difficult version because it indicates that the text has not been changed in the interest of later interpretation. Hence, "in her house" should have been chosen as the most difficult reading of the text, since in later times wo/men were not permitted to become leaders of local churches.

• Another step in the corrective method focuses especially on enhancing *biblical literacy* and *knowledge about wo/men* in the bible. Miriam Therese Winter shares in *WomanWord* that she discovered, to her great surprise, sixty-four wo/men mentioned in the Christian Testament, not counting references to groups of wo/men. She asks: Why is it that male apostles from the time of Jesus figure so prominently in the accounts of the early church, while women of the gospels are replaced with a whole new cast of female characters after Pentecost? Moreover, why is it that many Christians and Jews know very few names of biblical wo/men and do not celebrate these wo/men as their foremothers as they celebrate their forefathers? For instance, when students are asked to list at least a dozen biblical wo/men, few can pass the test. Many of them can recall Eve and Mary, the mother of Jesus; some might have heard about Jezebel or the "wo/man at the well"; and some might remember Mary Magdalene as the sinner and prostitute. Rarely, though, do they know anything, for instance, about Priska or Hulda. By contrast, even those without any religious training have no trouble naming the leading male figures of the bible.

This lack of general knowledge about the wo/men of Scripture is mostly due to the kyriocentric character of religious instruction and liturgical selection, since religious education and liturgical practices have decisively shaped Christian imagination and still do so. Marjorie Procter-Smith has pointed out that contemporary lectionaries tend to include wo/men associated with male heroes, while they omit texts about wo/men such as Rachel, Leah, Deborah, Judith, Tabitha, Lydia, Priska, or the daughters of Phillip.

To rectify this lack it becomes necessary to develop a remedial approach that can rediscover all the texts about wo/men to be found in biblical writings. Since most religious people in Catholic traditions know the bible in and through liturgical readings and the celebration of biblical feast days, the selection of liturgical *readings about wo/men* and ritual *celebrations of biblical wo/men* become an important remedial strategy for reshaping biblical interpretation and imagination.

• A remedial approach, however, does not restrict itself to the canonical writings. It also fosters *extra-canonical and cross-cultural* research about wo/men in antiquity. Scholars have rediscovered leading wo/men, e.g., in the Apocryphal Acts, in Gnostic writings, in the texts of the so-called church fathers, as well as in Jewish apocryphal, Rabbinic, and Greco-Roman literature and history. For example, they have discovered the Goddess Isis and many other Goddesses; they have found Sophia-Wisdom as a central figure in Jewish, Christian, and Gnostic literatures; they have learned about the Therapeutes, a spiritual Sophia-Wisdom group in Egypt which is mentioned by the Jewish philosopher Philo. Moreover, they have not restricted themselves to the study of texts, but have also searched extra-textual remnants for new information about wo/men. For instance, the archeological work of Bernadette Brooten on Jewish wo/men leaders and that of Ute Eisen on wo/men office holders in the early church has "unearthed" much information and decisively changed our knowledge about wo/men in ancient Judaism and Christianity.

• A corrective method of interpretation seeks not only to recover forgotten traditions about wo/men, but also to remove the centuries of kyriocentric interpretations that have covered up the original, supposedly true meaning of the biblical text. Feminist scholars have shown, for instance, that biblical commentaries have either neglected wo/men's presence in the text or distorted the original meaning of the female characters in biblical stories.

In response to those who quote the bible to support the socio-symbolic kyriarchal order, feminist revisionist interpretation asserts that the biblical texts themselves are not misogynist. Rather, biblical texts and commentaries have projected their kyriocentric cultural bias onto biblical texts and it is this bias that is used against wo/men. Consequently, the bible, correctly understood, actually fosters the liberation of wo/men.

Feminists who belong to communities believing in verbal inspiration often engage in a very fine-tuned exegesis of biblical texts in order to prove that the literal sense of the text, if it is understood correctly, provides a true and liberating meaning. Hence, a feminist remedial interpretation that explicitly works from the belief that Scripture speaks with di-

vine authority has taken center stage in feminist Christian, Islamic, and Jewish *apologetic* hermeneutics. The belief that the bible is the literal, inspired word of G*d and owes its existence to divine authorship and authorization assumes that one can peel away the kyriocentric layers of Scripture like a husk so that the revealed truth and essential meaning of the bible come to the fore. The full truth taught by the bible will emerge if and when wo/men are able to utilize the appropriate tools of interpretation and if and when men repent of their sexist prejudices.

• Another form of revisionist interpretation is the focus on *wo/men as biblical authors*. Scholars have argued, for instance, that the gospels of Mark (Paul Achtemeier) and John (Sandra Schneiders) were written by wo/men evangelists. Others have suggested that at least half of the Lukan material on wo/men must be ascribed to a special pre-Lukan source that owed its existence to a wo/man evangelist (Leonard Swidler). Still other scholars have argued that wo/men's traditions will surface in the gospels if they are read with the appropriate methodology (Elaine Wainwright). A century ago, the German scholar Adolf von Harnack argued that Priska was the author of the epistle to the Hebrews. Such suggestions of female authorship not only expand our historical-theological imagination, but also assert that wo/men have participated in articulating and shaping biblical traditions and texts.

One cannot assume, however, that wo/men have written liberating texts just because they were wo/men. The pastoral epistles, for instance, forbid leading wo/men to teach and have authority over men (1 Timothy 2:11), but instruct wo/men elders to be "good teachers" and to teach younger wo/men their kyriarchal household duties, "that the word of G*d may not be discredited" (Titus 2:3-5). Or, to give another example: as Elizabeth A. Clark has pointed out, in her Virgilian poem *Cento,* the fourth-century writer Proba elaborates biblical traditions in ways that depict wo/man's status as more negative than it actually is in the bible. Unlike the so-called church fathers, Proba does not extol asceticism but rather recommends traditional kyriarchal Roman values "of respect for parents and kin, sanctity of home, and marital chastity" as Christian values.

Instead of assuming an essential feminine style of thinking and writing that enhances the well-being of wo/men, one needs to critically explore whether and to what degree the kyriocentric text communicates kyriarchal values and visions through wo/men. One must also consider that, like men, wo/men have internalized cultural feminine values and that they consequently tend to reproduce the kyriarchal politics of otherness in their speaking and writing. Hence, a remedial interpretation of Scripture from wo/men's perspective does not suffice.

• Remedial or corrective interpretation often uses a method of *classification* that re-inscribes kyriarchal dualisms. After discussing and gathering textual information about wo/men, interpreters frequently catalogue and systematize the collected materials in a dualistic fashion. For instance, they isolate positive and negative statements about wo/men in order to point to the positive biblical teachings and traditions over and against the negative ones. Such positive texts and traditions about wo/men and the feminine are considered separate from "texts of terror" and the stories of wo/men's victimization.

Other scholars classify biblical statements about wo/men and feminine imagery about G*d either as positive, ambivalent, or negative. Whereas negative elements are said to permeate the Hebrew Bible and the intertestamental and post-biblical writings of Judaism and Gnosticism, negative elements in the Christian tradition—if acknowledged at all—are seen as limited to later Christian Testament writings and particularly the writings of the church fathers. Such a dichotomous classification favoring Christian—over and against Jewish—traditions perpetrates anti-Jewish attitudes and prejudices although its expressed intent is to reclaim the bible as a positive support for wo/men's emancipation.

• Other revisionist attempts underline not the negative role of wo/men in Judaism but rather the depravity of wo/men in Greco-Roman culture as an interpretive contrast. They claim that negative injunctions for Christian wo/men were necessary because of wo/men's depraved cultural socialization. For instance, one of the earliest feminist exegetical articles published by Antoinette Brown Blackwell in 1849 discusses texts such as 1 Corinthians 14 and 1 Timothy 2 that forbid wo/men to speak. She investigates whether the injunctions of these texts are rightly used against wo/men's speaking in public. Brown Blackwell tried to show that these two passages could not be used as "proof-texts" against wo/men. They do not prohibit wo/men's public teaching in general but only forbid a certain kind of faulty teaching.

In order to make her point, however, Brown Blackwell had to resort to two interlocking historical arguments: the depravity and low status of wo/men in the surrounding cultures of Judaism and Greco-Roman antiquity, and the misbehavior of church wo/men. She argued that the wo/men of the church had been kept in an "ignorant, degraded, and unchristian subjection." However, when the gospel of equality was preached to them, they were led into "the snare of the adversary" and attempted to teach and have authority over men.

Here emerges the problem that mars all revisionist approaches: in order to "save" the biblical text from its critics they often resort to blaming wo/men or their "depraved" cultures and religions rather than indict the misogynist texts of the bible.

Historical Reconstructive Methods

Historical studies seek to increase the distance between ourselves and the time of the text; they seek to increase our historical knowledge and enrich our imagination. At the same time, feminist historical reconstruction works to bridge the "chasm" between contemporary readers and the biblical text, a chasm that historical positivism has constructed. It seeks to displace the kyriocentric dynamic of the biblical text in its literary and historical contexts by re-contextualizing the text in a different socio-political-religious historical context in order to make the subordinated and marginalized "others" visible, and their repressed arguments and silences "audible" again. It thereby attempts to recover as wo/men's heritage both wo/men's religious historical agency and the memory of their victimization, struggle, and accomplishments.

• Until now only scant attention has been paid to the intellectual history of biblical interpretation by wo/men, which for the most part has had the remedial character I have been describing. Introductions to biblical interpretation still recount only the history of interpretation of elite white men but not that of "the others." Postcolonial biblical criticism has detailed how Eurocentric biblical-theological studies focus on the interpretive history and questions of white Euro-American men while neglecting the traditions and questions of African Americans or other cultural groups. We therefore lack sustained research into the history of biblical interpretation not only by African, Asian, or Hispanic Christians but also by wo/men of all cultures. In addition, writers of wo/men's religious history have not paid sufficient attention to the different ways black and white wo/men, for example, read the bible in the nineteenth century. Here, a rich store of knowledge is still to be discovered and awaits the feminist intellectual and social historian and interpreter.

• A history of biblical interpretation by wo/men would at the same time give us much insight into the ways wo/men have read and used the bible throughout the centuries and make us conscious of a rich feminist history now almost completely lost to us. Such a feminist intellectual history of biblical interpretation would document that feminist biblical interpretation is not a recent affair but spans all centuries and all cultures in which the bible was influential. It would not only reclaim wo/men's intellectual work, but also make clear that for centuries wo/men have been saying many of the things that feminists are now discovering. While there are many institutions dedicated to the discussion of men's ideas, there are almost none for wo/men's ideas. Hence, feminist scholars still have to build upon and elaborate the ideas of wo/men.

• At first, historical studies of wo/men in the bible or those of Jewish, Greek, or Roman wo/men were generally *topical-thematic* studies that understood kyriocentric texts and archeological artifacts about wo/men as descriptive source-texts of historical facts. A positivist "scientific" historical approach takes its sources as comprehensive and reliable data about wo/men in the biblical world. Texts are understood as "windows to" and "mirrors of" wo/men's reality in antiquity. Sourcebooks on wo/men in the Greco-Roman and Jewish biblical worlds assemble in English translation literary documents as well as inscriptions and papyri about wo/men's religious activities in Greco-Roman antiquity.

However, such a method re-inscribes the historical marginality of wo/men. Since textual and archeological source materials about wo/men's historical agency are very limited, scholarly and popular historical accounts tend to conclude that wo/men did not play a significant role in ancient history. Thus, although collections and translations of source materials provide helpful information, they nevertheless are in a certain sense pre-critical insofar as they obscure the fact that kyriocentric texts are ideological constructions and not reflections of reality. Consequently, they must be utilized with a hermeneutics of suspicion and placed within a feminist model of analysis and reconstruction.

• A feminist method of historical reconstruction conceptualizes wo/men's history not simply as the history of wo/men's oppression by men but as the story of wo/men's historical agency and struggles against kyriarchal subordination and oppression. In my book *In Memory of Her,* I sought to re-conceptualize the task of early Christian historiography as a reconstructive one. Such a reconstructive approach is not only indebted to epistemological explorations in feminist historiography but it can also be further theorized in light of discussions on the "New Historicism." It understands history not in a positivist sense but as a consciously constructive narrative, as the story of power relations and struggles. Recognizing the absence and marginalization of wo/men in kyriocentric texts, feminist historians have sought to articulate the problem of how to write wo/men back into history and how to capture the memory of wo/men's historical experience and contribution. The historian Joan Kelly has succinctly stated the dual goal of wo/men's history as both to restore wo/men to history and to restore history to wo/men. Wo/men have made socio-cultural contributions and challenged dominant institutions and values. They also have wielded destructive power and collaborated in kyriarchal structures of exploitation.

While at first glance feminist interpretation that focuses on biblical history seems to have very little to do with historical imagination, the shift in the theoretical understanding of historiography that has taken place has shown that history cannot be written without an ability for

imaginative reconstruction. Convinced of the power of images, today both feminist artists and feminist historians seek to create new interpretations of biblical texts about wo/men and to imagine them differently. One way to do so is to re-imagine them in their socio-historical contexts.

• Feminist scholars in religion have begun to open up many new areas of research by asking different historical questions that seek to understand the socio-religious life-worlds of wo/men in antiquity. Some of these questions are: What do we know about the everyday life of wo/men in Israel, Syria, Greece, Egypt, Asia Minor, or Rome? How did freeborn wo/men, slave wo/men, wealthy wo/men, or business wo/men live? Could wo/men read and write? Do we know of any wo/men philosophers, poets, or religious thinkers? What rights did they have? How did they dress? Which powers and types of influence did they gain through patronage? What did it mean for a wo/man of Corinth to join the Isis cult, the Synagogue, or the Christian group? What did imprisonment mean for Junia? How did wo/men in Philippi receive Luke-Acts?

Although many of these questions still need to be researched and might never be answered, asking them has engendered several important insights. For example, asking such questions has made it possible to rediscover Junia, the apostle; to document the history and leadership of wo/men in ancient Israel and Judaism as well as in early Christianity; to locate the household-code texts in Aristotelian political philosophy; and to subject Gnostic writings to gender analysis. Socio-historical studies have illuminated the daily life of wo/men in the ancient world and underlined the class divisions between wo/men.

However, insofar as historical studies do not sufficiently problematize the positivist assumption that kyriocentric source-texts are descriptive and reliable evidence for socio-historical reality, their focus on wo/men's history remains caught up in the marginalizing tendencies of the kyriocentric text, which subsumes wo/men under male terms.

• A feminist socio-rhetorical construction of early Christian history moves away from the method of isolating and focusing on texts *about wo/men* toward a theoretical elaboration of socio-political and cultural-religious historical models that allow one to place wo/men—freeborn and slave, Jewish and Greco-Roman, African and Asian, elite and poor—in the center of early Christian struggles and history. Texts about wo/men are not directly descriptive of wo/men's actual historical reality and agency. They are only indicators. Such texts bring to the surface the presence of wo/men and marginalize them at the same time.

Kyriocentric biblical texts tell stories and construct social worlds and symbolic universes that mythologize, reverse, absolutize, and idealize kyriarchal differences and, in doing so, obliterate or marginalize the his-

torical presence of the devalued "others." Biblical texts about wo/men therefore are like the tip of an iceberg intimating what is submerged and obfuscated in historical silence. They have to be read as indicators of the historical reality that they both repress and construct. As rhetorical texts, canonical texts and their interpretations construct a world in which those whose arguments they oppose either become the "deviant others" or are no longer present at all.

In order to displace the marginalizing dynamics of the kyriocentric biblical source-text or artifact, a critical feminist analysis takes the texts about wo/men out of their contextual frameworks and reassembles them like mosaic stones in a feminist pattern or design that does not recuperate but counteracts the marginalizing or oppressive tendencies of the kyriocentric text. To that end, one has to elaborate models of historical and socio-cultural reconstruction that can subvert the biblical text's kyriocentric dynamics and place the struggles of those whom it marginalizes and silences into the center of the historical narrative.

• Biblical readers are generally not aware that biblical histories are neither reports of events nor transcripts of facts but rather rhetorical constructions that have shaped the information available to their authors in light of their religious or political interests. The earliest attempt to chart Christian beginnings utilized a geo-political model of reconstruction. Luke-Acts tell the story of early Christian beginnings in such a way that the gospel moves from Galilee to Jerusalem. After Jesus' and the early Christian mission's rejection in Jerusalem, the gospel moves to the Greco-Roman world. Acts ends with the gospel's arrival in Rome, which was then the geo-political center of the inhabited world. This early Christian model has not only anti-Jewish but also imperialist and Eurocentric implications.

Some other reconstructive early Christian models are, for instance, the theological models of orthodoxy-heresy and of Jesus-apostolic succession. Confessional theological variations include both the Protestant model of rapid deterioration from Jesus and his first followers to early Catholicism, and the Roman Catholic growth model which assumes that early Christian beginnings contain the seeds for the development that climaxes in the Roman papacy. Such historiographical models are genderized insofar as they assume that the presence of wo/men's leadership in early Christian communities signals heresy or that Jesus chose only male apostles as his successors.

The reconstructive model of "background" and "center" is equally flawed. Reconstructions of early Christian wo/men's history construe Jewish or Greco-Roman wo/men's history as "background" in order to assert the liberated status of Christian wo/men over and against that of Jewish or pagan wo/men. They employ a Christian supremacist recon-

structive model. Equally gendered are sociological models that construct the opposition between charismatic equality and kyriarchal institution, male ascetic itinerant radicalism and familial love-kyriarchalism, or masculine honor and feminine shame, since such models perpetuate the dualistic framework of the Western cultural gender system.

Hence, feminist scholars who utilize sociological or anthropological reconstructive models must insist that such models be tested for their kyriocentric theoretical implications and kyriarchal limitations. Social-scientific frameworks that are not open to a feminist critique of ideology but are utilized by biblical scholars in a positivistic way do not displace the marginalizing dynamics of the kyriocentric source-text. On the contrary, they reify it.

• Finally, a critical feminist historical reconstructive approach challenges dominant scholarship by insisting that history must be written not from the perspective of the "historical winners" but from that of the silenced or marginalized. In order to achieve a historically adequate description of the socio-cultural and religious worlds of the bible, scholars can no longer limit their investigations to the history of Western elite men. Rather, they must re-conceptualize early Christian history so that the voices and struggles of the "vanquished of history" can be heard and become visible again.

Although a critical feminist reconstructive approach recognizes the provisionality and multiplicity of historical knowledges as particular, situated, and "embodied," it nevertheless does not abandon the claim to the relative objectivity and historical validity of its reconstructions. The objectivity and adequacy of such critical feminist historical reconstructions must be assessed in terms of whether and to what extent they can make present the historical losers and their arguments—that is, to what extent they can make visible the symbolic world-constructions of those who have been made "invisible" in kyriocentric texts. One is still able to disclose and unravel "the politics of otherness" constructed by the kyriocentric text because it is produced by a historical reality in which "the absent others" are present and active.

In order to reconstruct the past, feminist scholars therefore utilize wo/men's experience and feminist theoretical analysis of reality as a scientific resource and as a significant indicator of the reality against which our interpretations and reconstructive models are to be tested. They rightly argue that the relationship between kyriocentric text and historical reality cannot be construed as a mirror-image but must be decoded as a complex ideological construction.

Hence, a critical feminist rhetorical analysis seeks to break the hold of the sacred kyriocentric text and its unquestioned authority by resisting

its ideological directives and hierarchically arranged binary oppositions in order to unmask the kyriarchal politics of biblical texts and interpretations. By rejecting textual naturalization and by tracing the intimate interaction between kyriocentric text and socio-political reality, it seeks to undo the text's ideological power of persuasion. By elucidating not only the sexual but also the kyriarchal politics of biblical texts, such a critical analysis enables wo/men readers to resist the prescriptive rhetorics and attemptcd identity formation. By reading biblical texts against their kyriocentric grain such a critical feminist analysis dislodges texts from their kyriarchal frame in order to reconstruct their historical information differently. This calls for an increase in historical imagination.

Imaginative Interpretive Methods

From its inception, feminist interpretation has sought to actualize biblical stories in role-play, storytelling, bibliodrama, dance, and song. In order to break the marginalizing and obliterating tendencies of the kyriocentric text, feminists tell biblical stories in which wo/men are silenced or not present at all in a different key and with a *difference*.

• One of the earliest methods developed in feminist biblical interpretation was the method of personal identification with the wo/men characters of biblical stories whom it sought to revive through biblical storytelling. This method not only focuses on the wo/men characters of biblical stories, but also imagines wo/men characters in so-called "generic" stories that do not explicitly mention wo/men but allow for their presence. The storytelling might make explicit, for example, that not only the "sons of Israel" but also the daughters gathered at Sinai and were covenant partners, or that the audience of Jesus consisted not only of men but also of wo/men.

Whereas the retelling of biblical stories in Midrash or legend is quite familiar to Jewish and Catholic wo/men, it is often a new avenue of interpretation for white Protestant wo/men. Since African-Americans, who are predominantly Protestant, were forbidden to learn to read and write, their biblical interpretations have always imaginatively elaborated in story, sermon, and songs certain key figures (e.g., Moses) and paradigmatic events (e.g., Exodus) of the bible in terms of their hopes and struggles for liberation. It was especially the story of the liberation of Israel from the slavery of Egypt that fired the imagination of the spirituals. Faith became identification with the heroes and heroines of the Hebrew Bible and with the long-suffering but ultimately victorious Jesus.

• Renita Weems has suggested that despite negative experiences with the bible, African-American wo/men remain faithful to it because of

their love of stories. One way to tell a story differently is asking the *"what if"* question: What if Eve had given birth to Adam? What if Miriam had become the founder and leader of Israel? What if we had as many letters of Mary of Magdala as we have from Paul? What if Jesus had been born a wo/man? What if Mary had written the infancy stories? What if Divine Wisdom were to be worshiped by Jews and Christians? What if...?

Other techniques of storytelling *"otherwise"* include *interviewing* the writers of the gospels or biblical characters, such as questioning Moses about Miriam's fate; *telling the story* of the Exodus from the viewpoint of the granddaughter of Miriam; *writing a letter* to Paul or receiving one from the wo/man who anointed Jesus; inventing characters and letting them speak, as for instance the daughter of the Syrophoenician wo/man or a wo/man friend of Sarah or the wo/man who anointed Jesus. Other possibilities include writing different psalms: psalms of praise, curse, or pleading; writing wisdom sayings in the "I am" or "But I say to you" style; or writing makarisms (Blessed are the poor) or antitheses (It is written...but I say to you). It is important to keep in touch with our emotions and feelings when engaging in such storytelling or creative writing.

Other ways to tell a biblical story differently include dance, music, collage, painting, or body movement.

• Jewish feminists have rediscovered the ancient form of Midrash, which is one of the classic methods for interpreting biblical texts. Midrash can refer to either halachic or aggadic interpretation but mostly refers to the latter. *Halachah* specifically deals with legal materials, whereas *Aggadah* includes parables, stories, ethics, and homilies. Midrash thus is a particular kind of imaginative interpretation.

If interpreters use the bible's own language and share at least some of the Rabbinic assumptions, one can speak of Midrash, which is the Rabbinic method of coping with socio-political and theological change and of integrating this change into tradition. Feminist Midrash has a similar function. According to Gary G. Porton,[1] Midrash is based on the following basic assumptions:

1. Every part of the bible was written in a very precise way in order to teach. Hence, every nuance, grammatical variation, repetition, as well as the relative position of verses, is a clue to deeper understanding.

---

[1]Gary G. Porton, *Understanding Rabbinic Midrash* (Hoboken, N.J.: Ktav Publishing House, 1985).

2. Everything in the bible is interrelated. Hence, one can use a verse from one book to prove a point of interpretation of a text in another book although the two writings might have no apparent relationship.
3. It is possible and desirable to have multiple interpretations of a single verse.
4. Reason is not enough; it must be combined with faith. As a result, one might refute an interpretation by quoting a biblical verse that seems to contradict it.
5. Making Midrash is a sacred activity. It is a way to express our relationship with G*d. Study and interpretation lead to redemption of the world by bringing G*d's presence into it.

The basic theological presupposition underlying Midrash-making is the assumption that the bible is not the painting itself but more like the palette of colors that an artist used to create a painting. It provides the language, metaphors, stories, promises, and prophecies that are to be used to reflect on the new reality in which we find ourselves. Feminists study the biblical text and write modern stories in relation to it which incorporate their experiences and consciousness into Jewish tradition. Feminist Midrash puts wo/men's voice back into the text and retells the biblical story in a spirit of "tikkun olam," of mending or healing the world. It thereby creates an inclusive language and imagination that affirms all people and cherishes each person's G*d-given gifts.

• *Feminist bibliodrama,* another form of imaginative interpretation that has been developed primarily in Europe and widely practiced since the 1970s in bible groups and schools, churches, and workshops, has great affinity with the *Leitura Popular da Bíblia* developed in Brazil. This approach is also experiential and text-oriented; it is an open method of interaction between a biblical text and the experience and emotions of those engaging in the process of its interpretation.

This method seeks to make participants aware not only of the contradictions, poisonous elements, or violent experiences but also the life-affirming and emancipatory potentials in biblical stories and texts. It usually has four components: the reading or telling of a biblical text with special focus on certain words, emotional markers, or contradictions inscribed in the text; body work such as stretching and release of tensions, expressive movement, and physical exercises; imaginative dramatic processes of role-play, dialogue, inner imagination, and dramatic staging of the whole text or aspects of it that can extend over a couple of days; and "debriefing" during the last stage, in which a group tries to understand the interpretation given to the text and their reactions and emotions in re-

sponse to it. It is similar to *psychodrama*, but seeks for a deeper understanding of the biblical text rather than focusing on the insights and effects on the self-understanding and life-stories of the participants.

• Cultural methods of interpretation stress the importance of visual expression and pictorial elaborations of biblical wo/men's stories. Realizing that many wo/men in history were not (and still, today, are not) able to read and write, this approach points to the power of visual images, which replace the printed word for illiterate, barely literate, or post-literate contemporary audiences.

Artistic or popular depictions of biblical stories not only are a source of instruction but also shape the imagination of religious and societal communities. In medieval cathedrals one finds sequences of biblical stories that are called the "bible of the poor." Just as medieval and renaissance paintings depict biblical figures and stories in the colors and customs of their own times, so the paintings of biblical events by Nicaraguan peasants and the slide sequences of *Parables Today* told in the Basic Christian Communities in São Paulo, Brazil, are set within the socio-economic and political realities of the poor in Latin America. Such socio-cultural studies have explored countless variations in the depictions of Eve and Mary, the Mother of Jesus, and have rediscovered Martha, the wise virgin and dragon slayer in medieval art.

Furthermore, whereas some feminist artists have depicted the crucified Jesus as a wo/man or created images of God the Mother, others focus on wo/men of the bible. This approach has pointed to the traditional fascination of artists with the figure of Judith while it has problematized the figuration of female nakedness in the religious and cultural depictions of the Christian West.

In short, this strategy of cultural criticism is in the process of rediscovering a rich but also problematic cultural heritage by tracing the figure of Divine Sophia in literature and art or through rediscovering the image of Mary Magdalene in story, novel, visual arts, music, film, and drama.

Methods of Conscientization

Feminist consciousness-raising wishes to subvert the persuasive power of the kyriocentric text by placing wo/men in the center of attention. It thereby seeks to undo the immasculation (Judith Fetterly) that takes place in the process of reading. Since andro-kyriocentric language constructs human values and situations in grammatically masculine, so-called generic language and invites readers to identify with the central characters and protagonist of a story, it leads to the reader's internalization of elite male values and roles. In order to critically make conscious the ideo-

logical powers of the andro-kyriocentric texts, feminists have available various methods of analysis. Biblical narratives are more than descriptions of events. They urge their readers to inhabit the subject position offered to them by the text and to adopt certain values and perspectives. The silences, contradictions, arguments, prescriptions, and projections of biblical texts, as well as the bible's discourses on gender, race, class, and culture, must be unraveled to show their ideological inscription of the kyriarchal politics of otherness. Hence, feminist conscientization seeks to shift attention from the kyriocentric text to wo/men as reading subjects.

• Feminist reader-response criticism is a cultural practice that makes us conscious of the complex process of reading and enables us to learn how to read differently. By showing both how kyriarchal discourse constructs the reader and how gender, race, and class affect the way we read, such an approach underlines the importance of the reader's textual and socio-cultural location.

Reading and thinking in a kyriocentric symbol-system entice biblical readers to align themselves and identify with what is culturally normative, that is, culturally "male." Thus, reading the bible can intensify—rather than challenge—wo/men's embeddedness in the cultural kyriarchal discourses that alienate us from ourselves.

A feminist method of conscientization therefore seeks to foster methods of resistance that develop alternative visions to deconstruct, debunk, and reject the kyriocentric politics of the canonical text. For example, we can attend to a "wo/man's point of view" inscribed in biblical texts as well as to the ideological inscriptions of kyriocentric dualism and the politics of gender in cultural and religious texts.

Yet, by tracing out the feminine/masculine binary structures of the biblical text or by focusing on the "feminine" character constructs (e.g., mother, daughter, bride) of biblical narratives, structuralist and deconstructionist readings run the risk of re-inscribing rather than dislodging the dualistic gender politics of the text. To read the text against its kyriarchal grain and to become resisting readers, we need to develop a different radical egalitarian imagination.

The kyriocentric biblical text derives its seductive as well as its critical "powers" from its generic aspirations. For instance, wo/men may read stories about Jesus in a non-gendered way without paying much attention to the maleness of Jesus. Yet, if we read/hear such stories in a theological contextualization that emphasizes the maleness of Jesus, wo/men's cultural kyriarchal self-identity will be shaped as masculine identity in and through such a reading. Focusing on the figure of Jesus, the Son of the Father, "doubles" wo/men's oppression when reading the bible. In the act of reading wo/men suffer not only from the alienating division of self

against self but also from the realization that to be female is neither to be "divine" nor to be "a son of God." Yet, if we read such stories of Jesus in a radical egalitarian contextualization, such a radical democratic imagination can engender emancipatory readings.

• The method of imaginative identification with biblical wo/men also has serious limits. It can become effective for liberation only if it does not overlook the fact that wo/men characters are constructs of kyriarchal texts and authors. For instance, feminist imaginative reinterpretation of biblical texts sometimes argues openly for a gender-specific biblical hermeneutics in terms of Jungian archetypal psychology and cultural glorifications of femininity, motherhood, and true womanhood. Most of the time, however, such imaginative biblical recreations unconsciously reproduce the Western romanticist and individualist ideal of the "White Lady."

If imaginative biblical reinterpretation does not go hand in hand with a hermeneutics of suspicion but instead uncritically embellishes the wo/men characters in the kyriocentric text, it invites readers to positively identify with those feminine role models that the kyriocentric text constructs. Such a reinterpretation actualizes and reproduces the very images and myths of "true womanhood" from which it seeks to become free. Since popular books on "the wo/men of the bible" often utilize biblical stories about wo/men for inculcating the values of conservative womanhood, a feminist interpretation must approach not only the biblical stories but also its own re-dramatizations with a hermeneutics of suspicion. It needs to critically analyze not only the history of interpretation associated with these stories but also their function in the overall rhetoric of the biblical text and its contemporary contexts.

Since wo/men's stories are embedded in and structured by kyriarchal culture and religion, they must be subjected to a process of critical evaluation and displacement. A critical interpretation for liberation must question the emotions which kyriocentric stories evoke and the values and roles they project before it can re-imagine and re-create them in a feminist key.

• Kyriarchal biblical language is not only androcentric; it is also kyriocentric. Imaginative identification therefore leads not just to the wo/man reader's immasculation but also to her colonization. For instance, Chung Hyun Kyung notes that the biblical story of Jesus' suffering and death is held up as the model to imitate for Asian wo/men, whose lives are filled with suffering and obedience. She relates a story about a Korean Sunday school teacher whose life was threatened in a bout of domestic violence. The woman testified that she had experienced G*d's love through her husband's judgment. When she accepted that she had to obey her husband

as G*d's representative, her old self died and her new self was born. She concluded her testimony, to applause from the congregation: "There have been no arguments and only peace in my family after I nailed myself on the cross and followed God's will."

Such a reading of the central Christian biblical story, which identifies with the obedience and suffering of Jesus, not only reinforces the bible's cultural masculinizing tendencies but also inculcates kyriarchal submission and self-alienation in the interest of mental and psychological colonization.

• Our reading of generic kyriocentric biblical texts does not necessarily have to lead to kyriarchal self-alienation. Wo/men readers can de-activate the essentialist cultural-theological naturalized masculine/feminine gender framework in favor of an abstract, degenderized reading.

Empirical studies have documented that so-called generic masculine language [man; pronoun "he"] is read differently by men and by wo/men. Whereas men connect male images with such language, wo/men do not connect any images at all with the kyriocentric text but read it in a generic, abstract fashion. This is possible because of the ambiguity of generic, grammatically masculine language.

In each instance, wo/men have to decide whether or not they are addressed by a statement such as "all men are created in the image of G*d." In the absence of any clear contextual markers, such a statement can be understood either as generic-inclusive of wo/men or as masculine-exclusive. How readers decide on the meaning of such a generic text greatly depends on their range of experience. Fifty years ago readers would have concluded a sentence such as "all professors at Harvard Divinity School are..." with "white educated men." The presence of white wo/men and African or Asian faculty in theological schools—however small their numbers—no longer allows for such a "common-sense" conclusion.

When wo/men recognize their contradictory ideological position in a kyriocentric language system, they can become readers resisting the master-identification of the kyriocentric, racist, classist, and colonialist text. However, if this contradiction is not brought into consciousness, it cannot be exploited for change but leads to further self-alienation. For change to take place, wo/men and other nonpersons must concretely and explicitly claim as their very own the human values and visions that the kyriocentric text ascribes to "generic" elite, white men. Wo/men can do this by imagining a different world of equality and well-being.

• Carol Newsom, for instance, has interpreted Proverbs 1–9 in terms of discourse theory. The author of Proverbs 1–9 does not conceal the text's speaking subject but openly constructs the text as a communication between father and son. The speaking voice of the text lays claim to the au-

thority of the father, who sanctions notions of righteousness, justice, and equity, but who vilifies rival discourses, namely, the symbolic practices embodied by two wo/men, Wisdom and the Strange Woman.

In the process of reading, readers are continually invited or summoned (interpellated) to take the kyriarchal subject position of the son who submits himself to the authority of the father. In taking this subject position offered them by the text, wo/men readers identify themselves at one and the same time as subordinated male subjects and as female objects of speech. The subjectivity of wo/men readers—i.e., the ability to construct oneself as a subject in and through language—becomes fractured.

Yet wo/men readers can also resist the summons of the text by refusing to take on the subject position it offers and by identifying themselves with its dissident voices. In order to do so they need to imagine different subject positions drawing on their own experience to "hear these dissident voices into speech."

• We also can learn how to read differently by paying special attention to *narratological* features, as for example in the story of the Syrophoenician wo/man told in Mark 7, and ask questions such as: Who speaks? Who acts? Who is left out or silenced? What agenda is pursued? Is it one that supports the dominant social-cultural or religious order or one that goes against its grain? How are the characters drawn? Whose story is told more fully, and whose agenda is fulfilled in the story? Which characters are approved of and which are disapproved of? What is the setting of the story and the sequence of narrative events? To use narrative criticism for a close reading of a particular biblical text enables us to lay open the kyriocentric dynamic of the text for critical reflection.

• As we have seen, feminist interpretation at first strongly emphasized identification with the wo/men characters in a story such as, for example, that of the bleeding woman. Reader-response criticism has shown that such identification leads to the immasculation of wo/men. However, feminist analysis has paid less attention to the function of wo/men characters in kyriocentric stories. When men identify with a male in power such as Moses, David, or Jesus, the female characters in a story are the means by which the male reader is bonded with the male author. When we examine how a female character functions as such a "means of bonding" or as the "glue" that holds things together, then we can see that the wo/man character is often introduced in order to enhance the authority and power of the male protagonist.

For instance, many wo/men mentioned in the gospels are wo/men who have been healed by Jesus and their stories underscore how powerful

Jesus is. The author or narrator thus uses a wo/man character to gain power over readers so that they will agree that Jesus is a powerful teacher and prophet whose work fulfills the words of the prophets. In the process of reading, a disabled wo/man thus becomes doubly self-alienated because she realizes that she can never be like Jesus.

• From its beginnings, feminist interpretation has sought to undo the power of the kyriocentric text by placing wo/men in the center of attention. To demonstrate this, when reading gospel stories about Jesus and wo/men one can trace out the kyriocentric dynamic of the text in order to decenter Jesus and to center attention on the wo/man protagonist. Placing the Syrophoenician wo/man in the center rather than Jesus, for example, has engendered a rich variety of interpretations. Imaginatively moving wo/men from the periphery of the kyriocentric text can undo its unconscious, naturalized mechanisms of inscribing wo/men's self-alienation and second-class citizenship.

At the same time, we must be careful always to read from the perspective of multiply oppressed wo/men. Here it does not suffice just to decenter the leading men. We also need to decenter wo/men of high status and to refocus attention on their subordinates and dependents. For instance, focusing on Hagar rather than on Sarah has brought to the fore the prejudices and power relations that exist between wo/men. It also shows how the text endorses the kyriarchal value system and wo/men's second-class citizenship and status in patriarchal societies.

• Another means of decentering the kyriocentric text has been role reversal. You reverse, for instance, the roles inscribed in texts that speak about male protagonists such as the twelve and then read them as speaking about wo/men, in order to lift into consciousness the naturalized common-sense assumptions about masculine and feminine gender inscriptions constructed by the andro/kyriocentric text.

Although Christians believe that the humanity of Jesus and not his masculinity is salvific, the characterization of Jesus in male terms has become so much "common sense" that both male and female readers are shocked when the character of Jesus is changed, for instance, into a female Messiah. The pervasive masculinization of kyriocentric stereotypes thus becomes particularly obvious when the gender, status, ethnicity, or religious affiliation of Jesus is reversed and Jesus is seen as a wo/man surrounded by female disciples.

• In order to test out whether stories can be read in a generic way as speaking about wo/men disciples, we can, for example, read stories about the disciples and discipleship as speaking about male and female disci-

ples. In a next step we have to test out whether texts that speak only about men allow us to read them as speaking about human values that apply both to men and wo/men. If a text such as Mark 6:7, 12, "and he called to him the twelve and sent them out two by two.... So they went out and preached that men should repent..." still makes sense when read as referring to wo/men disciples, it can be understood in an inclusive fashion. If it does not make sense, then such a text must be marked as a kyriocentric text.

The same inclusive reading must be done with respect to high-status and low-status people as well as with respect to people of different cultural and religious affiliations. Or, we can ask, is it possible to reverse anti-Jewish texts so that the texts about Jews can be read as speaking about Christians, or that the texts about Romans can be read as speaking about colonized peoples, such as, for instance, Jews?

• If we carefully analyze the kyriocentric mechanisms and strategies of biblical texts, we can read them against their kyriarchal grain rather than taking such texts at face value. Since kyriocentric texts are projections of male elites seeking to persuade readers in the interest of kyriarchal domination and values, we must always read such kyriocentric texts against their persuasive intentions. Stories are never just descriptive but always also prescriptive. Hence, they must be analyzed not only for what they tell but also for what they presume or pass over in silence. Moreover, since they submerge subordinate others and eliminate them from the story, kyriocentric language and texts are to be read as the tip of the iceberg indicating what has been lost. We must search for the submerged and untold part of the story, its inscribed contradictions, silences, and persuasive strategies.

An effective way of reading against the grain is the method of "defamiliarization" (*Verfremdung* = making alien) developed by the writer Berthold Brecht, whose basic insight was that the knowledge of truth is possible only through critical thinking. The defamiliarization process makes a text or an idea that is "common sense," the rule, usual, and familiar unusual, unfamiliar, unexplainable, alien. One can either change the biblical text or its immediate context, or place the text into a different reading situation. For instance, one can change the beatitude "Blessed are the poor" and say "Blessed are the rich for money rules the world." Or one can read the text in terms of gender: "Blessed are poor wo/men and woe to rich men." Further, one can change the context and move the text from the Sermon on the Mount to the story of the Syrophoenician wo/man where it becomes part of her objection to Jesus: "You said blessed are the poor, but now you have forgotten it!" Finally, one can defamiliarize the text by spelling out the situation in which the text is heard today:

"Blessed are the poor—Never again Rwanda; Blessed are those who hunger and thirst for justice—Never again Auschwitz; Blessed are the peacemakers—Never again Baghdad and Kosovo."

• Yet another method of critical interpretation is to read consciously "as a wo/man" or "from a wo/man's perspective." If, in the first moment of feminist criticism, interpreters appealed to their experience as wo/men, and in the second moment they exposed the ideologies inherent in the andro-kyriocentric text and in malestream criticism, in the third moment interpreters can approach the text not as wo/men reading as men but as wo/men reading as wo/men. They must question how the text constructs masculine attributes and seek to revalorize the feminine so that wo/men readers can affirm their female identities and experiences. To this end they trace and deconstruct symbolic gender dualism and inscription. For instance, the story of the wo/man who praises the womb that bore Jesus and the breasts that suckled him (Luke 11:27-28) can be analyzed as follows:

Jesus	Woman
Those (people)	Womb/Breasts
Hear	Bore
Keep	Sucked [suckled]
Word of G*d	You [Jesus]
Word	Body
Native	Foreign
Speech	Silence
Male	Female

Positioned within such a dualistic interpretive gender framework, Jesus and the Wo/man become opposites. To align oneself with Jesus, the male, leads to the immasculation of wo/men readers. Such a process of immasculation leads wo/men readers to reject their bodily female identity in the process of reading.

Reading with such a dualistic interpretive gender lens gives one three choices: to naively identify as a wo/man with the kyriocentric constructs of the female characters; to identify in the process of reading as a man; or to affirm one's female identity by reading as a wo/man. However, all three modes of reading fail to allow us to break through the dualistic naturalized gender construction of the text. This can be done, I suggest, only if one relativizes the dualistic gendered rhetoric of the text in favor of a radical egalitarian reading.

• To make conscious the naturalizing powers of the kyriocentric text and to undo the naturalizing re-inscriptions even of feminist interpretations, one must read the text from an alternative ideological location. I have suggested the *ekklesia of wo/men* as such an alternative radical democratic space. This space allows wo/men readers to read from the radical democratic perspective of equality and to reclaim the human and divine qualities that rightly are theirs but which have been stolen from them in and through andro-kyriocentric language, culture, and religion.

However, such readings in the space of the *ekklesia of wo/men* must be done from different socio-political subject locations. Feminist biblical interpretations do not come in one shape and color. There are many different perspectives at work and many different socio-cultural religious locations shaping feminist interpretation: womanist, mujerista, Latina feminist, Africana feminist. There are readings from the perspective of Latin American, European, Anglo-American, Asian, and African wo/men; lesbian and queer readings; postcolonial readings that take the different forms of imperialism into account.

All these interpretive approaches insist on an articulation of the socio-political, global-cultural, and pluralistic religious locations and contexts of biblical texts and interpretations. In various ways they fashion new methods and models and offer a wealth of new cultural stories and resources for an emancipatory practice of interpretation that can support wo/men's struggle for justice, self-determination, and freedom.

• *Leitura Popular da Bíblia* is based on the Brazilian educator Paulo Freire's *Pedagogy of the Oppressed* and Augusto Boal's *Teatro Popular.* It takes the life-experiences of poor wo/men as its starting point and goal. It seeks to give them a "key for reading" the bible which makes the connections between their life and biblical life and puts their experiences in touch with the experiences of biblical people. The change of consciousness that results evokes a desire for new societal, personal, and religious structures.

Psychodrama is similar to the *Leitura Popular da Bíblia* insofar as it also has as its goal personal transformation. It opens doors to suppressed memories, forgotten experiences, and denied emotions; it helps participants to know and accept their own story and to understand it within a larger world drama, to see their role clearly and to affirm it or learn a new one. It enables participants to see as much of their problems and themselves as they can tolerate. When it gets too much, they can turn away and say, this is just a role I play, it is not me. It uses biblical stories as a process to heal.

Participants usually sit in a circle with empty chairs in the middle, one for each character in the story which is worked on. During the telling

of the story, the group is asked to allow the characters to speak to them: Who repulses you? With whom do you agree? Who fascinates you? With whom do you identify? Do you recognize people from your own life in the story? Do they evoke memories of times past? What kind of memories? What more would you like to know more about a character whom you find attractive or troubling? The group chooses roles freely and, depending on how much time is available, a few parts or the whole story is acted out. Rather than describe such a process I want to quote at length Evelyn Rothchild-Laeuchli, a therapist, who describes the effects on one participant in such a play:

> Amy sat in a chair, her body frozen, her hand clenched around a crumpled ball of Kleenex, and her face an unmoving mask. The only sign of the storm raging inside her was the tears that slid down her cheeks. She saw so many images: the flowers at her grandmother's funeral, her father throwing a chair in rage and her mother's face turned, unfocused seeing nothing. . . . The word incest spun in her head that would not attach itself to the bits of memory or the feelings in her body. If she could move, she knew she would scream or throw up. Finally she said, "I have to know, even if I die!" Amy was a member of a small group in a psychiatric hospital who had just played the story of Lot. Amy played Lot's wife, a wo/man without a name. Her husband Lot, faced with the angry and lustful men of Sodom, offered his two young daughters to be raped in place of the two angels who were his guests. He then fled G*d's wrath. . . . "But Lot's wife behind him looked back, and she turned into a pillar of salt" (Genesis 19:17-26). Later . . . Lot had intercourse with his two daughters. . . . For Amy a door had opened to memories and awareness. . . . Now at last, she was looking back into a childhood of violence and abuse—the burning city of Sodom . . . During the discussion of our play, someone said: "This is a horrible story. Why would G*d put such a terrible story in the Bible?" Amy answered simply, "It's the story of my life. Somehow I feel better that it's in the Bible." A pillar of salt is something precious—salt of the earth and salt of our tears—it is an example that nourishes the spirit of the community. Amy's courage to look back healed us and gave us hope.[2]

---

[2]Evelyn Rothchild-Laeuchli, "Lot's Wife Looks Back: Biblical Stories as Therapy and Play," in *Body and Bible: Interpreting and Experiencing Biblical Narratives*, ed. Björn Krondorfer (Philadelphia: Trinity Press, 1992), 191–192.

To end is not to conclude: I have sought to sketch out some of the key methodological steps and theoretical moves in feminist biblical interpretation. All these different methods can be used as single steps or braided together and used in the process and movement of a critical feminist interpretation for liberation. However, it must be noted that such feminist methods and approaches to biblical interpretation are not primarily accountable to the standards of the academy or the church. Rather, they are committed to the liberation movements of wo/men for justice and well-being. The following statement of Selma Bosch, a Brazilian farm worker, appropriately sums up and ends this chapter, challenging you to become involved not only in the spiraling dance of feminist biblical interpretation but also in the struggles of Wisdom "movements" for dignity, hope, justice, and well-being:

We have always read the bible. It was difficult, and I only began to understand the bible when I received a key for reading: About whom does the text speak; for whom does it speak?...If one reads the bible and understands it, then one has more hope. Then one stays in the community meeting and also in the Union meetings....However, sometimes one loses courage and one does not want to participate in the movements any longer. But then one remembers the midwives, Moses, Ruth, Joshua. If one sees the situation and the suffering, then one cannot remain quiet. Moreover, our bible is no longer a "clean" book. Since the moment when I began to understand the bible, I have written in it and made annotations to what I noticed. Most important is that the reading of the bible and the popular movements go hand in hand. I participate in the wo/men's farmworker movement. If one does not struggle, one can not achieve anything. The reading of the bible compels us to get involved and it helps us to understand ourselves better.[3]

---

[3]My translation of a statement quoted in Heloisa Gralow Dalferth/Claudete Beise Ulrich, "'Wie der Sauerteig, den eine Frau nahm,' Leitura Popular da Bíblia und Bibliodrama," in *In Spiralen Fliegen. Bibliodrama und TZI Aktuell,* ed. Margarete Pauschert/ Antje Röckemann (Münster: Schlangenbrut e.V., 1999), 23.

Deepening Movement

Elisabeth Schüssler Fiorenza, *Sharing Her Word: Feminist Biblical Interpretation in Context* (Boston: Beacon Press, 1998), 75–136.

Moving Steps

- What are the methods of interpretation you have learned? Are they different from the ways in which you read the bible? Do you think the same methods of interpretation should be used for interpreting the bible as you would use for reading literary or historical texts? Give arguments for and against such an assumption.

- Which of the corrective methods of interpretation do you use? Do you believe that the authority of the bible allows for only feminist corrective methods but not for reading practices that are critical and deconstructive? If so, is a critical feminist interpretation for liberation possible in the paradigm of remedial interpretation?

- Service and suffering are often seen as redemptive. What are the problems with such an understanding? When does a statement such as, for instance, "Take up your cross and follow me" become oppressive? How should we deal with oppressive texts? Should we cut them out of the bible, stop reading them, or...?

- This is an exercise in historical imagination. Recall who the following biblical wo/men were: Bathsheba, Bilhah, daughters of Phillip, Deborah, Dinah, Mary of Magdala, Jezebel, Sheba, Judith, Leah, Lydia, Sarah, Lot's wife, Hagar, Anna, Hannah, Elizabeth, Martha, Mary, Miriam, Phoebe, Priska, Rachel, Rebecca, Susanna, Pilate's wife (feel free to add other wo/men if you wish). Do not skip over the wo/men you do not recognize but browse your local library or the World Wide Web to search for information about them and critically assess this information. Choose one wo/man and "hear her into speech" by having her write a letter or give a speech.[4]

Movement Exercise

Choose one biblical text and try to analyze it with the help of worksheet 9. For further reading on a critical-rhetorical-emancipatory method, see my book *Rhetoric and Ethic: The Politics of Biblical Studies* (Minneapolis: Fortress Press, 1999).

---

[4]Thanks to Kim Smiley for this suggestion.

A Socio-Historical Rhetorical Model
of Feminist Interpretation

I. Socio-Ideological Rhetorical Analysis: Reading Against the Grain
[Hermeneutics of Experience, Systemic Analysis, Suspicion, and Evaluation]

1. Determine style, genre, plot, characters, focalization, argument of the text. What arguments about the texts are constructed by commentators? How do you evaluate them? Does the text allow you to construct a different argument or focus, e.g., does it allow you to place the wo/men characters—marked by race, class, education, culture, religion, gender—into the center of attention? What kinds of contradictions, tensions, and discrepancies does the text or do its commentators seek to overcome or explain away?

2. What is the social location, "perspective," or "point of view" inscribed in the text? What is your own social location and perspective? What is that of commentators? Can you construct the text's "point of view" from a perspective in the margins? What are the submerged or marginalized voices silenced by the text?

3. What is the exigency of the inscribed rhetorical situation? Why is the text constructed as it is? What is its goal and vision? What are the constraints which are placed on the inscribed author, audience, and reader? How does the text construct the interaction between inscribed author and audience, protagonist and other characters, present and past?

4. What are the "common-sense" assumptions made by yourself, commentators, and the text itself, e.g., references to custom, prescriptions, rules, doctrines, "self-evident" points, "everyday" understandings of reality, laws, regulations?

5. Trace the symbols, metaphors, allusions, symbolic world constructions of commentators and those inscribed in the text. Articulate the tacit, unspoken assumptions, perspectives, arguments, silences, missing information, presupposed values, exclusions and inclusions, vilifications and glorifications.

6. Explore the emotions, appeals, feelings, motivations, convictions, values, moral practices, piety, sympathies, and visions that are connected for you with the text, advocated by commentators, and evoked by the story or argument of the text itself. What scale of values do you bring to the assessment of the text? What are your criteria for deciding whether the text seeks to inculcate kyriarchal values and visions in its original setting or today?

II. Socio-Historical Rhetorical Analysis: Imagining a Different World
[Hermeneutics of Remembrance, Imagination, and Transformation]

1. What social, political, religious, *historical* markers do you find in the
    text? What is the social status of the main characters, author, and audi-
    ence inscribed in the text? Do we have information about them from
    other historical sources?

2. What kind of institutional and social locations and geographical, histor-
    ical, religious, political situations are evoked by the text? What institu-
    tional models of social interactions, e.g., family, domination, friendship,
    parties, associations, etc. are promoted as "common-sense" structures
    by the text, are used as a foil for the argument of the text, or can be
    amplified with information from other sources?

3. What can one say about the possible *historical*-rhetorical situation?
    What are the socio-historical models or images of interpreters for re-
    constructing the historical situation of the text? What sources do we
    have besides the text for reconstructing its historical settings?

4. What methods and modes of investigation allow one to trace the "ge-
    netic" history of the text? Please distinguish clearly the levels of histori-
    cal reconstruction in which you engage, e.g., the time of the historical
    Jesus, that of the Jesus movement in Palestine, missionary movement
    in the Greco-Roman cities, the early churches, contemporary interpre-
    tations.

5. Which agents, voices, and arguments are repressed in the text? How
    can one make them again visible and audible as partners in the *histori-
    cal* conversation, debate, and struggle—on the level of the text, of the
    stage of the tradition, or on the historical level? Do the contradictions,
    strains, or tensions in the text allow us to reconstruct a historical situa-
    tion different from that advocated by the text?

6. What are the dominant historical, sociological, and theological models
    for reconstructing the history of the first centuries C.E.? What role does
    historical imagination play in historical knowledge? Can this history be
    re-imagined as the history not only of the historical winners but also of
    the historical losers? Is success a legitimate theological, ethical, or reli-
    gious category? How does the text read when placed within different
    historical models of reconstruction or different imaginative models of
    transformation?

7. What are the values and visions inscribed in the text that can engender
    transformation of kyriarchal mindsets and structures? How has your
    understanding of the text changed in the process of interpretation?
    Does the text encourage greater dignity, independence, respect, and
    responsible citizenship of wo/men?

CHAPTER VI

Wisdom's Dance

Hermeneutical Moves and Turns

We have not arrived but come to the end of this book. Hence, it is time to catch our breath and review our moves and movements. As I have argued in the previous chapters, the fourth, emancipatory paradigm of biblical studies seeks not just to understand biblical texts and traditions but also to provide a space for transforming both wo/men's self-understanding, self-perception, and self-alienation *and* Western malestream epistemological frameworks, individualistic apolitical practices, and socio-political relations of cultural colonization. By analyzing the bible's power of persuasion, it is meant to engender the self-understanding of biblical interpretation as a critical feminist praxis against all forms of domination.

Liberation theologies of all colors have not only pointed to the perspectival and contextual nature of scientific knowledge and biblical interpretation, but also asserted that biblical scholarship and theology are—knowingly or not—always engaged for or against the oppressed. Hence, a multiplex liberationist feminist framework is needed that allows the non-persons (to use an expression of Gustavo Gutiérrez) to be subjects of interpretation and historical agents of change. Since the fourth, rhetorical-emancipatory paradigm understands biblical studies as public discourse, it seeks to engender critical feminist conscientization and systemic ethico-political analysis.

Throughout this book we have seen how malestream paradigms of interpretation provide frames of meaning and "regimes of truth" that organize the relations between text, contexts, and us as readers. Whenever we read/hear/interpret a biblical or any other text, we read/hear/interpret it by engaging one or more of these paradigms of interpretation. But whereas the malestream paradigms of interpretation do not call for a critical hermeneutical self-consciousness, the emancipatory paradigm makes explicit the hermeneutical lenses with which it approaches the text. While

the other paradigms conceal the fact that they also operate within socio-political and religious analytic frameworks, the emancipatory paradigm openly confesses that it seeks to engage in biblical interpretation for the sake of conscientization. Hence it acknowledges the analytic lenses or eyeglasses—that is, the theoretical frameworks—that it deploys in the process of reading.

Religious biblical identity that is shaped by Scripture must in ever-new readings be deconstructed and reconstructed in terms of a global praxis for the liberation of all wo/men. Cultural identity that is shaped by biblical discourses must also be critically interrogated and trans-formed. Hence, it is necessary to re-conceptualize the traditional spiri-tual practice of discerning the spirits as a critical ethical-political prac-tice. As interpreting subjects, wo/men readers learn in a critical spiraling dance of interpretation to reclaim their spiritual authority for assessing both the oppressive and the liberating imagination of particu-lar biblical texts and their interpretations. They reject the epistemologi-cal blueprints and methodological rules of the "master" that marginalize and trivialize wo/men.

If you have followed me in these chapters on the road to the open house of Wisdom-Sophia, you will have realized that feminist biblical interpretation is a complex and exhilarating process. Feminists have used different rhetorical metaphors and comparisons for naming such an emancipatory process of interpretation: "making visible," "hearing into speech," "finding one's voice." I myself have favored metaphors of move-ment such as turning, walking, way, dance, ocean waves, or struggle. Since Plato attacked rhetoric as "mere cookery," I sometimes have borrowed this metaphor and spoken of biblical rhetorical interpretation as baking bread, mixing and kneading milk, flour, yeast, and raisins into dough, or as cooking a stew, utilizing different herbs and spices to season the pota-toes, meat, and carrots, which, stirred together, produce a new and differ-ent flavor.

However, as I pointed out in the introduction, the metaphor of the cir-cle dance seems best to express the spiraling moves and movements of Wisdom at work in feminist biblical interpretation. Dancing involves body and spirit, it involves feelings and emotions, and it takes us beyond our limits and creates community. Dancing confounds all hierarchical order because it moves in spirals and circles. It makes us feel alive and full of energy, power, and creativity. As Lillalou Hughes so powerfully puts it:

> The circle of the dance is an enacted symbol....Circles connote
> the smallest and largest elements of our world, from tiny cells to
> planets....In dancing the circle we experience our bodies as part

of that dynamism of life—we experience the depth of our being.
... The sacred dance traditions of the world endeavor to repeat the
encounters with the divine. By dancing the human-divine encounter humans are put in touch again with their creative origin.
... For the dancer the scheme of the round dance is based on total
participation, a rapt concentration of one's whole being while stepping along the perimeter of the circle as it turns around.[1]

While the classic "hermeneutical circle" seems to be closed, a critical
feminist hermeneutics moves in spiraling circles and circling spirals.
Moving in spirals and circles, feminist biblical interpretation is ongoing;
it cannot be done once and for all but must be repeated differently in different situations and from different perspectives. It is exciting, because in
every new reading of biblical texts a different meaning emerges. By deconstructing the kyriarchal rhetoric and politics of inequality and subordination inscribed in the bible, feminist interpreters are able to generate
ever-fresh articulations of radical democratic religious identities and emancipatory practices. Such an emancipatory process of biblical interpretation has as its "doubled" reference point the interpreter's contemporary
presence and the biblical past.

After having introduced some of the methodological steps and explored the theoretical space and horizon of feminist biblical interpretation
in the preceding chapters, in this concluding chapter I want to crystallize
my proposals by charting seven hermeneutical moves or strategies of interpretation.

Whether one thinks of the emancipatory interpretive process as baking bread or walking in the way of Wisdom, as a hearty "stew" or a joyful
"dance," crucial hermeneutical ingredients, spices, or moves in a critical
process of interpretation and rhetorical analysis are: a hermeneutics of experience, domination and social location, suspicion, critical evaluation,
creative imagination, re-membering and reconstruction, and transformative action for change. These hermeneutical practices are not to be construed simply as successive independent methodological steps of inquiry
or as discrete methodological rules or recipes. Rather, they must be understood as interpretive moves or hermeneutical movements that interact
with each other simultaneously in the process of "making meaning" out
of a particular biblical or any other cultural text in the context of the globalization of inequality.

Like the socio-political analytic that I have elaborated in chapter 4,
so also the following hermeneutical movements in the hermeneutical

---

[1]Lillalou Hughes, "Circle Dance," in *An A to Z of Feminist Theology,* ed. Lisa Isherwood and Dorothea McEwan (Sheffield: Academic Press, 1996), 30.

"dance," or the "strategic flavorings" of a rhetoric of liberation, work on
the following two different levels of interpretation:

- the language-systems, ideological frameworks, and socio-political-
  religious locations of *contemporary interpreters* living in kyriarchal systems of domination, and
- the linguistic and socio-historical systems of *biblical texts* and
  their effective histories of interpretation.

An ethics of interpretation strategically engages these hermeneutical
"moves," "dance steps," or "seasonings" as rhetorical discursive practices
on both levels in order to displace literalist doctrinal, positivist-scientific,
and relativist free-for-all de-politicized academic as well as popular hegemonic practices of interpretation. Most important, this interpretive process
or "hermeneutical dance" commences not by focusing on malestream texts
and traditions but by placing wo/men as biblical interpreters and readers in
the center of its movement. It seeks to recast interpretation not in positivist
but in rhetorical terms. It does not deny but rather recognizes that religious
texts are *rhetorical* texts, produced in and by particular historical debates
and struggles.

The rhetorical character of Scripture was understood in Christian medieval interpretation, which used the notion of the four different senses of
Scripture. It also has been appreciated in Jewish understandings of the
bible. In his book *The Midrash: An Introduction,* Jacob Neusner argues
that the Rabbis considered the bible not strictly as a source to be interpreted but as

> [serving] a purpose defined not by Scripture but by a faith under
> construction and subject to articulation. Scripture formed a dic-
> tionary, providing a vast range of permissible usages and intelli-
> gible words.[2]

He likens the bible to a palette of colors that an artist uses to create a
painting, but it is not the painting itself. In order to reflect on their experience after the destruction of Jerusalem and the Temple, as well as to construct a system of meaning, the Rabbis used the bible as a language.
Some believed that the Torah was written in black fire on white fire and
that the white spaces around the black letters held meanings yet to be discovered. As Naomi Hyman points out, this belief provides a space for
feminist interpretation.

---

[2]Jacob Neusner, *The Midrash: An Introduction,* (Northvale, N.J.: Jason Aronson,
1990), xi.

Jews of today write Midrash for the same reasons our ancestors did: It is our prayer, our plea and our affirmation. It is the way we insist that our voices be heard while at the same time giving honor to a tradition that has sustained us even as it pushed us aside. We write because we want our children to have stories that are both Jewish and feminist. We write because in the writing, we find places for ourselves in the white spaces between the black letters.[3]

Such a feminist biblical interpretation engages in an emancipatory rhetorical process that argues for the integrity and indivisibility of interpretive discourses as well as for the primacy of the contemporary starting point for feminist interpretation. To that end, it engages in a hermeneutical dance of deconstruction and reconstruction, of critique and retrieval that takes place on the level of both the text and interpretation. Thereby, it seeks to overcome the hermeneutical splits between sense and meaning, explanation and understanding, critique and consent, distanciation and empathy; between reading "behind" and "in front of " the text; between the present and the past; between interpretation and application, realism and imagination. To paraphrase Naomi Hyman, feminist Wisdom interpretation moves, spirals, turns, and dances in the places found in "the white spaces between the black letters." Its spiraling circle dance, I suggest, engages the following seven basic hermeneutical moves and movements.

A Hermeneutics of Experience

As a critical process of conscientization and emancipation, the spiraling dance of biblical interpretation begins with a hermeneutics of experience. From their beginnings, feminist theory and theology have understood experience as a central category and norm. Recognizing that wo/men's perspectives and experiences had not been included in the articulation of Western culture or Christian theology, feminist scholars sought to listen to and explore wo/men's experiences of oppression and liberation. Traditionally, theological statements such as "The bible is the revealed Word of G*d" have been used as norms for judging wo/men's experience. Now, feminist theologians are insisting that it is the experience and agency of wo/men that should be given priority in biblical reading. Hence, they seek not only to articulate the experience of contemporary wo/men but also to search for the experience of biblical wo/men.

---

[3]Naomi Hyman, *Biblical Wo/men in the Midrash: A Sourcebook* (Northvale, N.J.: Jason Aronson, 1997), xviii.

However, very soon the concept of wo/men's experience came to be problematic in two ways. Wo/man's experience was often understood in universalist essentialist terms, although it was articulated mostly with respect to white middle-class wo/men. Wo/men's experience is as variegated and as complex as are the wo/men articulating it. Some might object against such a pluralization of wo/men's experience, noting that wo/men also share some common experiences, such as giving birth or being raped or battered. Nevertheless, to essentialize these female experiences as "feminine" is to overlook the fact that even these experiences differ, since gender is always inflected by race, culture, class, age, and ethnicity.

In religion the experience common to wo/men has been the historical experience of exclusion and silencing on grounds of gender. Hence, feminist theology began with wo/men naming their experiences of silencing and exclusion as well as articulating their experiences of the sacred and the Divine. Soon, however, feminist theologians realized that wo/men's experiences of the Divine are also shaped and deformed by cultural and doctrinal kyriocentrism. Consequently, experience must be analyzed in systemic socio-political and theological terms. Wo/men's experience is socially constructed and coded in kyriocentric language, a coding that is dualistic and asymmetric: male-positive, female-negative, white-positive, black-negative, elite-positive, subaltern-negative, West-positive, Orient-negative, Christian-positive, Jew/Muslim-negative. Therefore, the reading of kyriocentric biblical texts reinforces wo/men's experiences of inferiority and second-class citizenship as divine revelation.

Hence, wo/men's experience as a criterion and norm had to be qualified with the concept of "feminist experience." Feminist experience begins with a "break-through" or "aha" experience of cognitive dissonance. Reading "feminist" or reading "otherwise" is possible only when experience is named differently. Hence, the objective and goal of feminist biblical interpretation, as I have argued here, is not just a better understanding of the bible but *conscientization,* which makes us aware of how our experience is determined by and yet also differs from the cultural-religious standard of what is "normal" or "common sense."

By beginning with the socio-cultural religious experiences of the marginalized and colonized, of those wo/men traditionally excluded from interpreting the bible, from articulating theology, and from shaping communal Christian self-understanding, feminist liberation interpreters change the starting point of traditional biblical interpretation. The goal in particular is to learn something about the experiences of wo/men's struggles at the bottom of the kyriarchal pyramid of domination and exploitation, because their situation lays open the fulcrum of oppression and dehumanization threatening every wo/man. Victories in the struggles of

multiply oppressed wo/men in turn reveal the liberatory presence of G*d in our midst.

In short, a critical feminist, ethical-political, emancipatory-rhetorical analysis begins not simply with individualized and privatized experience but rather with a critical reflection on how experience with the biblical text is shaped by our socio-political location. It also asks about the experiences of wo/men and their cultural locations inscribed in the biblical text. Hence, a hermeneutics of experience critically renders problematic the social-religious and intellectual locations not only of biblical interpreters but also of biblical texts, and it does so in relation to global struggles for survival and well-being. Therefore the feminist category of experience, in my view, has the following four crucial components:

- Experience is mediated linguistically and culturally. There is no "pure experience" that can be distilled from its kyriocentric contexts and texts.
- The personal is political. Personal experience is not private but public; it is socially constructed in and through race, gender, class, heterosexuality, ethnicity, age, and religion.
- Since personal experience is determined socially and religiously, it demands critical analysis and reflection that can explore the social location of experience.
- Experience is a hermeneutical starting point, not a norm. Only certain experiences, namely the experiences of struggle and liberation for justice and radical equality, can be articulated as feminist norms.

A hermeneutics of experience approaches a text by asking for readers' experience in relation to the text. Does it resonate with one's individual experiences? What kinds of group experiences are triggered by the text? Is the text familiar because it has been central to the group to which one belongs? Is this text part of the interpreter's heritage or is it alien? Do one's experiences suggest a certain interpretive approach to the text? Since their experiences have been oppressive and self-alienating, post-biblical feminists engage in a purely deconstructive reading. Since their experiences of biblical reading have not just been negative but have inspired their self-affirmation and struggles for liberation, Jewish or Christian feminists have sought to develop critique but also an appreciation of the bible.

Similar questions must be asked with respect to the experience inscribed in texts to be interpreted. What kinds of experiences does the text evoke? What kinds of experiences are inscribed in the text? What kinds of emotions and sentiments are espoused by the text? Whose experience

stands in the center and whose experience is ruled out, silenced, or marginalized? What is the emotional persuasive tenor of the text? If wo/men are mentioned, are their textual experiences constructed in kyriocentric rather than in radical egalitarian terms? Does the experience inscribed in the text "resonate" with our own experiences? These and similar questions seek to identify and name both our experiences when reading the text and those inscribed in the biblical text itself. As we saw in the story of Amy recounted in chapter 5: if the biblical text evokes negative experiences that "resonate" and amplify our own experiences of violence, we need courage and strength to continue the dance of interpretation. Engaging the experiences evoked by the text can work as a catalyst for articulating and coming to terms with our own experiences of self-esteem or inferiority, of strength or violence.

A Hermeneutics of Domination and Social Location

A critical interpretation for liberation, therefore, does not simply ask for the experiences of wo/men with a particular text and its interpretation. It also reflects on how our social, cultural, and religious location has shaped our experience with and our reaction to a particular biblical text or story. To that end, feminist interpreters engage in the critical *analytics of domination* that I have discussed in chapter 4. The kind of systemic analysis we adopt will crucially determine our interpretation. For instance, you will read the story of the wo/man with a hemorrhage differently depending on whether you engage in a Thomistic, Aristotelian, Freudian, capitalist, anarchist, postcolonial, or feminist analysis. Moreover, a feminist liberationist approach insists that analytic frames of interpretation cannot be emancipatory if they privilege cultural femininity, the religious text itself, or other malestream doctrinal, theological, spiritual, or theoretical frameworks as hermeneutical frameworks and spaces from which to read, rather than prioritize wo/men's struggles against multiplicative structures of oppression.

Hence, a feminist hermeneutics insists on a systemic analysis that is able to disentangle the ideological (religious-theological) functions of biblical texts for inculcating and legitimating the kyriarchal order. At the same time, it seeks to underscore and explain the potential of biblical texts for fostering justice and liberation in the radical democratic horizon of the *ekklesia*. Such a systemic analysis of the socio-cultural and political-religious structures of domination identifies not only contemporary situations of domination but also those inscribed in the biblical texts. A critical feminist analytics of domination can do this because it has been formulated to investigate modern political structures of domination as well as the kyriarchal structures of antiquity inscribed in biblical texts.

Patricia Hill Collins has suggested three interdependent questions with which to evaluate such social-analytic categories:

- Does this social theory speak the truth to people about the reality of their lives? Whose knowledge counts, whose standards are used, and who is discredited? Who decides what counts as knowledge and how are knowledge and truth validated?
- What is the stance of a social theory toward freedom, and what pragmatic strategies does it suggest to achieve its vision of emancipation? What is its theory of emancipation and does it facilitate political action?
- Does a critical social theory move wo/men to struggle and how effectively does it provide moral authority for emancipatory praxis? Does it engender the search for justice as an ongoing principled struggle that resists disciplinary power relations and gives meaning to everyday life?[4]

With the help of such a critical feminist analytic, you can first question your own social location and participation in kyriarchal power relations. In so doing, you become conscious of how your experiences are constructed by and you yourself construct your self-identity in terms of gender, race, class, religion, or nationalism. However, social location must not be mistaken for an identity category but rather must be understood as a group category. As we have seen, wo/men are slotted by birth into the group categories "feminine" or "masculine," "black" or "white," "American" or another nationality, belonging to the "upper crust" of society or to the "serving population." These categories assign identity slots to us according to group category. We find ourselves to be members of a gender group that we experience as "given," rather than as historically and socially constructed. Individuals cannot simply opt out of group identities because social constructs such as sex, gender, race, class, or ethnicity are "common sense," "naturalized," and inscribed on the body.

Whether you understand yourself primarily as a wo/man, or as black, or as a foreigner, or as working-class depends on which group status functions as the nodal point for the structural subject positions into which you are born and in which everyone is implicated. For instance, if you are an upper-middle-class, white wo/man in a kyriarchal society you will understand yourself primarily in gender terms; if you are black or Asian in such a society you might define yourself primarily in racial terms rather than in gender or class terms; and if you are an Indian or African wo/man

---

[4]Patricia Hill Collins, *Fighting Words: Black Women and the Search for Justice* (Minneapolis: University of Minnesota Press, 1998), 398–399.

you will tend to see yourself first in colonialist terms rather than in race or gender terms. Thus, our individual identities are always constructed and pressures are exerted on us to identify with such social markers. If we refuse to do so, social censure and punishment will follow.

A hermeneutics of social location critically reflects on the social location of both interpreters and texts as a "choreographic" system within kyriarchal power relations. Their common location within relations of domination constitutes social groups. Hence, it is not difficult to see how class-only, gender-only, and race-only conceptual frameworks constitute social groups and why within binary thinking, elites control the masses, men control wo/men, whites control blacks, and Euro-Americans control the colonies. However, an "adding-on" or "adding-up" approach does not suffice to conceptualize our social location as, for instance, black, elite, colonialized, educated wo/men. Such an adding-on approach does not suffice because it is not able to comprehend and articulate how race, gender, class, and ethnicity mutually construct and multiply each other. The intersectionality of the structures of domination construct, for example, white wo/men as a group that occupies a distinctive social location, and at the same time such intersectional processes construct white wo/men's collective self-definitions and actions within the group in a kyriarchal manner. Race, sexuality, class, gender, and nationality are not personal attributes of individuals that they can choose or reject; rather, they are structural power relations.

Intersectionality does not describe an actual pattern of social organization but serves as an interpretive framework for comprehending how intersections of race, gender, class, sexuality, and ethnicity shape any group's experiences across specific social contexts. Different groups will experience such structures of domination differently depending on their social location within the kyriarchal pyramid of economic, political, and ideological power relations. These power relations are kept in place by institutional mechanisms such as separation and exclusion and/or family affiliation and inclusion. For instance, elite wo/men have been excluded from the public realm and secluded in the private sphere. As a group, wo/men have been defined by family affiliation, which serves as the glue that naturalizes structures of domination. Thus kyriarchal group power works through segregated spaces as well as through emotional identification.

A hermeneutics of domination makes it possible for us to critically reflect on how relations of domination are operative as socially assigned categories and identity slots and as the range of options within these group identity slots that individual wo/men can choose in constructing their unique identities as individuals. It also makes it possible to examine how we as individuals act in specific situations, how we negotiate our

lived experience, and how we access cultural knowledge such as the bible to construct individual expressions of self within socially defined categories. It helps us explore how these different expressions of self- and group-identity are at work in the process of interpretation as well as in the process of textual formation. It also assists us in seeking possibilities and ways of transforming such socially defined categories of domination.

A Hermeneutics of Suspicion

As biblical readers we are taught to approach the bible with a hermeneutics of respect, acceptance, consent, and obedience. Instead of cultivating a hermeneutics of appreciation and consent, I have argued, a critical feminist interpretation for liberation develops a hermeneutics of suspicion that places on all biblical texts the warning "Caution—could be dangerous to your health and survival." Texts such as "If a man lies with a male as with a woman, both of them have committed an abomination; they shall be put to death" (Leviticus 20:13) or "It was one of them, their very own prophet who said: 'Cretans are always liars, vicious brutes, lazy gluttons.' That testimony is true..." (Titus 1:12) cannot be approached with a hermeneutics of empathy, appreciation, and consent but must be approached with a hermeneutics of suspicion.

Such a hermeneutics of suspicion does not take the kyriocentric text and its claim to divine authority at face value, but rather investigates it as to its ideological functions in the interest of domination. Emotionally, it might be difficult to engage in such a hermeneutics of suspicion either because you have internalized biblical authority as unquestionable taboo or your experiences with the bible have been positive and edifying. Hence, before you can fruitfully engage in a hermeneutics of suspicion, you need to work through your emotions, anxieties, and fears, and to ask what stake you have in upholding a hermeneutics of appreciation and consent.

A hermeneutics of suspicion is so threatening because it challenges and demystifies the structures of domination that are inscribed in the biblical text, in our experience, and in contemporary contexts of interpretation. It may make you feel uneasy and anxious because it breaks a taboo to scrutinize not only the presuppositions and interests of interpreters and those of biblical commentators but also the kyriocentric choreography of the biblical text itself. However, a hermeneutics of suspicion must not be misunderstood as peeling away layers of debris in order to recover a pre-given ontological reality that is understood in essentialist terms. A hermeneutics of suspicion must not be mistaken for a hermeneutics of discovery, which assumes that there is some order in the world that can be discovered if one becomes aware of the various disguises used to cover up the Truth and distort reality.

Kyriocentric language, I have argued, does not cover up but constructs reality in a certain way and then mystifies its own constructions by naturalizing them. Hence, a hermeneutics of suspicion is concerned with the distorted ways in which wo/men's actual presences and practices are constructed and represented in and through kyriocentric language and media. Kyriocentric texts, literary classics and visual art, works of science, anthropology, sociology, or theology do not cover up reality "as it is." Rather, they ideologically-rhetorically construct reality in the interest of domination insofar as kyriocentric texts produce the invisibility and marginality of wo/men as a "given" fact and "common-sense" reality. If we want to change such rhetorical-ideological textual practices, their kyriocentric character must be exposed and they must be dislodged from their contexts of domination. Consequently, a hermeneutics of suspicion is best understood as a deconstructive practice of inquiry that denaturalizes and demystifies linguistic-cultural practices of domination rather than as working away at the layers upon layers of cultural sediments that hide or repress a "deeper truth."

A hermeneutics of suspicion has the task of disentangling the ideological functions of kyriocentric text and commentary. It does not assume a kyriarchal conspiracy by the classics and their contemporary interpreters but insists that wo/men do not, in fact, know whether we are addressed by grammatically masculine generic texts. Hence, wo/men always have to think twice and to ask whether or not we are meant. Such a hermeneutic must be applied

- to grammatically masculine kyriocentric texts in order to unravel their ideological functions;
- to kyriocentric stories. One must analyze the "point of view" of the story, which expresses the ideological-rhetorical aims of the narrative as well as asks how it represents its wo/men characters;
- to contemporary commentaries and interpretations of the text as well as to its history of interpretation;
- to our own "common-sense" assumptions, pre-understandings, prejudices, and value systems. It must scrutinize our theoretical frameworks and interpretive goals as well as our social location and function in relations of domination.

In short, since readers align themselves with the dominant voice and model presented by the kyriocentric text, a hermeneutics of suspicion critically analyzes such dominant strategies of meaning making. In addition, it must draw out and make manifest masculine/feminine, superior/inferior, we/others roles and values inscribed in the text. It engages in a conscious articulation of the ideological strategies of the text and makes

apparent the text's interaction and resonance with our experience and cultural value-system. Finally, it seeks to determine and circumscribe the rhetorical situation and context in which the text was formulated and operates today.

A Hermeneutics of Critical Evaluation

A hermeneutics of ethical and theological evaluation presupposes and completes a hermeneutics of suspicion. It is necessary because texts are always held in context; they have a multiplicity of meanings. Hence, this hermeneutic seeks to assess the rhetorics of texts and traditions as well as those of contemporary discourses in terms of a feminist liberationist scale of values. Just like a hermeneutics of suspicion, a hermeneutics of critical evaluation is difficult to practice for those interpreters who have been socialized into a hermeneutics of trust and/or obedience toward the scriptural texts. While a hermeneutics of trust and consent, which is advocated by the doctrinal paradigm of interpretation, reads the bible for guidance and edification and obediently accepts its teachings on submission, a critical feminist hermeneutics of evaluation seeks both to make conscious the cultural-religious internalizations and legitimizations of kyriarchy and to explore the values and visions that are inscribed as counter-cultural alternatives in biblical texts. It consents only to the authority of those texts that have passed through a critical hermeneutics of suspicion and have been assessed in a concrete particular situation to function as emancipatory.

A critical theo-ethical hermeneutics evaluates biblical texts and interpretations in terms of a feminist scale of emancipatory values and visions that may be inspired by, but are not necessarily derived from, the bible. For instance, Sheila Redmond has pointed out that the biblical values of suffering, forgiveness, purity, need for redemption, and obedience to authority figures prevent recovery from child sexual abuse and continue to disempower their victims. If such values that prevent recovery are espoused by a biblical text, they must be named and made conscious as kyriocentric values that perpetuate suffering and abuse, and therefore must be judged for their possibly debilitating effects in particular situations where such abuse exists or is remembered. Accordingly, a hermeneutics of evaluation seeks to adjudicate the oppressive tendencies as well as the liberating possibilities inscribed in biblical texts, their function in contemporary struggles for liberation, and their "resonance" with wo/men's experience. It does so not once and for all but again and again in particular social locations and situations.

A hermeneutics of evaluation, however, does not categorize biblical texts and traditions in a dualistic fashion either as oppressive or as emancipatory. Rather, it seeks to adjudicate again and again how biblical texts

function in particular situations. Its criterion or standard of evaluation, the well-being of every wo/man (which includes the principle of human rights as wo/men's rights), must be established and reasoned out in terms of a systemic analysis of kyriarchal domination. For theological reasons, such a hermeneutics of proclamation insists that biblical religions must cease to preach kyriarchal texts as the "word of G*d," since by doing so we continue to proclaim G*d as legitimating kyriarchal oppression. Instead, it argues, biblical religions must articulate visions of well-being that proclaim the Divine as a power for liberation.

A hermeneutics of evaluation has a double reference point. The first is *cultural-ideological*. Language and texts are not self-enclosed systems of signs but have performative power: they either legitimize or challenge power structures, serve to "naturalize" or to interrupt hegemonic world-views, or function to inculcate dominant or emancipatory values. The key question of a hermeneutics of evaluation is: What does a text *do* to those of us who submit to its world of vision and values? As a consequence, a critical hermeneutics of evaluation seeks to make us conscious both of the cultural-religious forms of the internalizations and legitimizations of kyriarchy and of alternative radical-democratic, counter-cultural values and visions inscribed in the text. It assesses how much a text encodes and reinforces structures of oppression and/or articulates values and visions that promote liberation. For such an assessment, we have to articulate an emancipatory scale of values that can but need not be derived from the bible. Rather, it is to be articulated in the emancipatory struggles to survive and change kyriarchal structures.

The second reference point for a hermeneutics of evaluation is *religious-theological*. In a Christian context, biblical texts are understood and proclaimed as the Word of G*d. Canonization compels us to make sense out of texts in such a way that we can accept, consent, and submit to them. A hermeneutics of submission and consent understands canonical authority as kyriarchal authority that requires subordination. Such an understanding of canonical authority in terms of the logic of kyriarchal identity fosters exclusion and vilification of the other. Canon is understood either as the criterion, standard, or rule, as *norma normans et non normata*—a norm that is to be obeyed and not evaluated—or as a cultural classic that is more like the constitution than a set of individual laws: a collection of interpretive paradigms, metaphor or parable, model, type, or frame of meaning that gives shape and form to our values and beliefs.

This understanding of biblical authority is derived from the Latin *auctoritas,* which means the authority of the lord/master/father/husband who requires obedience, submission, and consent. However, canonical authority also can be understood as radical democratic creative authority in the sense of authorship that recognizes a plurality of meaning and

truth. In such an understanding, the root sense of authority is derived from the Latin verb *augere,* which means to augment, enhance, initiate, originate, or authorize. An understanding of canonical authority in the sense of *augere*—augmentation, creativity, and enhancement—is the authority of radical democracy that invites debate, risk, vision, empowerment, and transformation rather than obedience and submission. It engages in the spiritual practice of the discernment of the spirits that is possible only in the alternative space to kyriarchy, in the radical democratic space of the "imagined community," the *ekklesia of wo/men.* Hence, the *ekklesia of wo/men* is the radical democratic center and theo-ethical horizon of a critical feminist biblical interpretation in the open house of Divine Wisdom.

A Hermeneutics of Creative Imagination

A hermeneutics of creative imagination in turn seeks to generate utopian visions that have not yet been realized, to "dream" a different world of justice and well-being. The space of the imagination is that of freedom, a space in which boundaries are crossed, possibilities are explored, and time becomes relativized. What we cannot imagine will not take place. The imagination is a space of memory and possibility where situations can be re-experienced and desires re-embodied.

Because of our imaginative abilities, we can put ourselves into other people's shoes, relate to their feelings, and participate in their deliberations and struggles. Historical imagination allows us to see wo/men's struggles in the past and to make the connections to our own. The following Midrash on Myriam, the prophetic leader of the Exodus who was smitten with leprosy because she insisted that God had spoken not only through Moses but also through her (Numbers 12:1-16), eloquently makes this point.

Myriam's Vision[5]

It's night time, the moon is shining and I catch sight of a desert flower blooming before me. I focus on its beauty, the stillness of the night, trying to grasp onto a strand of quiet, an oasis from the rage that has been coursing through me. I think about the irony— how beautiful G*d's creation, yet the tremendous injustice in the world. The very quality that made me strong enough to save Moses by speaking to Pharaoh's daughter, to lead the people by the sea, to fight against injustice is being squashed. The humiliation of being sent outside of the camp, like one sends a child

---

[5] I am grateful to Chris Schüssler-Fiorenza for permission to print her Midrash.

having a tantrum away from the table. And the rumors that were started, becoming stronger every day until they take on a truth of their own. That it was G*d who punished me, that G*d sent me away and turned me into a leper. A message to silence women who want to speak directly, honestly, to speak their minds openly instead of relying on their sexuality, relying on tricks, relying on sweetness. An implicit threat that this is what will happen to you if you challenge the status quo. An idolization of Moses and his laws, so that to challenge him or them becomes a challenge to G*d. I hate being silenced.

I want to tell my story.

I was not struck down by G*d for challenging Moses. Our fight was not about Moses' wife nor was I punished for *lashon hara* (evil tongue). Instead it was about conflicting visions for community, a power struggle, a political battle. The difference between a community based on Moses' "Don't go near a woman" (a false relaying of G*d's words) and a community where men and women are equals, working together to create a just community, sharing power and opportunity, leaving behind the legacy of slavery.... As I relive the vision of community that I, along with other women and men, have been working so hard to realize, I grow angry again.

And then I have a vision...

I see women struggling for freedom and equality, and then being pushed back, and then rising again. This stretches out over thousands of years. I feel despair. Despair that the struggle seems never ending. That women will have to recreate the wheel over and over again. But seeing further, a glimmer of hope arises. I see that there will always be strong women who will continue the struggle. And that as long as we are struggling there is always the hope, the dream, the possibility of realizing our vision of a more just world.

Because of the imagination we are able to tell the story differently, to see history in a new light. Because of the imagination we are able to conceive of change, of how situations can be altered. Historical imagination, like all other imagination, is absolutely necessary for any knowledge of biblical texts and worlds. Imagination enables us to fill in the gaps and silences, and thereby to make sense out of a text. Usually we see the power of imagination embodied in art, music, literature, and dance but not in science, since we generally assume that science works only with deductive, rational, logical arguments. However, such an assumption is incorrect insofar as science always works with hypotheses and models that depend on in-

formed imagination. Imagination mines the unconscious as a store of feelings and experiences as well as a depository of common-sense practices and codes. These unconscious presuppositions determine scientific thought and decide how we read texts, reconstruct history, and imagine the past.

A hermeneutics of imagination retells biblical stories, re-shapes religious vision, and celebrates those who have brought about change. To that end it does more than utilize historical, literary, and ideology-critical methods, which focus on the rhetoric of religious texts and their historical contexts. It also employs methods of storytelling, role-play, bibliodrama, Midrash, pictorial arts, dance, meditation, prayer, and ritual for creating a "different" religious imagination, methods which were discussed in chapter 5. One such imaginative practice is the retelling of biblical stories and the rewriting of biblical texts in poetic interpretation and song. In her CD entitled *Dancing Sophia's Circle,* Colleen Fulmer, for instance, braids together biblical Wisdom texts and their echoes in the gospel of John into an invocation of Divine Wisdom-Sophia:

O Wisdom Sophia
The Power and splendor of G*d
Feed our hungry souls at your abundant table.
I am the way, the truth and the life,
Come to me, come to me
I am the Light that shows you the way
Come to me, come to me
I am the vine, the source of your growth
Come to me, come to me
I am living water that quenches your thirst
Come to me, come to me...
I am living Bread that gives you strength
Come to me, come to me...
I am the life poured into your hearts
Come to me, come to me
I am the resurrection and life
Come to me, come to me
I am the Life of all creation
Come to me, come to me.[6]

Imaginative role-play is another feminist spiritual practice of imaginative interpretation. It is a process of encounter between a biblical text

---

[6]Colleen Fulmer, *Dancing Sophia's Circle: Original Songs Exploring and Celebrating the Great Wisdom-Sophia Tradition* (Loretto Spirituality Network, 725 Calhoun Street, Albany, CA 94706).

and a group of people who use their imagination and dramatic capabilities to identify with and enter a biblical scene with all the senses, emotions, heart, and reason. Insofar as imaginative role-play establishes identity with the characters of the kyriocentric text and historicizes them, it is in danger of re-inscribing "common-sense" understandings of gender, race, class, or heterosexuality and bringing to the fore repressed emotions and experiences that are kyriarchically saturated. Hence it calls for critical reflection and debate.

Since our imagination and utopian visions are always both informed and deformed by past experiences and present socio-political locations, such imaginative role-play cannot simply be applauded but must be discussed with a hermeneutics of suspicion and evaluation. In order to thwart the powers of the kyriocentric text that lead to self-alienation, wo/men identifying with the characters and storyline must dislodge the text from its original context and make its kyriocentric dynamic conscious. For example, I never ask groups to role-play Jesus in order to gain some emotional and imaginative distance from this central figure of the gospel stories. Instead, we place the wo/men characters into the center of attention. Such a hermeneutical move does not mean that we should identify with the wo/men characters of the kyriocentric text. Rather, it means that we have to approach them with a hermeneutics of suspicion and evaluation before we can re-imagine them in the radical democratic horizon of the *ekklesia of wo/men.*

The following suggestions for role-playing the story of the wo/man anointing Jesus illustrate this creative, imaginative method for filling in the gaps and blank spaces:

1. Please read your gospel text of the story about a wo/man anointing Jesus (Mark 14:3-9 and parallels).

2. Identify the main characters: What would you like to know about them? Write down your questions and interview the characters.

3. Interview the gospel writer: Why did s/he write the story down as s/he did? What interests come to the fore?

4. Prepare to role-play the following characters:
    the gospel writer/storyteller
    the wo/man
    the house owner or host
    the poor
    the disciples
    a neighbor
    the granddaughter of the wo/man

Reader-response criticism has pointed out that we "make meaning" in the process of reading by imaginatively filling in the gaps, fissures, and breaks in the text with reference to our experience and knowledge. Jewish hermeneutics has imagined that the Shekhinah, the Divine Presence, dwells in the blank spaces between the letters of the word. In the process of storytelling or role-playing, our imagination, so to speak, seeks to make present Divine Wisdom in the "blank spaces" between the biblical wo/men and our own lives. Hence, every enactment is different. Retelling biblical stories and re-imagining biblical characters in creative imagination and play is a catalytic process that liberates us from the false images that we have made.

A Hermeneutics of Re-Membering and Reconstruction

A hermeneutics of re-membering and re-construction works not only to increase the distance between us and the time of the text but also to increase our historical knowledge and imagination. Hence, a hermeneutics of historical reconstruction questions the "chasm" that historical positivism has constructed between contemporary readers and the biblical text. At the same time, it seeks to displace the kyriocentric dynamic of the biblical text in its literary and historical contexts by re-contextualizing the text in a socio-political-religious historical model of reconstruction that aims at making the subordinated and marginalized "others" visible, and their repressed arguments and silences "audible" again. It thereby attempts to recover wo/men's religious history and the memory of their victimization, struggle, and accomplishments as wo/men's heritage.

Such a hermeneutics of remembrance utilizes constructive methods of re-visioning insofar as it seeks not only for historical retrieval but also for a religious reconstitution of the world. It seeks these things in and through a recovery of the forgotten past both of wo/men's victimization and of their struggles for survival and well-being. With postmodern thinkers, it is fully conscious of the rhetoricity of its own reconstructions but nevertheless insists that such work of historical remembrance is necessary in support of wo/men's struggles for survival and transformation today. If lack of a written history is a sign of people's oppression, then feminists and other subaltern scholars cannot afford to eschew such rhetorical and historical re-constructive work.

A rhetorical and historical method of critical reconstruction does not understand texts as windows to the world or as mirrors of the past; it does not read historical sources as objective data and evidence of how things really were. Neither does it understand historiography as a transcript and report of "what actually happened," or mistake its scientific models of reconstruction as descriptions of reality. Rather, it remains conscious of the

fact that all three phases of historiography—documentary research, explanation, and writing—must be rooted in a hermeneutics of suspicion, critical evaluation, and historical imagination. Historical understanding depends on analogy. It is narrative-laden and amounts to a remaking and retelling of reality; it is not reality itself nor a record of what actually happened. History and memory of the past always imbricate imagination and are imbricated by it.

A hermeneutics of historical reconstruction and re-membering should not be used to avoid a hermeneutics of critical theological/ideological evaluation. Its constructive moment must be undergirded by a hermeneutics of suspicion and critical analysis. However, a hermeneutics of reconstruction has not only a deconstructive but also a constructive task. It relies on a scale of values and a world of vision that must be justified and validated in public discourse and debate. It does not understand history writing as a transcribing of events but as the "logic of the probable." Hence, it eschews textual positivism that understands the text as window to the world, as reflection of and reference to historical reality, treating its sources as objective data and evidence of how things really were. It also eschews historical positivism, which understands history as a depiction of reality. In this view, historiography is a transcript and report of "what actually happened."

Instead, a hermeneutics of remembrance and reconstruction subscribes to rhetorical realism, which understands history as the possible and probable. The writing of history has three phases: documentary research, explanation, and writing. All three phases must be subjected to a hermeneutics of suspicion and critical evaluation.

Historiography, as mentioned, is narrative laden; it is a remaking and retelling of reality but not reality itself. It involves selection, weighing, interpretation, and validation of documents. Moreover, history writing depends on style, intention, and composition, on how one tells the story. Hence, historiography also needs to utilize a hermeneutics of experience, systemic analysis, and imagination because explanation depends on the historian's experience and adjudication of probability.

Furthermore, historiography is a theory of action that assumes continuity between the "history makers," between those who make history and those who write history. The subjects and objects of history writing are people who *make* history. Historical actors and writers share not only a single spatio-temporal framework of dating and periodization but also a single field of action. Historians depend on the "making" of real historical actors for their own "history making" (Ricoeur). History becomes *their* story. In short, historians are "history makers" who write history in terms of their own experience and vision of the real.

In making history, historians rely on theoretical models of historiography that understand history as identity-formation, as memory, as an

account of the historical winners, as heritage, or as reconstruction. In the writing of early Christian history, several reconstructive theological models have been employed. Among these are the *supersessionist model,* which claims that Christianity is superior to and the fulfillment of Judaism; the *apostolic succession-hierarchical model,* which maintains that an unbroken chain of succession exists between Jesus and the hierarchy today; the *orthodoxy-heresy model*, which claims that orthodoxy preceded the aberrations of heresy; the (Protestant) *pristine origins-deterioration model*, which assumes a "golden age" in the beginning that very soon declined into the sinful structures of the church; and the (Catholic) *growth-development model*, which understands early Christian beginnings as the seed that developed into the wonderful tree of the Roman Catholic Church. Hence, it is important that you identify the reconstructive model that undergirds your own historical understanding of early Christian beginnings. You then need to interrogate your historical knowledge using a hermeneutics of suspicion and discern how much it informs your experience, in order to see how much you have invested in it.

In my own work I have argued that a feminist historiography must replace the andro-kyriocentric malestream models of world construction with a radical egalitarian model of re-membering. History writing therefore can be likened to making a quilt, fitting all the bits and pieces of information into a new design and model. With such a displacement of the positivist model of historiography, transforming it into a historical discourse that can be likened to quilt-making, I have sought to open up the possibilities of wo/men's historical presence and awaken the capacity to envision alternatives to the kyriarchal past and its struggles. This requires new hermeneutical assumptions that can correct the andro-kyriocentric tendencies of our historical sources.

- *First,* we must assume that wo/men were present and active in history until proven otherwise. Hence, we have to read kyriocentric texts in an inclusive fashion unless it is explicitly stated that wo/men were not present.
- *Further,* texts and injunctions that seek to censure or limit wo/men's behavior must be read as prescriptive rather than as descriptive of reality. If wo/men are forbidden from a certain activity, we can safely assume that they might actually have engaged in it so much that it became threatening to the kyriarchal order.
- *Finally,* texts and information must be contextualized in their variegated cultural and religious environments and reconstructed not only in terms of the dominant ethos but also in terms of alternative social movements for change.

In sum, to remember is to assert historical existence and to claim historical subjectivity. Such historical remembrance recaptures biblical traditions as wo/men's traditions of struggle, survival, and vision. It reclaims wo/men's historical heritage. History writing envisioned as "quilting" feminist history becomes a transformative praxis. The task of a hermeneutics of remembrance is aptly characterized by the Caribbean writer Michelle Cliff:

> To write as a complete Caribbean woman, or man for that matter, demands of us retracing the African past of ourselves, reclaiming as our own, and as our subject a history sunk under the sea, or scattered as potash in the canefields, or gone to bush, or trapped in a class system notable for its rigidity and dependence on class stratification. On a past bleached from our minds. . . . It means realizing our knowledge will always be wanting. It means also, I think, mixing in the forms taught us by the oppressor, undermining his language and coopting his style and turning it to our purposes.[7]

A Hermeneutics of Transformative Action for Change

The critical interpretative process or "hermeneutical dance" has as its goal and climax a hermeneutics of transformation and action for change. As we have seen, it seeks to alter relations of domination that are legitimated and inspired by kyriarchal biblical religions. To that end, it explores avenues and possibilities for changing and transforming relations of domination inscribed in texts, traditions, and everyday life. Such work stands accountable to those wo/men who struggle at the bottom of the kyriarchal pyramid of discrimination and domination. It also seeks to articulate religious and biblical studies as a site of social, political, and religious transformation.

When seeking future vision and transformation, we can only extrapolate from present experience, which is always predetermined by past experience. Hence, we need to analyze the past and the present in order to articulate creative visions and transcending imaginations for a new humanity, global ecology, and religious community. Yet I submit that only if we are committed to work for a different, more just future, will our imagination be able to transform the past and present limitations of our vision. As Toni Morrison so forcefully states in her novel *Beloved:*

---

[7]Michelle Cliff, "A Journey into Speech," in *The Graywolf Annual Five: Multicultural Literacy,* ed. R. Simonson and S. Walker (Saint Paul: Graywolf Press, 1988), 59.

She did not tell them to clean up their lives or to go and sin no more. She did not tell them they were the blessed of the earth, its inheriting meek or its glory bound pure. She told them that the only grace they could have was the grace they could imagine. That if they could not see it, they would not have it.[8]

The shared spiritual wisdom/Wisdom visions of biblical religions have the power to evoke potent emotions and creative responses and thereby create the sense of community necessary to sustain contemporary visions and struggles for an alternative society and world. Biblical studies, therefore, must be refashioned in such a way that they can contribute to the formation of a Wisdom/Spirit-space of courage, hope, and vision in our variegated struggles for justice. The sub-discipline of biblical theology also needs to be re-visioned in such a fashion that it can contribute to the articulation of a Spirit-center of global dimensions.

To sum up my explorations: a critical rhetorical-emancipatory process of interpretation challenges practitioners of biblical studies and readers of the bible to become more theo-ethically sophisticated readers by problematizing both the modernist ethos of biblical studies and their own socio-political locations and functions in global structures of domination. At the same time, it enables them to struggle for a more just and radical-democratic *cosmopolitan* articulation of religion in the global cosmopolis or *ekklesia of wo/men*.

In order to comprehend the contours of such a paradigm shift in the self-understanding of the discipline of biblical studies, I have argued that one must move from a scientist-academic to a critical public ethos of discourse that is fueled by reflection on issues arising from wo/men's confrontation with injustice. Such a shift and transformation of biblical studies would be able to skillfully negotiate the Scylla of "what the text meant" and the Charybdis of "what the text means today" by focusing on ethical-theological biblical visions of justice and well-being for every wo/man on the globe.

A transformation of this kind gestures toward a biblical theology that is no longer dependent on modernist and positivist historicism for its criteria. While biblical theology still would need to reason historically insofar as it still must read biblical texts as rhetorical texts in particular historical contexts, it nevertheless would be freed to ask central ethical-political and theological questions: What kinds of values and visions do biblical texts and their contemporary interpretations advocate? Do they value theological visions that contribute to the well-being of everyone in the global *cosmopolis* or do they reinforce the languages of domination and hate as theo-logical?

---

[8]Toni Morrison, *Beloved* (New York: Knopf, 1987), 88.

A critical rhetorical method and hermeneutical process of wisdom/ Wisdom's spiraling dance of interpretation that seeks to serve public theological deliberation and religious transformation is not restricted to Christian canonical texts but can be and has been explored successfully by scholars of traditions and scriptures of other religions. Moreover, it is not restricted to the biblical scholar as expert reader. Rather, it calls for transformative and engaged biblical interpreters who may or may not be professional readers. It has been used in graduate education, in parish discussions, in college classes, and in work with illiterate wo/men. The Swiss theologian Regula Strobel sums up her pastoral experience with people who, in parish bible study groups, have engaged or "danced" the "dance" of interpretation. She writes that people who have worked with my critical multifaceted wisdom/Wisdom process of interpretation have changed in an impressive way. In the beginning they still sought the authority of the theologian, who was to decide how a biblical text is correctly understood and interpreted. Increasingly they learned to understand themselves as subjects not only of biblical readings. On the basis of their experiences they have formulated what was liberatory and what was oppressive. They eschewed the pressure to derive all decisions from the bible or the attitude of Jesus. For they experienced as meaningful and supportive as the criterion for decision and action everything that contributes to the liberation and life in fullness of wo/men and other disadvantaged persons. Thereby they could read even ambiguous bible texts and be nourished by the liberating aspects without taking over the oppressive ones.

In and through such a critical rhetorical process of interpretation and deliberation, religious and biblical studies are constituted as public discourses that can be critically investigated and become sites of struggle and conscientization in the radical democratic horizon of the *ekklesia* and *basileia*. Patricia Hill Collins has dubbed such a praxis of change and transformation "visionary pragmatism." Feminist visionary pragmatism points to an alternative vision of the world but does not prescribe a fixed goal and end-point for which it then claims universal truth. I have tried to articulate such visionary pragmatism in this book as Wisdom spirituality.

In such a process of imaginative pragmatism, one never arrives but always struggles on the way. This process reveals how current actions are part of a larger, meaningful struggle. It demonstrates that ethical and truthful visions of self-affirmation and community cannot be separated from the struggles on their behalf. One takes a stand by constructing new knowledge and new interpretations. While vision can be conjured up in the historical imagination, pragmatic action requires that one remain responsive to the injustices of everyday life. If religion and biblical interpretation are worth anything, they must inspire such visionary pragmatism in the everyday struggles for justice and the well-being of all.

I want to end by pointing to the method of transformation that Rebecca Alpert has proposed. She points out that the greatest single struggle facing Jewish lesbians and gay men is coming to terms with Leviticus 18:22 (see also 20:13) which commands: "Do not lie with a male as one lies with a wo/man; it is an abomination." This text is read on Yom Kippur and then twice during the annual cycle of Torah readings. It is part of the Torah, the five book of Moses which traditionally are believed to be the words of G*d written down by Moses. Thus, these words are considered to be not just a record of the past but a declaration of G*d's will for the people. No law revealed in the Torah can ever be annulled or voided.

She suggests three hermeneutical methods to deal with this text. The first is to stay within the system and look at Midrash to see how traditional interpretation re-directed it; the second is to read it in a historical fashion and thereby make it a text of the past that has no authority for today, and the third is to confront it, allowing it to face our anger and outrage, and to make it an instrument of transformation:

> In our encounter with Leviticus, we experience the pain and terror and anger that this statement arouses in us. We imagine the untold damage done to generations of men, women, and children who experienced same sex feelings and were forced to cloak or reflect them.... We remember how we felt when we first heard these words and knew their holy source. And we get angry—at the power these texts have had over our lives, at the pain we have experienced in no small part because of these words. ... Then, if we can, we grow beyond the rage. We begin to see these words as tools with which to educate people.... We begin to use these very words to break down the silence that surrounds us ... each of us can tell the story of what this prohibition has meant in our lives—how we have struggled with it, and where we are on the road to resolution.... In this way, we can transform Torah from a stumbling block to an entry path.[9]

Continuing in wisdom/Wisdom's Ways of Justice

Both you and I have come to the end of this book, but I hope that the "dancing" has just begun. Whether you engage the bible or the newspaper, interpretation, like dancing, involves body and soul, feet and vision;

---

[9]Rebecca T. Alpert, "In God's Image: Coming to Terms with Leviticus," in *Voices of the Religious Left: A Contemporary Sourcebook,* ed. Rebecca T. Alpert (Philadelphia: Temple University Press, 2000), 221.

it requires moving and movement; it means creating and participating in a movement of Wisdom's friends, and it asks that we get involved in a wisdom/Wisdom movement for change and transformation. It involves moving out of kyriarchal relations of domination and into the radical democratic space of Divine Wisdom; it means engaging multicultural and multireligious grassroots democratic movements for the well-being of all; it means initiating and getting involved in consciousness-raising wisdom/ Wisdom groups, in the *ekklesia of wo/men,* which all over the world envisions, debates, and puts into practice such a radical democratic future of well-being for everybody without exception. I hope we will meet on Wisdom's ways and movements toward justice that span all four directions and never end their spiraling-circling dance!

> O Wisdom of the East O Wisdom of the East
> Sophia, Sophia
> Come breathe in us Come breathe in us
> Sophia, Sophia
> O Wisdom of the South O Wisdom of the South
> Sophia, Sophia
> Come shine in us Come shine in us
> Sophia, Sophia
> O Wisdom of the West O Wisdom of the West
> Sophia, Sophia
> Come live through us Come live through us
> Sophia, Sophia
> O Wisdom of the North O Wisdom of the North
> Sophia, Sophia
> Come root in us Come root in us
> Sophia, Sophia
> (Colleen Fulmer)

Deepening Movement

Elisabeth Schüssler Fiorenza, *But She Said: Feminist Practices of Biblical Interpretation* (Boston: Beacon Press, 1992), 51–76.

Moving Steps

- Consider the road to wisdom/Wisdom you took by working through this book. How do you plan to continue in Wisdom's ways? Are you able to "dance" the hermeneutical dance with its diverse moves, repetitions, and steps? Can you name the stumbling blocks that you found on your way and identify three turns which you really enjoyed?

- Did you change in the process of reading and debating this book? If so, how? Did your understanding of yourself, of the bible, of biblical authority, or of feminism change? List words or think of metaphors or bring things to your meeting that could characterize and image such transformations.

- Choose one biblical text such as the story of Martha and Mary (John 11-12) and try to work on it from the perspective of each of the seven hermeneutics elaborated in this chapter. List five questions to be asked in each of the seven movements of interpretation.

- Write a poem, song, ritual, litany, or story that celebrates Divine Wisdom as giving revelation and inspiration to Her people. How do you feel inspired by Her? How is the bible inspired by Her? How has your spirituality changed because of your work with this book?

Movement Exercise

1. Discuss worksheet 10 on the "Queen of the South."

2. Continue to "dance" by utilizing worksheets 12–18 on hermeneutical movements in each of your next sessions.

The Queen of the South Will Rise[10]

I am the Queen of the South. I come from Latin America and the ends of the earth. I speak for all those who are poor and marginalized. My presence has made the story of the people of the South a story of hope. My people are often seen as the dregs of society—if there is a street cleaner, if there is a person who is spat upon, if there is a person who is removed from the centers of power, these are my people. We are removed from those centers of power that reside in your North—we are the small people, the people who in your eyes are not worthy to receive your attention. You see us as dirty and unclean; you look down upon us as if your station on this earth raises you above us; you wipe us away with the wave of your hand. Our skin is darker, in fact to you it may even look heathen. We come from jungles, from untamed, uncivilized places so far from your home. We are the people of the South, the lost and mysterious, the poor and uneducated, the outcast and unknown.

I am the Queen of the South. Though you may spit upon my mantle, I stand here for all of my people and hold the wisdom and power of the ages. Many prophets have called upon me and recognized my power. Oh, yes, you may look sideways at my people but do not doubt our wisdom. I heard of Solomon in the North and came to test his wisdom and wit. I left my southern lands, my home, and my comfort to find out just how true the knowledge of the North is. It is he who held my arm and who did not want to let go. He knew my power and he recognized my wisdom as larger than his own.

Solomon was not alone among my prophets. Jesus too called upon my name. He proclaimed that "the Queen of the South will rise at the judgment with the people of this generation and will condemn them" because they exploit the common people. I am the Queen of the South, I am the queen who rises with the people of this generation for judgment. It is we who hold the wisdom of the ages. For we come from the ends of the earth to listen to the Wisdom treasured by Solomon. It is we who can recognize the spirit from within. It is we who trust life while Jesus' audience asks for signs and confirmation. It is we who can bring liberation to the downtrodden or condemnation to the wicked.

---

[10]This is a somewhat revised text which was prepared by Elizabeth Zachry, Patrick Tiernan, Pushpa Joseph, and Julie Cedrone for a group project on "Latina Feminist Theology and the Queen of Sheba" (Luke 11:29-32) in Gospel Stories of Wo/men, Fall 2000.

Though our faces may appear unclean, it is we who embody the life-giving spirit of Divine Sophia. While others may rely on their prayers and pious deeds, we stand in judgment of this world of power and hierarchy. It is your North that may look to our South for a different knowledge—a wisdom that is from G*d and for a community which is not like the one you have built. We are the people of the Queen from the South, the dark people of hope.

I am the Queen of Wisdom, the Queen of the South. I was present from the beginning of time, in all peoples, a free gift to anyone who wishes to partake. My abode is in the dark and labyrinthine depths within each human heart, the quintessential though infinitesimal atom in all creation. I am accessible to all, in and through all. I make myself manifest through a great variety of languages—languages that spread the wonder of diversity and the delight in variety, uniting and dancing in the under-standing of hope.

I am the Queen of Wisdom. I delight in liberating people, in particu-lar the ones who are downtrodden and oppressed. I call them mine and I set my table for them to relish. I shout my message in the public places. Wisdom refuses to be silenced. I am the Queen of Wisdom. I reside in the dangerous memories of my people—memories of pain and torture—and with my skillful touch I transform these memories into well springs of power, a power that will nourish and sustain the wo/men people of the South in their struggle for bread and respect. That is the nature of wis-dom/Wisdom. She will rise in all her fury, yet she is silent as the spring that flows forth from the bosom of the earth, to flow into the sea of life. My hands—Wisdom proclaims—have known the weariness of labor, but I will not drop down in fatigue so that the trees will flourish and plants will blossom. My touch is a life-giving touch.

I am the Queen of Wisdom and I am on a journey. By nature I am ad-venturous and am capable of wonderful feats. I have a mine of treasures stored in my inner resources and I delight in displaying them whenever the need arises. With these treasures I venture out to encounter any situa-tion that has within it the potential to set my power free. I meet with road-blocks and impediments, but they do not paralyze me, because my en-ergy is inexhaustible; its source is the combined struggles of my people.

I am the Queen of Wisdom, and I have been a topic of discussion since the beginning of time. I have been bruised and slain, and each time I rise anew, I regain a new life, a new energy. I resurrect, in all, filling the receiver with courage and strength to continue on her journey. They try to extinguish the flames of new life but I continue to burn brighter and higher, ascending from the valleys, scaling the mountains, till I become a beacon torch sparkling and glowing in the wilderness. I am the Queen of Wisdom, the Queen of the South.

Biblical Interpretation as a Site of Struggle for Liberation

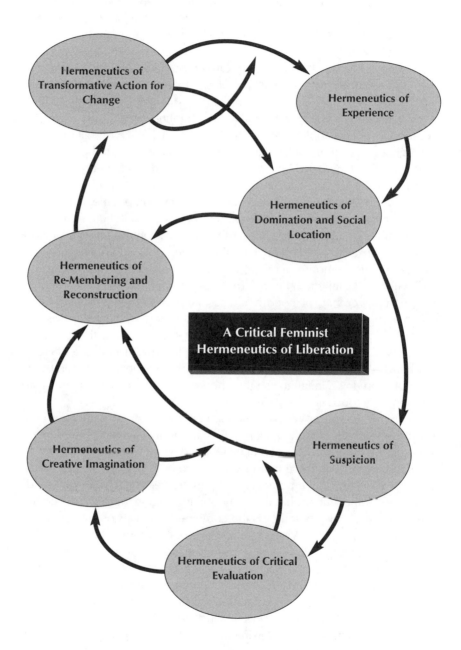

Hermeneutics of Experience

1. "Women's experience" has been understood as a central category and norm. Recognizing that wo/men's perspectives had not been included in the doing of theology and that doctrinal statements such as "The bible is the revealed word of God" were used as norms for judging wo/men's experience, feminist scholars searched for the experience of biblical wo/men.

2. Problem: "Woman's experience" was understood in essentialist universal terms, but wo/men's experience is as variegated and as multiple and complex as there are wo/men.

3. Nevertheless, wo/men have some experiences in common although they may experience them differently. Certain experiences, such as battering or rape, are experiences common to wo/men although they are not the same since gender is inflected by race, culture, and class.

4. In religion the common experience of wo/men has been that of exclusion, silencing, and marginalization. Hence, feminist theology began with wo/men claiming and naming our own experience. But soon feminist theology had to distinguish between wo/men's experience and feminist experience.

5. Feminist experience: Begins with a "break-through" or "aha" experience or "cognitive dissonance."

6. Feminist experience must be analyzed in systemic terms. Experience is socially constructed and coded in kyriocentric language. Linguistic kyriocentric coding is dualistic and asymmetric: male positive – female negative; white positive – black negative; elite positive – subaltern negative; West positive – Orient negative; Christian positive – Jew/Muslim negative. Reading androcentric biblical texts inculcates wo/men's negative self-understanding, inferiority, and second-class citizenship as divine revelation.

7. Reading "otherwise" is possible only when experience is changed from hegemonic to feminist experience and named differently. The goal of feminist biblical reading is not just understanding but *conscientization*, i.e., making us aware of how our experience is determined and how we are nevertheless different from the cultural/religious standard. This is possible only if we struggle for an alternative experiential "space" from which to read.

8. The feminist category of experience has four crucial components:
    a. Experience is mediated linguistically and culturally. There is no "pure" experience.
    b. The personal is political. Personal experience is not private but public. It must be recognized that experience is socially constructed in and through gender/race/class/ethnicity.
    c. If personal experience is determined socially and religiously, it demands critical analysis and reflection which can explore social location and status.
    d. Experience is a theological entry or starting point, not a norm. Only a certain experience, i.e., the experience of struggle and liberation, can be articulated as a feminist norm.

Hermeneutics of Domination and Social Location
Socio-Cultural Analytics

1. *Systemic Analysis*

a. Socio-cultural analytics: world-view-intellectual tool for understanding reality

b. A critical feminist socio-cultural analytic—not just wo/men's experience

c. Applies to both our own world and the world of Scripture: grid or lens

Objection:
Those who have supported the idea of a feminist standpoint epistemology [FSE] see feminism as a *replacement* for male-centered knowledge. This option is anti-pluralist, in the sense that somewhere along the line it must claim cognitive as well as political superiority for feminist knowledge and wo/men's experience.

2. *Basic Category of Analysis: Patriarchy*

a. Rule of the Father of the household

b. Violent overthrow of matriarchy

c. Dualism, especially of gender: androcentrism

d. Same domination of all wo/men by all men

Objections:
a. Does not take the experience of racism into account

b. Does not see that wo/men have different social status positions which depend on the men with whom they are associated

c. Does not take into account that patriarchy has been abolished in modernity

d. Does not take into account that patriarchy is different in different cultures and changes over time

3. *Category of Analysis: Kyriarchy—Rule of the Lord/Master/Father/Husband*

a. Kyriarchy as a socio-political multiplicative system of domination: destabilization of the category of "woman"

b. Kyriocentrism as socio-cultural discursive system securing domination —justification for the exclusion of wo/men

c Classic patriarchal kyriarchy and democracy: household

d. Modern fraternal kyriarchy and democracy: nuclear family

4. *Theological Elaboration: Structural Sin*

a. Not individual [Eve] but collective ["Original Sin"]
b. Institutionalized injustice and collective discrimination
c. Not recognized as injustice because it is justified by religious-cultural symbols, value-systems, and discourses; kyriocentric theology: common sense
d. Produces a consciousness that is self-alienated and collaborates in its own and others' dehumanization and oppression because it is seen as intentioned by G*d

Repentance
a. Conscientization—examination of conscience
b. Personal rejection of structural sin
c. Con-version—a turning around
d. A new socio-theological self-understanding and vision of the world: the *ekklesia of wo/men*

Hermeneutics of Suspicion

Label the bible: "Caution—could be dangerous to your health and survival!"

1. *Necessity for a Hermeneutics of Suspicion*
a. Andro-kyriocentric language
b. "Naturalizing" function of kyriocentrism
c. The "common-sense" character of oppression
d. What kind of G*d do we proclaim?

2. *Basic Conditions for a Hermeneutics of Suspicion*
a. Systemic analysis of domination
b. Distinction between systems of domination and ideological legitimization
c. Recognition of domination which is made natural and common sense by cultural-religious texts and symbols
d. Theological analysis: domination as structural sin

3. *Areas of Investigation*
a. The subjects of interpretation and their socio-political religious location
b. Commentaries and traditions of interpretation and their effective history
c. Kyriocentric texts and symbol systems and their ideological functions
d. Kyriarchal contexts of texts and interpreters

4. *Objections to and Misunderstandings of a Hermeneutics of Suspicion*
a. It is apologetics which circumvents the literal meaning of the texts.
b. It is said to look for a deeper truth which it seeks to uncover: phallogocentrism.
c. Texts do not have definite meanings—only contexts are kyriocentric or kyriarchal.
d. It is tainted by Enlightenment rationalism and atheism. Biblical authority requires trust and obedience rather than suspicion.

- Do you agree with these objections? Why? Why not?
- Do they reflect understanding of a feminist hermeneutics of suspicion?
- Why can one not simply trust and obey the bible?
- Why does the theological authority of the bible require a hermeneutics of suspicion?

Hermeneutics of Critical Evaluation/Proclamation

– A hermeneutics of evaluation for proclamation presupposes and completes a hermeneutics of suspicion.
– A hermeneutics of evaluation is necessary because texts always mean in context; they have a multiplicity of meanings.

A hermeneutics of evaluation has a double reference point:
  I. Questions of ideological assessment: **Cultural**
  II. Questions of biblical authority: **Theological**

I. AS CULTURAL-IDEOLOGICAL HERMENEUTICS

Language and texts are not systems of signs closed in themselves but have performative power: legitimization or challenge of power structures; "naturalization" or interruption of hegemonic world-view; internalization of dominant or emancipatory values: *What does a text do to us if we submit to its world of vision and values?*

Hence, a critical feminist hermeneutics of evaluation seeks
1. to make us conscious of
   • the cultural-religious internalization and legitimizations of kyriarchy
   • the radical democratic, counter-cultural, alternative values and visions inscribed in the text
2. to assess how much a text
   • encodes and reinforces structures of oppression
   • articulates values and visions that promote liberation
3. to articulate a feminist, i.e., emancipatory, scale of values which
   • can but need not necessarily be derived from the bible
   • must be articulated in emancipatory struggles for survival and for changing kyriarchal structures

When analyzing a biblical text, feminist critical analysis pays special attention to
   • "point of view" which expresses the ideological-rhetorical aims of a text; readers align themselves with the dominant voice, values, and characters of the text (e.g., the Syrophoenician wo/man)
   • drawing out and underscoring superior/inferior, we/others, masculine/feminine roles and values inscribed in the text and actualized in the act of reading
   • explicitly articulating the "point of view" or ideological strategy of the text in terms of our cultural value-systems and to making the text's interaction with this system explicit
   • determining and circumscribing the rhetorical situation and context in which the text operates today (e.g., anti-Judaism)

II. AS RELIGIOUS-THEOLOGICAL HERMENEUTICS

In a Christian context, biblical texts are understood and proclaimed as the word of G*d, although biblical scholarship has amply documented that they are the words of historical men.

Understanding of auctoritas = *authority as*

1. *Kyriarchal Authority*
   • Authority of lord/master/father/husband: obedience/submission/consent
   • Logic of identity/exclusion/vilification
   • Canon is standard/rule/criterion, as norm that can not be changed
   • Historical critical scholarship formulates a canon within the canon
2. *Radical Democratic Authority*
   • Derived from the verb *augere* = augment/enhance/initiate/originate
   • Plurality of meanings and truth
   • Critical evaluation rather than obedience
   • Logic of radical democracy = debate/risk/change/vision/inspiration

Canonical Authority in Christian Communities

Canonization compels us to make sense out of texts in such a way that we can accept, consent, and submit to them. It asks for a hermeneutics of obedience.

1. *Malestream Proposals*
   • **Evangelical**: Plenary inspiration/hierarchy of truth; Scripture interprets Scripture
   • **Methodist:** Scripture/tradition/experience/reason are authoritative
   • **Lutheran:** Canon within the canon: "What brings forth Christ"
   • **Roman Catholic:** Scripture/doctrine/liturgy/tradition/hierarchy, sense of believers; criterion: "What is revealed for the sake of our salvation"
   • **Historical-Critical-Theological:** Meant-means/interpretation-application

2. *Feminist Liberationist Proposals*
   • Authorization by Scripture – Scripture as language
   • Scripture as context – our lives as text/dialogical imagination
   • Scripture interprets Scripture: normative principle
   • Correlation between situation and text/principles and norms
   • Reading Scripture for the sake of conscientization and inspiration

3. *Discerning the Spirit(s)*
   • Scripture as a site of struggle over meaning
   • Scripture as inspiration in ever-new situations
   • Critical analysis of inscribed structures/values/visions
   • Criteria of evaluation derived from the experience of wo/men struggling at the bottom of the kyriarchal pyramid for survival and well-being
   • Goal: strength and power in the struggles for liberation and transformation

Hermeneutics of Creative Imagination

- The space of the imagination is that of freedom. This is a space in which boundaries are crossed. In the imaginary space, time becomes relativized and possibilities open up. The space of the imagination is the space of memory and possibility where longings and desires are expressed and events can be re-experienced.

- Usually we see the power of imagination embodied in art, music, literature, or dance but assume that science works only with rational, logical, deductive thought. Such an assumption is incorrect, because science works with hypotheses and models that depend on informed imagination. Stress on purely logical and cognitive operations represses emotions, feelings, and perceptions and therefore makes for bad history or theology.

- Thanks to our imaginative abilities we can put ourselves into another person's position and relate to that person's feelings, deliberations, and struggles. With our imagination we are able to conceive of change and see how situations can be altered. Historical imagination is absolutely necessary for any understanding of biblical texts. It enables us to fill in the gaps and empty spaces and thus to make sense out of the story.

- Historians who write history or exegetes who interpret historical texts depend on their imagination to "make history," to see the people of the past as history makers and as historical agents.

- Imagination relies not just on information but also on the unconscious as a store of repressed feelings and experiences as well as of common-sense practices and codes. Our unconscious assumptions determine our rational thought, how we read texts and reconstruct history.

- The imaginative retelling of biblical stories not only establishes identity with the androcentric characters and historizes but also enacts common-sense, taken-for-granted cultural and religious understandings and brings to the fore repressed emotions and experiences. Hence, it calls for a hermeneutics of suspicion.

Hermeneutics of Re-Membering and Re-Construction

I. Hermeneutics of Re-Construction

1. A hermeneutics of memory **should not be used to avoid a hermeneutics of critical theological/ideological evaluation**. Its constructive moment must be undergirded by a hermeneutics of suspicion and critical evaluation.

2. A hermeneutics of re-membering and re-construction is **not only a deconstructive but also a constructive hermeneutics and relies on historical imagination and a scale of values and a world of vision** which must be justified and validated in public discourse: e.g., analytic of kyriarchy and radical democracy.

3. A hermeneutics of memory must not be undergirded by liberal pluralism (assuming that everything goes) but **critical re-membering. Analytic concepts and models of reconstruction are important.** History depends on our images and models of the past which we derive from the present (analogy).

II. Texts and Artifacts as Sources of History

1. Textual Positivism: Text as Window to the World

Text as window to, reflection of, and reference to historical reality

Sources are objective data and evidence of how things really were

2. Historical Positivism: History as Depiction of Reality—What Actually Happened

Historiography is transcript and report of actual events and of "what actually happened"

3. Historical Constructivism

History is narrative-laden—a remaking and retelling of reality but not reality itself

4. History as the "Logic of the Probable": Reconstituting the World

Rhetoricity of the texts and sources—reading against the grain

History as identity-formation/history as memory—account of the historical winners

Historiography must be adequate both to the sources **and** to those historically silenced or marginalized

III. Models of Historical Reconstruction

1. Theological Models of Early Christian History

Judaism-Christianity: Supersessionist Model
Apostolic Succession: Hierarchical Model
Orthodoxy-Heresy: Truth-Falsehood Model
Pristine Origins Deterioration Model
Growth and Development Model
Historical Jesus Model

2. Feminist Models

Focus on Women in the Bible
Women's History
Feminist Gender History
Feminist Multicultural History
Feminist Multicultural History of Struggle

Hermeneutics of Transformative Action for Change

I. Areas in Need of Liberation and Transformation

- Kyriocentric language and text
- Kyriocentric symbol systems
- Kyriarchal structures
- Common-sense assumptions
- Languages of hate
- Biblical authority
- Biblical texts of terror
- Prejudices/kyriocentric frameworks/mindsets
- Ourselves
- Our society
- Our religious communities

*[Please give concrete examples—
brainstorm to name other areas in need of transformation]*

II. Transforming Biblical Texts

1. Identifying with historical wo/men rather than with kyriocentric biblical texts

2. Inclusive reading: inserting wo/man or female into androcentric texts

3. Reversal: reversing male and female, rich and poor, etc. characters

4. Placing multiply oppressed wo/men in the center—constructing an alternative perspective to that of kyriocentrism

5. Articulating the perspective of the most marginalized and dehumanized wo/men

6. Reading the wo/men passages as the tip of an iceberg—reconstructing for the submerged part of the story

7. Reading the kyriocentric text not as descriptive but as a prescriptive projection of male elites

8. Critically analyzing female characters as exchange objects which are the means by which readers are bonded to the elite male protagonist (Emily Cheney)

9. Reading against the grain: mapping kyriarchal relations inscribed in the text and constructing an alternative story-text-image

10. Hearing the silenced and forgotten into speech (Nell Morton)

EXPLANATION OF TERMS (GLOSSARY)

Laura Beth Bugg

Androcentrism – Literally "male-centeredness" (from the Greek word *aner* = "male"). A linguistic and cultural system that understands male/man as the norm and wo/men as secondary, peripheral, and deviant.

Androgyny – From the Greek words for "man" (*aner*) and "woman" (*gyne*), androgyny is a synthetic term and social ideal that combines traditional masculine and feminine qualities and virtues but still privileges the male.

Anti-Judaism – Prejudice against, hostility toward, or defamation of Jewish people and Judaism, whether through negative stereotyping, persecution, or vilification for the purpose of elevating another group or tradition (for example, Christianity).

Apocalypse/Apocalypticism – Ancient writings such as the Book of Revelation that consist of visions and revelations, received by a prophet or seer, sometimes in the form of dreams, regarding the future or heavenly realm. Apocalypticism is a theological outlook and social movement.

Apocalypse of John – Also called the Book of Revelation; the last book in the Christian bible.

Apocrypha/Apocryphal – Books that have not been accepted into the Jewish or Christian canon.

Archeology – The scientific study of ancient cultures on the basis of their material remains such as monuments, artifacts, buildings, pottery, and fossil relics.

Archive – A collection of historical documents and materials, but in French philosopher Michel Foucault's sense; also the conditions and rules by which it is possible to know something at a specific historical point in time.

Athena – Greek Wisdom and Warrior Goddess who is said to have been born from the head of her father, Zeus, the highest God.

Binary Thought – An either-or way of thinking about reality or a view that divides concepts into two mutually exclusive categories (man/ woman, white/black, reason/emotion) rather than looking for overlaps and commonalities.

Canon – From the Greek for "reed" or yardstick, a canon is generally a criterion, law, or rule and, more specifically, a list, especially of sacred writings preserved as normative.

Capitalism – An economic system based on private ownership of the means of production and characterized by large differences between rich and poor, "developed" and "underdeveloped" countries.

Class – In its most general sense, a group of persons who share a common placement in a capitalist economy and a common socio-political and cultural status in a society.

Colonialism – The exercise of imperialist power by which one nation obtains control over another, creating a relationship of dependency (the weaker on the stronger) and exploitation, in which the resources of the subordinate nation are used to enrich the dominant one. Unequal relations are maintained by means of economic, political, social, cultural, and religious control.

Conscientization/Consciousness-raising – A process in which an individual or group names and understands the structures of internalized oppression and begins to become free of them.

Critical Social Theory – Bodies of knowledge and sets of institutional practices that theorize about the social in defense of social and economic justice.

Deconstruction – A critical theory and constellation of methods that question assumptions about identity, truth, and perceived norms. This is done chiefly through identifying binary opposites or dualisms and revealing how the primary, positive term determines the second term in a negative fashion in order to assert its own positivity.

Diatessaron – An attempt by ancient Christians to telescope, or compile, the four gospels now deemed canonical into one unitary document.

Discourse/Discursive – In general, the process of engaging in communication and verbal exchange and the verbal interchange of ideas. In the writings of the French philosopher Michel Foucault, discourse refers not to language in the sense of linguistic system or grammar but to a well-bounded body of social knowledge. Such cultural systems, as for instance scholarly disciplines such as medicine or biblical studies, are constituted through various discourses to which not all people have equal access.

Ecofeminism – Ecological feminism—a variety of feminist positions—makes the connections between the domination of nature and the domination of wo/men and

seeks to find ways and visions for ending the exploitation of both nature and wo/men.

Ekklesia – The radical democratic assembly of free citizens who gather in order to conduct critical debate and to determine their own communal, political, and spiritual well-being. When found in the Christian Testament (New Testament) the word is translated as "church."

Ekklesia of Wo/men – Since throughout history full citizenship and democracy were restricted to elite males, it is necessary to qualify *ekklesia* with wo/men in order to overcome its kyriocentric determination.

Emancipation/Emancipatory – Liberation or deliverance from dependence, subjection, slavery, control, or any form of oppression. The emancipatory hermeneutical paradigm engages in biblical interpretation for the sake of conscientization.

Enlightenment – An eighteenth-century Western intellectual and social movement that believed humanity was emerging from the "dark age" of superstition and ignorance into a new era of scientific rationality, reason, and social justice. It emphasized the use of reason in the examination of previously accepted ideas and institutions.

Epistemology – From the Greek for "knowledge," epistemology refers to the study of the ways in which knowledge is articulated and made possible. It sets standards that are used to assess what we know and why we believe what we believe. "Epistemological Privilege" is the notion that experience of struggles against oppression (for example, that of poor women) provides a different knowledge and calls for different standards of knowledge.

Essentialism – The notion that individuals or groups have inherent unchanging characteristics and that universal claims can be made about any group (for example, wo/men) or individual regarding such characteristics. Essentialism neither comprehends the differences between wo/men nor recognizes that essences are constituted by structures of domination.

Exegesis – A method of critical textual analysis or philological and historical explication of a text, in particular a verse-by-verse investigation and explanation of a text.

Femininity/Feminine – A set of qualities, rules, and ideals governing female behavior and appearance that are internalized in and through education, enforced through fashion and cosmetics, and believed to be innate, although they are socially, culturally, politically, and religiously constructed.

Feminism – A movement and theory for the economic, social, political, and religious equality, rights, and dignity of all wo/men. It is focused on the struggle of wo/men against domination, exploitation, oppression, and dehumanization.

Gender – A grammatical classification system as well as a culturally shaped set of qualities and attributes determining the difference between male and female. While sex and gender can be distinguished, they are both socially constructed.

G*d – Elisabeth Schüssler Fiorenza's way of writing "God" that acknowledges the insufficiency and inability of human language to adequately name the Divine. It seeks to indicate that G*d is ultimately unnamable and ineffable.

Gnosis/Gnosticism – From the Greek word for knowledge (*gnosis*), Gnosticism is a complex and probably inadequate term for a varied religious movement and its literature. Central to its system of ideas among others is the claim to secret, esoteric knowledge and the belief in the dual nature of the cosmos (light/dark, good/evil, mind/body, etc.) and the Divine.

Gospel Harmony – A synthesis of the four canonical gospels of Matthew, Mark, Luke, and John into one unified text (for example, the *Diatessaron*). This process seeks to eliminate or reconcile theological or textual differences through the creation of a single, authoritative document.

Gynecentrism/Gynaikocentrism – Has been coined in opposition to androcentrism. Gynecentrism is a theoretical perspective that posits women/ females (in Greek, *gyne*) as paradigmatic and argues that women, as superior in essence to men, should be dominant in the social order.

Hegemony – A form of social organization that diffuses power throughout the social system such that multiple groups police themselves and suppress each other's resistance and dissent, thereby depoliticizing it. Hegemony is a web of relationships, functions, and experiences that allow an elite ruling power to remain in a position of authority.

Hermeneutics – From the Greek word *hermeneuein*, which means to interpret, exegete, explain, or translate. Hermeneutics refers to both the theory and practice of interpretation.

Heterosexism – The assumption that compulsory heterosexuality is the only normal mode of erotic behavior and that marriage and sexual orientation toward men is the only normal behavior for wo/men. Both as an institution and an ideology, heterosexism is an essential element in the maintenance of structures of domination.

Historical Criticism – The study of historical sources in order to determine events in history as they might have occurred and how knowledge about them is transmitted. In attempting to answer questions of historicity, many tools and methodologies are employed, among them source, form, redaction, and social-historical criticism, as well as the evaluation of material remains (archeology).

Historiography – The act of writing history that involves three phases—documentary research, explanation, and writing—in the composition of historical nar-

rative. Because it involves the selection, weighing, interpretation, and validation of documents, it is a remaking and retelling of reality, but not a transcript of "what actually happened."

Household Codes – A term for texts (e.g., Colossians 3:18–4:1; Ephesians 5:22–6:9; 1 Peter 2:18–3:7; 1 Timothy 2:11-15, 5:3-8, 6:1-2; and Titus 2:2-10, 3:1-2) inculcating the submission of subordinated groups. Household codes are found in Jewish and Greco-Roman philosophical writings, the Christian Testament and other early Christian writings. They articulate relations of domination between wife and husband, slave and master, child and father, community and empire in which the socially weaker groups (wives, slaves, children, and Christian community) are to submit to and obey the stronger group (lord, father, husband, slave-master, and imperial authorities), which is often one and the same person or group.

Immasculation – First coined by the feminist literary critic Judith Fetterly, immasculation refers to the internalization of and identification with man/male in and through texts and language.

Inspiration/Verbal Inspiration – From the Latin *inspirare* = to breath in, to inspire. Like the wind, the Holy Spirit is believed to "breathe life" into people. Verbal inspiration, a dogmatic term, asserts that every word in Scripture is inspired, speaks with divine authority, and is without error because it owes its existence to divine authorship and authorization.

Isis – An Egyptian Wisdom Goddess who had widespread appeal in the Greco-Roman world. She is called upon as the holy and eternal Divine Savior of the human race who is "beneficent in cherishing mortals" and proclaims a universal message of salvation. All the different nations and peoples used divine titles derived from their own local mythologies when they called on Isis, the many-named, who is one but encompasses all.

Kyriarchy – A neologism coined by Elisabeth Schüssler Fiorenza and derived from the Greek words for "lord" or "master" (*kyrios*) and "to rule or dominate" (*archein*) which seeks to redefine the analytic category of patriarchy in terms of multiplicative intersecting structures of domination. Kyriarchy is a socio-political system of domination in which elite educated propertied men hold power over wo/men and other men. Kyriarchy is best theorized as a complex pyramidal system of intersecting multiplicative social structures of superordination and subordination, of ruling and oppression.

Kyriocentrism – The cultural-religious-ideological systems and intersecting discourses of race, gender, heterosexuality, class, and ethnicity that produce, legitimate, inculcate, and sustain kyriarchy.

Literary Criticism – A set of methodologies that approach texts as literary documents. Among them are "New Criticism," which focuses on the language and in-

ternal structures of the literary work rather than on the historical setting of the text, and "Narrative Criticism," an analysis of how the story is told, with attention to plot and character analysis.

Malestream – A term marking the fact that history, tradition, theology, church, culture, and society have been defined by men and have excluded wo/men. Frameworks of scholarship, texts, traditions, language, standards, paradigms of knowledge, and so on, have been and are male-centered and elite male dominated.

Materialist Feminist Criticism – A theory and method that focuses on the material conditions for the construction of sexuality and gender in cultural texts and discourses. It expands Marxist analysis of the material conditions of oppression to include heterosexuality, gender, race, and other social divisions.

Methods of Biblical Interpretation – Are historical, literary, hermeneutical, practical, psychological, and rhetorical.

Midrash – Derives from the Hebrew root *daled-resh-shin* which means "to seek out," to examine, and to investigate. Midrash originally was an oral method of commentary on the Hebrew Scriptures dealing with both *Halakah* (legal materials) and *Aggadah* (narrative materials, parables, stories, ethics, and homilies). More generally, Midrash refers to modern attempts to wrest meaning from biblical texts in order to integrate social, political, theological change into tradition and to put subjugated voices back into the text through alternative imaginative interpretation.

Mujerista – A neologism coined by the Latina ethicist Ada María Isasi-Díaz as an alternative expression for feminist focusing on the oppression and liberation of Latina/Chicana/Hispanic wo/men. It gives preference to the lived experience of Latinas in the U.S. and insists on their moral and religious agency.

Nationalism – Devotion to a particular nation, its interests and culture, and the conviction that its history, systems, traditions, and values should be preeminent. Also, the resulting identity constructed and asserted by a nation under "foreign" or non-national domination.

Neologism – The creation and employment of new words, or the new use or re-definition of existing ones.

Orthodoxy – A combination of the Greek words for "right/correct" (*orthos*) and "opinion" (*doxa*), this is adherence to approved, conventional, accepted, or customary doctrines and beliefs. It stands in contrast to heterodoxy or heresy. (Also the name of a Christian denomination.)

Patriarchy – Literally means the rule of the father and is generally understood within feminist discourses in a dualistic sense as asserting the domination of all men over all women in equal terms. The theoretical adequacy of patriarchy has been challenged because, for instance, black men do not have control over white

wo/men and some women (slave-mistresses) have power over subaltern women and men (slaves).

Positivist Science – A philosophical theory and scholarly discourse which holds that truth is known through the observance of natural phenomena and that the tools of science can represent factual reality. Historical positivism understands history as an accurate reflection and depiction of reality. It assumes that science can discover universal truth.

Postcolonialism – The social, political, economic, cultural, and religious theories and practices that arise in response and resistance to colonialism. Postcolonialism emerges in opposition to colonialism (see entry above) as a critical vantage point from which to struggle against imperialism.

Postmodernism – A mix of diverse and sometimes opposing theoretical approaches. It rejects modern universalist theories, seeks to destabilize power relations, recognizes multiplicity and diversity, and questions the notion of "scientific" positivist knowledges and singular meanings by stressing particularity, difference, and heterogeneity.

Praxis – Both established practices, customs, and/or uses and the theories sustaining them; it means ideas that inform practices and practices that shape ideas. Feminist biblical interpretation is an emancipatory praxis.

Rabbi/Rabbinic – Means "master," a Jewish religious leader especially trained and qualified to expound and apply the Torah.

Race/Racism – A classification of human beings into a common grouping on the basis of biological/physical characteristics. Racism is a system of unequal power and privilege and an ideology which holds that, based on race, groups can be ranked hierarchically with regard to intelligence, ability, and so on, and may thus be discriminated against. Racial segregation is a fundamental organizing principle of racism. Racism can be exercised as institutional racism, scientific racism, everyday racism, and personal racism.

Radical – From the Latin *radix* = root. Outside of the usual or customary, departing from the norm, or affecting revolutionary change. May also mean the root or foundation of a thing.

Radical Democracy – The envisioned social-political counter-system to kyriarchy (see entry above), radical, that is grassroots, democracy means equal citizenship and decision-making powers and radical, or total, economic, cultural, political, and religious equality, freedom, and well-being for all without exception. It envisions relations and institutions that are truly participatory and egalitarian.

Reconstruction – A method of re-membering, recovering, reclaiming, and restoring that seeks to deconstruct the kyriocentric dynamic of a text and to recontextu-

alize it in a different interpretive framework. It tries to make the subordinated and marginalized others "visible" and their repressed arguments and silences "audible" again by displacing the kyriocentric text and by reframing it in a hermeneutic context of struggle.

Rhetoric – Not simply to be understood in the colloquial sense of stylistic figure and ornament, linguistic manipulation, deceptive propaganda, or "mere" words, rhetoric/rhetorical inquiry assumes that biblical texts and interpretations are argumentative and persuasive discourses that involve authorial aims and linguistic-symbolic strategies as well as audience perception and construction. It acknowledges that the interpretation of texts and the production of meaning are determined by particular socio-political-historical locations and political-cultural-religious interest and power.

Roman Empire – The period of Roman rule following the Republic and typically dated from the time of the first emperor, Augustus, in 27 B.C.E., to Romulus Augustulus, the last Western emperor, deposed by the Goths in 476 C.E. At its peak, the Empire reached from the Persian Gulf in the east, across North Africa, and as far west as Germany and Britain.

Scientific Racism/Sexism – A specific body of knowledge about blacks, Asians, indigenous people, Latinas/os, or wo/men that is designed to prove the inferiority of these groups. It is produced within biology, anthropology, psychology, sociology, theology, and other academic disciplines and public discourses.

Semiology/Semiotic – The study of meaning in the forms of language, or of the relationship between signs and symbols. Semiotics comprises semantics (the study of meanings: signs and what they refer to), syntactics (the relation holding among signs), and pragmatics (the relationship between signs and their human users). Semiotics is based on the work of the French linguist Ferdinand de Saussure and means the system of interpreting signs and the methodology based on how these signs and symbols function to create meaning. The French feminist Julia Kristeva uses the term "semiotic" to describe the pre-oedipal stage of child development.

Social Location – Is constituted by the kyriarchal systems of race, gender, class, ethnicity, religion, or age that determine the social position and identity of individuals. It is a group rather than an identity category, since social positions are assigned to individuals through group categories and are not voluntary.

Sola Scriptura – From the Latin, meaning "Scripture alone." A hermeneutical principle particularly associated with Martin Luther and Reformed theologians, which asserts that only Scripture but not church tradition and authority is to be regarded as authoritative and binding.

Sophialogy – From the Greek *Sophia* = Wisdom/wisdom and *legein* = to speak, say, sophialogy is coined in analogy to theology or sociology and means the teaching and practice of wisdom/Wisdom.

Structuralism – The claim, made most notably by French social theorists such as Claude Lévi-Strauss, that there is a dualistic pattern or structure underlying every event/text that can be discovered and known through analysis.

Subaltern – Secondary or lower in status or position; subordinate. A term coined by postcolonial discourse.

Synoptic Gospels – From the Greek *synoptikos*, "to see together," this term refers to the first three canonical gospels, Matthew, Mark, and Luke, and to the ways in which they show similarities and differences in narrating the life, death, and resurrection of Jesus.

Synoptic Problem – The problem of understanding the relationship between the gospels of Matthew, Mark, and Luke by comparing their similarities and differences. The so-called Two-Source Theory is the generally accepted solution to the problem. It holds that both Matthew and Luke used Mark and a hypothetical source Q (from German *Quelle* = source) which can be reconstructed from the agreements between Matthew and Luke.

Talmud – Meaning instruction or study, is the authoritative body of Jewish tradition consisting of Mishnah (authoritative legal tradition) and Gemara (the learned commentary upon Mishnah). It exists in Palestinian (early fifth century) and Babylonian (late fifth century) forms.

Third World/Two-Thirds World – A geopolitical term used to indicate countries that are not in the so-called "First World," the economically privileged countries of North America, Japan, Australia, New Zealand, and western Europe (Communist eastern Europe was the "Second World"). In response to the hierarchical implications of "Third World," the term "Two-Thirds World" was introduced to acknowledge the greater portion of the world's citizens who do not live in economically privileged countries.

Torah – Meaning teaching, path, or way, commonly refers to the Five Books of Moses, the Pentateuch. It also can encompass the whole Jewish text tradition including the Bible, Mishnah, Tosefta, the Babylonian and Jerusalem Talmuds, Midrash, and commentaries. In a more general sense, it can mean the totality of revelation or the Jewish way of living which is informed by these texts.

Translation – The process of a transfer of or rendering into another language that involves an interpretation, via the analysis and experience of a translator. It is not a transcription, but depends on the intellectual framework and socio-political location of the translator and interpreter.

Wisdom-Sophia – The Greek word for wisdom/Wisdom, Sophia, a divine female figuration who appears in the Wisdom literature of the Hebrew Bible and Apocrypha, such as Proverbs, Ecclesiastes, and Sirach as well as in the Christian Testament.

Wo/man-wo/men – A way of writing proposed by Elisabeth Schüssler Fiorenza meant to indicate that the category "wo/man-wo/men" is a social construct. Wo/men are not a unitary social group but are fragmented by structures of race, class, ethnicity, religion, sexuality, colonialism, and age. This destabilization of the term "wo/men" underscores the differences between wo/men and within individual wo/men. This writing is inclusive of subaltern men who in kyriarchal systems are seen "as wo/men" and functions as a linguistic corrective to androcentric language use.

Womanist – First coined by writer Alice Walker, "womanist" refers to African-American feminists as feminists of color. The experience of black women is central, as is the struggle for survival of a people.

Women's Liberation Movement – In general, a centuries-old social movement for the emancipation of wo/men. Specifically, a social movement re-emerging in the late 1960s (and popularly called "Women's Lib") that struggles to achieve for all wo/men the rights, benefits, and privileges of equal authority and citizenship, which are denied to them by kyriarchal societies and religions.

Basic Reference Library

The following bibliographic recommendations are resources and tools of feminist interpretation which you might find helpful on your journey with *Wisdom Ways*.

Aquino, María Pilar, and Elisabeth Schüssler Fiorenza, eds. *In the Power of Wisdom: Feminist Spiritualities of Struggle*. London: SCM Press, 2000.

Bach, Alice, ed. *Wo/men in the Hebrew Bible*. New York: Routledge, 1999.

Brooten, Bernadette J. *Women Leaders in the Ancient Synagogue*. Atlanta: Scholars Press, 1982.

Büchmann, Christina, and C. Spiegel, eds. *Out of the Garden: Women Writers on the Bible*. New York: Fawcett Columbine, 1995.

Burrus, Virginia. *Chastity as Autonomy: Women in the Stories of the Apocryphal Acts*. Lewiston, Me.: E. Mellen Press, 1987.

Cady, Susan, H. Taussig, and M. Ronan. *Wisdom's Feast: Sophia in Study and Celebration*. New York: Harper, 1989.

Cady Stanton, Elizabeth, ed. *The Original Feminist Attack on the Bible: The Woman's Bible,* facsimile edition. New York: Arno Press, 1974.

Capel Anderson, Janice, and S. Moore, eds. *Mark & Method: New Approaches in Biblical Studies*. Minneapolis: Fortress Press, 1992.

Cheney, Emily. *She Can Read: Feminist Reading Strategies for Biblical Narrative*. Valley Forge, Pa.: Trinity Press, 1996.

Chopp, Rebecca S. *The Power to Speak: Feminism, Language, and God*. New York: Crossroad, 1989.

Christ, Carol, and J. Plaskow, eds. *Weaving the Visions*. New York: Harper & Row, 1988.

Clark Wire, Antoinette. *The Corinthian Women Prophets: A Reconstruction Through Paul's Rhetoric*. Minneapolis: Augsburg Fortress Press, 1990.

Demers, Patricia. *Women Interpreters of the Bible*. New York: Paulist Press, 1992.

Eisen, Ute. *Women Officeholders in Early Christianity: Epigraphical and Literary Studies*. Collegeville, Minn.: The Liturgical Press, 2000.

Fuchs, Esther. *Sexual Politics in the Biblical Narrative*. Sheffield: Sheffield University Press, 2001.

Gamble, Sarah, ed. *The Routledge Critical Dictionary of Feminism and Post-feminism*. New York: Routledge, 1999.

Haskins, Susan. *Mary Magdalen: Myth and Metaphor*. New York: Harcourt, 1993.

Hyman, Naomi M. *Biblical Women in the Midrash: A Sourcebook*. Northvale, N.J.: Jason Aronson, 1997.

Ilan, Tal. *Integrating Women into Second Temple History*. Tübingen: J. C. B. Mohr, 1999.

Isherwood, Lisa, and Dorothea McEwan, eds. *An A to Z of Feminist Theology*. Sheffield: Academic Press, 1996.

King, K. L., ed. *Images of the Feminine in Gnosticism*. Studies in Antiquity and Christianity. Philadelphia: Fortress Press, 1988.

Krondorfer, Björn. *Body and Bible: Interpreting and Experiencing Biblical Narratives*. Philadelphia: Trinity Press, 1992.

Kwok Pui-lan, and Elisabeth Schüssler Fiorenza, eds. *Women's Sacred Scriptures*. Concilium. Maryknoll, N.Y.: Orbis Books, 1998.

Lerner, Gerda. *The Creation of Feminist Consciousness: From the Middle Ages to the Eighteen-Seventies*. New York: Oxford University Press, 1993.

————. *The Creation of Patriarchy*. New York: Oxford University Press, 1986.

Levine, Amy-Jill. *"Women Like This": New Perspectives on Jewish Women in the Greco-Roman World*. Atlanta: Scholars Press, 1991.

Mays, James L., ed. *Harper's Bible Commentary*. New York: Harper Collins, 2000.

————, ed. *Harper's Bible Dictionary*. New York: Harper Collins, 1993.

Meeks, Wayne, ed. *The Harper Collins Study Bible: New Revised Standard Version with the Apocryphal/Deuterocanonical Books*. New York: Harper Collins, 1993.

Meyers, Carol, and others. *Women in Scripture: A Dictionary*. Boston: Houghton Mifflin, 2000.

Newsom, Carol A., and S. H. Ringe, eds. *Women's Bible Commentary: Expanded Edition*. Louisville: Westminster John Knox Press, 1998.

Pardes, Ilana. *Countertraditions in the Bible: A Feminist Approach*. Cambridge, Mass.: Harvard University Press, 1992.

Robins, Wendy S., ed. *Through the Eyes of a Woman: Bible Studies on the Experience of Women*. Revised edition. Geneva: WCC Publications, 1995.

Romney Wegner, J. *Chattel or Person: The Status of Women in the Mishnah*. New York: Oxford University Press, 1988.

Russell, Letty, and J. S. Clarkson, eds. *Dictionary of Feminist Theologies*. Louisville: Westminster John Knox Press, 1996.

Schaberg, J. *The Illegitimacy of Jesus: A Feminist Theological Interpretation of the Infancy Narratives*. San Francisco: Harper & Row, 1987.

Schottroff, Luise, S. Schroer, and M. T. Wacker. *Feminist Interpretation: The Bible in Women's Perspective*. Minneapolis: Fortress Press, 1998.

Schüssler Fiorenza, Elisabeth. *Bread Not Stone: The Challenge of Feminist Biblical Interpretation*. Tenth anniversary edition. Boston: Beacon Press, 1995.

————. *But She Said: Feminist Practices of Biblical Interpretation*. Boston: Beacon Press, 1992.

————. *In Memory of Her: A Feminist Reconstruction of Christian Origins*. Tenth anniversary edition. New York: Crossroad, 1994.

————. *Jesus: Miriam's Child and Sophia's Prophet*. New York: Continuum, 1994.

————. *Jesus and the Politics of Interpretation*. New York: Continuum, 2000.

————. *Rhetoric and Ethic: The Politics of Biblical Studies*. Minneapolis: Fortress Press, 1999.

————. *Sharing Her Word: Feminist Biblical Interpretation in Context*. Boston: Beacon Press, 1998.

————, ed. *The Power of Naming: A Concilium Reader in Feminist Liberation Theology*. Maryknoll, N.Y.: Orbis Books, 1996.

————, ed., *Searching the Scriptures: A Feminist Commentary*. New York: Crossroad, 1994.

————, ed. *Searching the Scriptures: A Feminist Introduction*. New York: Crossroad, 1993.

Segovia, Fernando, and M. A. Tolbert, eds. *Teaching the Bible*. Maryknoll, N.Y.: Orbis Books, 1998.

Selvidge, Marla. *Notorious Voices: Feminist Biblical Interpretation 1500–1920*. New York: Continuum, 1996.

Shepard Kraemer, Ross. *Her Share of the Blessings*. New York: Oxford University Press, 1992.

————, ed. *"Maenads, Martyrs, Matrons, Monastics" : A Source Book on Women's Religion in the Greco-Roman World*. Philadelphia: Fortress Press, 1988.

Sugirtharajah, R. S., ed. *Voices from the Margins: Interpreting the Bible in the Third World*. Maryknoll, N.Y.: Orbis Books, 1991.

Suskin Ostriker, Alicia. *Feminist Revision and the Bible*. Oxford: Blackwell, 1993.

Trible, Phyllis. *Texts of Terror: Literary-Feminist Readings of Biblical Narratives*. Philadelphia: Fortress Press, 1984.

Wainwright, Elaine M. *Towards a Feminist Critical Reading of the Gospel According to Matthew*. Berlin: de Gruyter, 1991.

Washington, Harold C., S. L. Graham, and P. Thimmes, eds. *Escaping Eden: New Feminist Perspectives on the Bible*. Sheffield: Sheffield Press, 1999.

Weems, Renita. *Just a Sister Away: A Womanist Vision of Women's Relationships in the Bible*. San Diego: Lura Media, 1988.

————. "Reading Her Way Through the Struggle." In *Stony the Road We Trod: African American Biblical Interpretation,* edited by Cain Hope Felder, 57–80. Minneapolis: Fortress Press, 1991.

West, Gerald. *Biblical Hermeneutics of Liberation: Models of Reading the Bible in the South African Context*. Maryknoll, N.Y.: Orbis Books, 1995.

Winter, Miriam Therese. *WomanWord: A Feminist Lectionary and Psalter: Wo/men in the New Testament*. New York: Crossroad, 1990.

INDEX

abolitionist movement, 84

academy, the: feminist biblical interpretation's relation to, 91; and the lack of disadvantaged women in biblical studies, 10; marginalization of feminist biblical studies in, 10–11; postmodernism and, 43; technical language of, 7–8; on women in the 1960s, 82–83

Achtemeier, Paul, 141

African-Americans, 10, 55, 148–49

Aggadah, 149

allegorical method of bible reading, 39

Alpert, Rebecca, 189

androcentrism, 114–15

androgyny, 124–25

anthropology, 113, 147

anti-Judaism, 48, 66, 142, 146

apocalyptic traditions, 27n.8

apocrypha, 23n.6

apostolic succession-hierarchical model, 185

archeology, 144

Arendt, Hannah, 87

Aristotle, 122

Athena, 24, 70

augere/auctoritas, 49

Bakhtin, Mikhail, 9

Basic Christian Communities, 151

Beauvoir, Simone de, 82n.4, 85, 112

bible, the: doctrinal-revelatory paradigm of reading, 38–40; false assumptions about the formation and reading of, 65–70; feminist rejection of, 64–65; fetishism of, 67–68; hermeneutic-cultural paradigm of reading, 41–43; rhetorical-emancipatory paradigm of reading, 43–49; scientific-positivist paradigm of reading, 40–41; starting point of feminist interpretation of, 89–90; synopsis of present work's understanding of, 4; the taboo of criticizing, 71–75; two models of language in, 29. *See also* feminist biblical interpretation; *and other specific types of interpretation*

biblicism, 40

bibliodrama, 150–51

Black theology, 85

Boal, Augusto, 159

Bosch, Selma, 161

Brecht, Berthold, 157

Brock, Rita Nakashima, 126

Brooten, Bernadette, 140

Brown Blackwell, Antoinette, 142

Butler, Ella, 6

Cannon, Katie G., 21, 55

canon: different churches' versions of, 23n.6; formation of, 65, 138–39; hermeneutics of critical evaluation and, 178

capitalism, 10, 45

Castelli, Elizabeth, 9

change. *See* transformation

Chokmah, 22, 24, 25–26

Christian Testament: term discussed, 22n.4

221

228

social location and, 172–75; a
hermeneutics of experience and,
169–72; a hermeneutics of re-
membering and reconstruction
and, 183–86; a hermeneutics of
suspicion and, 175–77; a
hermeneutics of transformative
action for change and, 186–89;
overview of, 43–49; on power,
47–48; summarized, 52
Rich, Adrienne, 61
Ricoeur, Paul, 184
role-playing, 150, 181–83
role reversal, 156
Roman empire, the, 120
romanticism, 26
Rothchild-Laeuchli, Evelyn, 160
Rousseau, Jean Jacques, 7n.7
Ruach, 22, 23

Sapientia, 23, 24, 25–26
Sarah, 156
Saving, Valerie, 126
Schneiders, Sandra, 141
scientific paradigm: bible reading
and, 40–41; as contrary to conscientization, 94–95; correctives to
modernity fostered by, 42; pedagogy of, 33–34. See also scientific-positivist paradigm
scientific-positivist paradigm: colonialism and, 45; grassroots
democracy and, 97; on 1 Corinthians 14, 47, 48; overview of,
40–41, 51. See also scientific
paradigm
scientism, 41
The Second Sex (Beauvoir), 82n.4
second-wave feminism, 84–85
self-sacrifice, 94
Seneca, 33
sex, 112–14. See also gender
Shekhinah, 22, 23, 24
sin, 110–11
social analysis: complex systemic,
117–24; dualistic categories of,
112–17; primary categories of,

107–12; reasons for a feminist,
102–7. See also social location
socialist-Marxist feminism, 117
social location: group-forums and
differences in, 16; hermeneutics
of, 172–75; kyriocentrism and,
122–24; overview of a complex
systemic analysis of, 117–18; primary categories of analysis of,
107–12; reasons for a feminist social analytic of, 102–7; rhetorical
biblical reading and, 96–97; of
women in antiquity, 145; worksheet for taking an inventory of,
100. See also social analysis
social-scientific models, 147
Society of Biblical Literature, 11
socio-historical rhetorical method of
feminist interpretation, 163–64
sola scriptura, 39
Sophia: controversy surrounding understandings of, 26; European
feminists on, 26; the Goddess and,
24; Jewish Scriptures on YHWH
and, 25; recent scholarship on,
25–26
Spelman, Elizabeth, 108
Spirit, the: the bible and, 67–68; gender of, 138; traditional theologies
on, as masculine, 22
spirituality, 1–2
Stanton, Elizabeth Cady, 64
storytelling, 148–49, 179–81
Strobel, Regula, 188
structural position, 106–7, 119
structural sin, 110–11
subject position, 106–7, 119
Suchocki, Marjorie, 126
superiority/inferiority, 87, 88, 94
supersessionist model, 185
supremacist model, 146
Suskin Ostriker, Alicia, 35–36
Swidler, Leonard, 141
symbolic mother concept, 35
Syrophoenician wo/man, the, 39,
156, 157
Talpade Mohanti, Chandra, 128

but also for his careful editing of the manuscript. His expert advice was greatly appreciated in the last stages of manuscript completion. I also want to express my thanks to Roberta Savage for the cover design and to production coordinator Catherine Costello for shepherding the manuscript through the various stages of production.

As always, I am in debt to Francis and Chris. Words are not enough to convey how much I treasure their unfailing support and unqualified love.

Acknowledgments

Many people have contributed to the ideas in this book. Since 1985 I have taught—first at the Episcopal Divinity School and then at Harvard University Divinity School—courses on Feminist Biblical Interpretation (affectionately called FBI by students). I have also learned a great deal from the participants in my workshops on Feminist Biblical Interpretation in India, the Philippines, Brazil, Chile, Switzerland, Australia, New Zealand, South Africa, and the U.S. I am grateful to have had the opportunity to lecture on Feminist Biblical Hermeneutics during a guest professorship at the Humboldt Universität in Berlin in 1997 and at the Protestant Theological Faculty in Heidelberg in 1999. With deep gratitude I dedicate this book to the many students and colleagues facilitating and participating in these workshops and classes.

Special appreciation and thanks are due to the students as well as to my teaching facilitators Melanie Johnson-DeBaufre and Deborah Whitehead in my 1999 Feminist Biblical Interpretation and in my 2000 Gospel Stories of Wo/men class. I was privileged to discuss with them parts of as well as the whole manuscript. Hence, I want to express my deep-felt gratitude for all their suggestions, enthusiasm, and insights. It is my hope that they have benefited as much from this process as I have from their critical feedback.

For their work and suggestions I also want to thank my research assistants Emily Neill who keeps me in good graces with the library, Lyn Miller who read the first draft of the manuscript, and Laura Beth Bugg who worked through its final draft and collaborated in assembling the glossary. My faculty assistant Hilary Muzingo typed some class lectures in preparation for this book. After she left, Chanta Bhan and Gail Morgan kept the office afloat during the final stages of the project. I am grateful to all three of them for their assistance and work.

Finally, without the untiring patience and persistent urging of my editor, Robert Ellsberg, this work would never have been completed. Years ago, Robert asked me to write a small 100-page introduction to feminist biblical hermeneutics and over the years he again and again inquired as to the progress of the manuscript. I am grateful not only for his persistence

CONTENTS

To the Participants
in my courses and workshops on
Feminist Biblical Interpretation
and
Gospel Stories of Wo/men

With appreciation for their critical questions, challenging insights,
and creative group projects

Founded in 1970, Orbis Books endeavors to publish works that enlighten the mind, nourish the spirit, and challenge the conscience. The publishing arm of the Maryknoll Fathers and Brothers, Orbis seeks to explore the global dimensions of the Christian faith and mission, to invite dialogue with diverse cultures and religious traditions, and to serve the cause of reconciliation and peace. The books published reflect the views of their authors and do not represent the official position of the Society. To learn more about Maryknoll and Orbis Books, please visit our website at www.maryknoll.com.

Manufactured in the United States of America

Library of Congress Cataloguing-in-Publication Data

Schüssler Fiorenza, Elisabeth, 1938–
    Wisdom ways : introducing feminist biblical interpretation / Elisabeth Schüssler Fiorenza
      p. cm.
    Includes bibliographical references and index.
    ISBN 1-57075-383-0 (pbk.)
    1. Bible—Feminist criticism. I. Title.

BS521.4 .S39 2001
220.6'082—dc21

                                                2001036547

Wisdom Ways

Introducing Feminist Biblical Interpretation

Elisabeth Schüssler Fiorenza

ORBIS BOOKS

Maryknoll, New York 10545

Wisdom Ways